* * *

TABLE OF CONTENTS

FORWARD

"Hitler's sex life has always been the topic of speculation. Some of his followers believe that he is entirely immune from such impulses. Some believe that his sex life is perfectly normal but restricted. Others believe that nothing happens when he is alone with girls." (Nizkor Project: 1943)
His detractors secretly believed that he was a chronic masturbator or that he derived his sexual pleasure through voyeurism. Everyone who knew him had an opinion, even if they were afraid to express it. Many believed that he was sexually impotent. Others, and these were perhaps in the majority, believed that he was either asexual or homosexual.
The truth is Adolf Hitler was all of these things at different stages in his life: asexual with a mother fixation, homosexual with a string of male companions and casual lovers, a voyeur and pornographer who enjoyed coprophilia and urophilia; a man with strong sadomasochistic urges and finally a reluctant heterosexual attracted to women much younger than himself - Catholic convent-educated girls he could easily manipulate and dominate. (Ibid.)
He managed to be all these things even though he had only one testicle - medical term 'cryptorchidism' - which was left undiagnosed until Hitler was 35 years old.

PART ONE: HITLER'S ASEXUAL PHASE

CHAPTER 1: INCEST, VIOLENCE, CRIMINALITY & INSANITY

ADOLF HITLER'S father, Alois Schicklgruber [Hitler] (b.1837-d.1903) had three wives, seven or possibly eight children, one separation and one divorce, at least one birth outside marriage, two births directly after his second and third weddings, one wife 14 years older than him, another 24 years younger, and his last, 23 years younger than him.

His first wife was the daughter of a superior, his second a waitress, and his third, Adolf Hitler's mother, was a servant who was also his foster-daughter and first cousin.

Before Adolf Hitler's parents, Alois Sr. and Klara Poelzl (b.1860-d.1907) could marry, they were obliged to get an episcopal dispensation from the Catholic Church because they were related to each other through shared grandparents.

In his petition [Linz registry 6.911/11/2 1884] dated October 27, 1884, Alois Sr. wrote unflatteringly of his intended bride, Klara: "the bride is without means and it is therefore unlikely that she will ever have another opportunity of a good marriage".

He included the family tree for both his and Klara's side of the family and all of their ancestors had the surname "Hiedler" [Hitler].

The Linz Episcopate declared itself "not competent" to issue the dispensation and forwarded the application to Rome where it was eventually granted by a Papal decree. None of this was ever mentioned by Hitler in his autobiography Mein Kampf (1925).

In fact, when he came to power in 1933, German newspapers and other media outlets were strictly forbidden from speculating on his ancestry.

Hitler's father, Alois Sr.

Adolf Hitler's father Alois Sr. was the illegitimate son of a 42-year-old housemaid, Anna Schicklgruber. He was born in Strones, near, Dollersheim, in Austria in 1837. His baptismal certificate left a blank space for where his father's name should have been. His mother Anna married a fifty-year-old miller, Johann Georg Hiedler in May 1842. She died in 1847 and Alois was raised by his uncle, Johann Nepomuk Hiedler. [The name Hiedler is a variation of Hitler which means "peasant smallholding"].

Alois Sr. left home at the age of thirteen to serve as a cobbler's apprentice. Later, he moved to Vienna where he was trained in crafting leather. He did not enjoy the work and in 1855 he joined Austria's Imperial Customs Service. He spent the remainder of his working life as a proud customs officer in the towns along Austria's western border with Germany.

Dr. Louis L. Snyder (Iron Fist in Germany: 1932) said: "His appointment to this post meant that Alois had moved several steps upward in the social scale from his peasant origins. Resplendent in his uniform with its shiny gold buttons, gold-rimmed velvet cap and pistol at his belt, he appeared to be a paragon of lower-middle-class respectability." At the age of 40, he changed his surname from Schicklgruber to Hitler so he could inherit money from his uncle.

In 1876, during his first marriage to Frau Glasl-Hoerer, Alois Sr. invited his 16-year-old cousin, Klara Poelzl to live with them as their "foster daughter". Frau Glasl was 14 years older than Alois, in very poor health, and because of her age, unable to have children. Their marriage was not a happy one and they separated but did not divorce, because as Catholics, they were not allowed to do so. His first wife died in 1883 by which time Alois had already had a child out of wedlock.

UPSTANDING CITIZEN: Alois Sr. was very proud of his uniform;
he had a photograph taken wearing it every year

Alois's second wife, Franziska Matzelsberger knew her husband had a roving eye and did not want his pretty cousin and foster daughter Klara Poelzl living in the house with them. She was sent to Vienna to work as a maid. Franziska gave birth to two children, Alois Jr. and Angela, but her health rapidly declined due to tuberculosis.

Klara returned to Alois's home to look after his bedridden wife and their two children. Franziska died in August 1884.

Then on January 7, 1885, six months after the death of his second wife, Alois Sr. married the young woman he had always called "niece" who was already pregnant with their first child. It was hardly a love match, and long after their wedding,

Klara could not break the habit of calling her husband "Uncle".

Repercussions of incest
Most children have two sets of grandparents, one maternal and one paternal, but in Adolf Hitler's case, he only had one set. The situation was further complicated by the fact that Klara Poelzl's mother Johanna (nee Hiedler) Poelzl, who lived all her life in the small town of Spital, was also born with the surname "Hitler". Alois Sr. and Klara's first three children died in infancy, Gustav (b.1885-d.1887), Ida (b.1886-d.1888) and Otto (1887) who only lived for three days.

HER HUSBAND'S COUSIN: Klara Poelzl before her marriage to Alois

Klara's fourth child, Adolf was born on April 20, 1889 on Easter Saturday in Braunau-am-Inn, Austria [a town on the German border]. Klara gave birth to another son, Edmund in 1894 but he lived for only six years. The sixth and final child of the marriage, Paula, was born in 1896.
Of Klara and Alois's six children, only Adolf and Paula lived to adulthood.

Savage beatings
Alois Sr. was a strict father who savagely beat his son Adolf if he did not do as he was told.
Dr. Louis L. Snyder (Iron Fist in Germany: 1932) said: "Adolf feared his father, a

hard and difficult man who set the pattern for the youngster's own brutal view of life. This sour, hot-tempered man was master inside his home, where he made the children feel the lash of his cane, switch, and belt. Alois snarled at his son, humiliated him, and corrected him again and again. There was deep tension between two unbending wills. It is probable that Adolf Hitler's later fierce hatreds came in part from this hostility to his father."

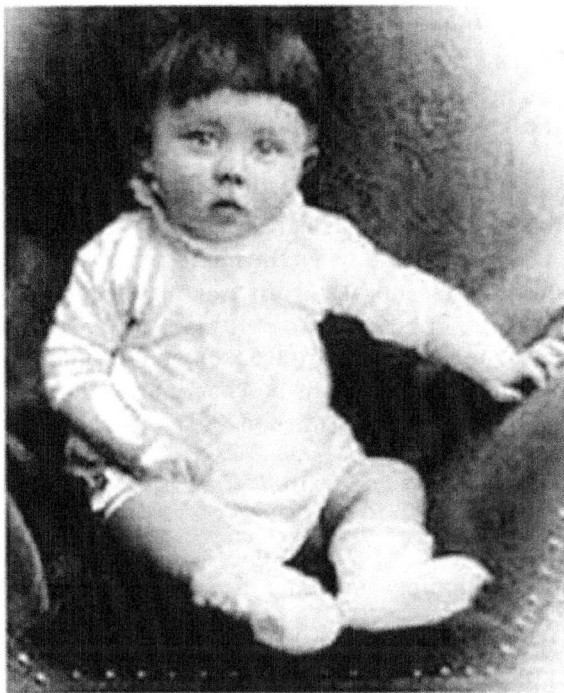

BABY FROM HELL: Adolf Hitler as a toddler, 1890

In his autobiography Mein Kampf [My Struggle] 1925, Hitler tried to give the impression that all was well in his childhood. His opening sentence described his parents as "faithful" and "devoted":
"In this little town on the river Inn, Bavarian by blood and Austrian by nationality, gilded by the light of German martyrdom, there lived, at the end of the 1880's, my parents: the father a faithful civil servant, the mother devoting herself to the cares of the household and looking after her children with eternally the same loving kindness."
But he soon contradicted the idyllic picture he had created earlier.
"Things end badly indeed when the man from the very start goes his own way and the wife, for the sake of the children stands up against him. Quarreling and nagging set in, and in the same measure in which the husband becomes estranged

from his wife, he becomes familiar with alcohol.

When he finally comes home drunk and brutal, but always without a last cent or penny, then God have mercy on the scenes which follow. I witnessed all of this personally in hundreds of scenes and at the beginning with both disgust and indignation." (Ibid.)

Years later, Hitler's nephew, William Patrick Hitler said he heard from his father (Alois Jr.), that Alois Sr. used to beat the children unmercifully. On one occasion, he beat his eldest son into a state of unconsciousness and on another occasion beat Adolf so severely that he left him for dead.

"He was somewhat of a drunkard and often his wife or one of the children would have to bring him home from the taverns. When he reached home a grand scene would take place during which he would beat wife, children and dog indiscriminately."

Hitler later said: (Hitler Speaks: 1939): "After reading one day in Karl May that the brave man gives no sign of being in pain, I made up my mind not to let out any sound next time I was beaten. And when the moment came. I counted every blow." Afterward he proudly told his mother: "Father hit me thirty-two times and I did not cry".

[The books of Karl May, an ex-convict from Saxony, entertained him until his dying day. Hitler was devoted to the gratuitous butchery perpetrated by the white American hero, Old Shatterhand, as he decimated the ranks of the evil Ogellallah Indians with clever brutality.

A full collection of May's novels were found in the Fuhrer bunker in Berlin after Hitler's suicide.]

According to Arthur H. Mitchell (Hitler's Mountain: 2010) when Hitler stopped reacting in pain to the whippings his father gave him, the corporal punishment stopped.

In M.M. Dunning's Psychological Effects of Child Abuse (2004) the author concluded that: "Hitler's father's mission was to prevent him [Adolf] from going down the same path as his older half-brother [Alois Jr.] who went to prison for theft. As a result he was particularly strict with him."

Dunning said: "There is substantial proof that child abuse has severe psychological effects that cannot be reversed. Many victims of child abuse often become offenders in violent crimes."

Impotent as a heterosexual

Dr. Walter C. Langer and his psychiatric research team (Nizkor Project: 1943) concluded that Hitler's aggressive fantasies towards his father reached such a point that he became afraid of his father's retaliation. [Note the Nizkor Project was conducted on the orders of the Overseas Secret Service, a forerunner of the CIA.]

"The retaliation he most feared was that his father would castrate him or injure his genital capacity in some way, a fear which is later expressed in substitute form in his syphilophobia [fear of syphilis]."

They said: "In abandoning the genital level of libidinal development, the individual becomes impotent as far as heterosexual relations are concerned. It would appear, from the evidence, that some such process took place during his early childhood."

American psychologist, Andrea Antczak has also concluded that by the time Hitler reached adolescence his sexual identity was totally confused and that many of Hitler's later "peculiarities" resulted from his abused childhood.

In her essay, "The Psychological Development of Adolf Hitler" (2010), she said: "His early years, through to his adolescence were encompassed by a negative environment that instilled in him hatred, anger, confusion and self-loathing." (Antczak: 2010)

FATHER & SON: A young Adolf sits on his father's knee but he only had eyes for his mother

"There is substantial proof that child abuse has severe psychological effects that cannot be reversed. The effects include aggressiveness, hostility, and poor relationships with peers and the opposite sex".

"The combination of the excessive affection from his mother and severe hatred towards his father resulted in a form of Oedipus complex." (Ibid.)

She concluded: "When reviewing Hitler's childhood from the eight stages of life, it is clear that he was unable to complete any of the stages successfully, I think it's safe to say that by the time he completed his adolescent stage, he suffered from identity confusion."

Antczak also claimed that this confusion and his intense hatred of his father fueled his murderous hatred during the Holocaust.

In such circumstances, [to the child] the whole world appears as extremely dangerous, uncertain and unjust.

"The result was that an unusual amount of bitterness against the world and the people in it became generated for which he could find no suitable outlets." (Nizkor Project: 1943)

Adoring mother
By contrast, Klara Hitler adored her son and loved him beyond all else.
She was 23 years younger than her husband Alois Sr. and they had little in common. She knew only too well his past history with women; that he lacked a loving disposition and spent most of his spare time in the taverns or gossiping with neighbors. "This meant that the affection which might normally have gone to her husband now found its way to her son Adolf". (Ibid.)
She had already lost three infants and feared she might lose yet another, so she did everything she could to grant her son Adolf's every wish. She even protected him from her husband's beatings by throwing her body in the way of the blows. She also did her best to please the brutal man she had married without much success.
Hitler's only childhood friend, (The Young Hitler I Knew: 1953), August Kubizek said:
"Alois Hitler's marriage with Klara was described by various acquaintances as very happy, which was presumably due to the submissive and accommodating nature of the wife. Once she said to me 'What I hoped and dreamed of as a young girl has not been fulfilled in my marriage;' and added resignedly, 'But does such a thing ever happen?'"
He said: "Even more than from Frau Hitler's occasional hints, one could gather this from her weary, drawn face. She told me once that Adolf was a very weak child and that she always lived in fear of losing him, too. Perhaps the early death of the [first] three children was due to the fact that the parents were blood relations. I leave it to the experts to give the final verdict."

Adoring son
In return, Adolf Hitler adored his gentle and indulgent mother and Kubizek described their relationship in almost ominous terms:
"She, who forgave him everything, was handicapped in the upbringing of her son by her boundless love for him." (Ibid.)
Their love for each other would have consequences. It expressed itself in Hitler's peculiar sexuality, his lifelong mother fixation and in his strange idea of intimacy with both sexes. (More in the next chapter,)

School days
When Hitler was three, the family moved to Passau, Germany where he acquired the distinctive lower Bavarian dialect, rather than Austrian German. In 1894 the family relocated to Leonding (near Linz), and in June 1895, when Adolf Hitler was six years old and about to start primary school, his father retired from government service.
For the next four years, he moved restlessly from one district to another near Linz,

buying and selling farms, raising bees, and spent much of his time getting drunk in local inns.

Even after he had retired, Alois Sr. continued to wear his civil service uniform when he appeared in public.

He was scrupulous about his appearance and when he spoke to his neighbors he did so in a condescending way perhaps looking down on them as "mere peasants" The Nizkor Project authors noted that he insisted on being addressed by his former civil service title "Herr Oberoffizial Hitler" even after retirement.

"If anyone happened to omit a part of it, he would call attention to their omission. He carried this to the point where, he became a source of amusement to the other villagers and their children."

"At home, he demanded that his children address him as 'Herr Vater' instead of using one of the intimate abbreviations or nicknames that children commonly do." (Ibid.)

FIRST DAY AT SCHOOL: Hitler, aged 6, poses in a sailor suit before starting primary school

Shortly after his father's retirement in1895, Hitler attended the local Volksschule (a state-owned school) in nearby Fischlham where three grades met in the same room and were taught by the same teacher. In spite of the fact that he had to change schools several times because of his father's restlessness, he did well in his studies.

He later said (Mein Kampf:1925): "It was at this time that the first ideals took shape in my breast. All my playing about in the open, the long walk to school, and particularly my association with extremely husky boys, which sometimes caused my mother bitter anguish, made me the very opposite of a stay-at-home. And though at that time I scarcely had any serious ideas as to the profession I should one day pursue, my sympathies were in any case not in the direction of my father's career."

His father's efforts at being a farmer ended in failure, and in 1897, the family moved to Lambach where Hitler was sent to a grade school run by Benedictine monks. The eight-year-old Hitler took singing lessons, performed in the church choir, and even considered becoming a priest. But things did not work out very well and he was expelled from the monastery (whose main spire bore a large swastika symbol) because he was caught smoking in the school grounds.

In 1898, the family returned permanently to Leonding.

All of the report cards from the time he entered school until he was eleven years old, show an almost unbroken line of "A's" in his school subjects. Hitler later referred to "this happy time" when "school work was ridiculously easy, leaving me so much free time that the sun saw more of me than my room".

He was also popular with other pupils and was much admired for his leadership qualities.

*ODDBALL: Hitler, aged 12; the boys in school shunned him
and called him "loser" and "odd ball"*

Rebellion

But at the age of eleven, the bottom fell out of Hitler's world and from a straight "A" student he suddenly dropped to a point where he failed in almost all his subjects and had to repeat the year. This was immediately after his younger brother Edmund died from measles in 1900.

According to the Nizkor Project (1943) Hitler "changed from a confident, outgoing, conscientious student to a morose, detached, sullen boy who constantly fought with his father and teachers".

His father Alois was incensed when Hitler told him that instead of joining the civil service he was going to become an artist.

Hitler said in Mein Kampf (1925): "Then barely eleven years old, I was forced into opposition for the first time in my life. Hard and determined as my father might be in putting through plans and purposes once conceived, his son was just as persistent and recalcitrant in rejecting an idea which appealed to him not at all. I did not want to become a civil servant. Neither persuasion nor serious arguments made any impression on my resistance. I did not want to be a civil servant: no, and again no. All attempts on my father's part to inspire me with love or pleasure in this profession by stories from his own life accomplished the exact opposite. I yawned and grew sick to my stomach at the thought of sitting in an office, deprived of my liberty; ceasing to be master of my own time and being compelled to force the content of a whole life into blanks that had to be filled out. The problem became more difficult when I developed a plan of my own in opposition to my father's. And this occurred at the early age of twelve. How it happened, I myself do not know, but one day it became clear to me that I would become a painter, an artist. There was no doubt as to my talent for drawing."

Konrad Heiden said that during Hitler's early adolescence, his rebellion against his father was at the forefront of many of his actions: (Hitler's Rise to Power: 1944) "He was not Austrian, he was not a dutiful son, he was not loyal and obedient, he was not even very conscientiously devoted to the Catholic religion of his country. A persistent legend relates that at the age of fourteen he spat out the Host at communion in protest." (Ibid.)

Much later, Nazi propaganda minister Joseph Goebbels said Hitler was "deeply religious but totally anti-Christian". He thought the Catholic church was too "meek" and apparently admired the Muslim faith for its strict adherence to rules and its control of the faithful.

Hitler began his secondary schooling on September 17, 1900. The attention he had received from his village teacher was now replaced by the more impersonal treatment of a number of teachers responsible for different subjects.

Ignoring his son's desire to attend a classical high school so he could become an artist, Alois sent his son to the Realschule in Linz.

Hitler rebelled against this decision, and in Mein Kampf said that he did poorly in school, hoping that once his father saw "what little progress I was making at the technical school he would let me devote myself to my dream".

Dr. Walter C. Langer et al said: "Competition was much tougher in the larger secondary school and his reaction to not being top of the class was to stop trying." His father who still had high hopes his son would follow him into the Austrian civil service was furious. However, Hitler was a stubborn child and attempts by his parents and teachers to change his attitude were met with failure. His bad behavior culminated in disgrace.

ARTFUL: Line drawing by Hitler of the family home in Leonding

Guilty of indecent assault

Hitler's first sexual "indiscretion" occurred at the Linz Realschule when he was 12 years old. At this tender age, he committed an offense against a "little girl" recorded in German as "Sittlichkeitsvergehen" which translates as an "act of indecency" or "indecent assault".

"Just what the sexual indiscretion consisted of, we do not know, but Dr. Bloch, who remembers that one of the teachers in the school told him about it, felt certain that he had done something with a little girl. He was severely censured for this and barely missed being expelled from school. It is possible he was ostracized by his fellow students and this was the reason he changed schools the following year." (Nizkor Project: 1943)

No doubt, his male teachers and school principal gave him a severe warning about his behavior. He may have received a thrashing from the principal. He had brought the name of the school into disrepute. His father Alois was still alive, and when word got to him, there is no doubt young Adolf received a severe beating from his belt or whip. The incident with the little girl would have stayed in his memory. Bad behavior had its consequences. In later life, he derived considerable pleasure from sadomasochistic practices.

After he had sexually assaulted the little girl, Hitler lost his popularity with other pupils. The boys in his own class were no longer willing to accept him as one of their leaders. They called him "oddball" and "loser". They laughed at him behind his back and avoided contact with him whenever possible.

As Hitler liked giving orders, he began to spend his time with younger pupils from the lower classes.

He enjoyed re-enacting battles from the Boer War and his favorite game was playing the role of a commando rescuing Boers from English concentration camps. He also enjoyed taking shots at rats with an air gun. (spartacus-educational.com: 2015)

"He would come to school with Bowie knives, hatchets, etc., and was always trying to initiate Indian games in which he was the leader.

The other boys, however, were not greatly impressed by him and his big talk; he gave every indication of being lazy, lived in a world of fantasy, talked big but did nothing of merit." (Nizkor Project: 1943)

While the teacher was explaining new material, Hitler read Karl May books which he kept concealed under his desk.

"He was forever antagonizing his teachers and the other boys. He has tried to create the impression [in Mein Kampf] that he was a leader and that he deliberately sabotaged his own education; the truth is that he was unpopular among his classmates as well as most of his teachers who considered him lazy, uncooperative and a trouble-maker." (Ibid.)

Honest-to-God lunatics

Hitler only worked at the subjects he was interested in, that is, Art and History, and he simply ignored other subjects for which he received marks ranging from "unsatisfactory" to "failing".

He later said of his teachers (Hitler Speaks: 1939): "Most of my teachers had something wrong with them mentally, and quite a few of them ended their days as honest-to-God lunatics."

"They had no sympathy with youth; their one object was to stuff our brains and turn us into erudite apes like themselves. If any pupil showed the slightest trace of originality, they persecuted him relentlessly, and the only model pupils whom I have known have all been failures in later life."

For at least one of his teachers, Dr. Eduard Huemer, the feeling of malevolence was mutual. In 1923 he said: [during Hitler's trial for treason]: "I can recall the gaunt, pale-faced youth pretty well. He had definite talent, though in a narrow field. But he lacked self-discipline, being notoriously cantankerous, willful, arrogant, and bad-tempered. He had obvious difficulty in fitting in at school. Moreover he was lazy, his enthusiasm for hard work evaporated all too quickly. He reacted with ill-concealed hostility to advice or reproof; at the same time, he demanded of his fellow pupils their unqualified subservience, fancying himself in the role of leader."

Another teacher, a Professor Gissinger said: "As far as I was concerned, Hitler left neither a favorable nor an unfavorable impression in Linz. He was by no means a leader of the class. He was slender and erect, his face pallid and very thin, almost like that of a consumptive, his gaze unusually open, his eyes brilliant."

His father's death

Hitler's father Alois Sr. died suddenly in the Gasthaus Stiefler pub in Linz on January 3, 1903.

Years later, Paula Hitler told US intelligence officers matter-of-factly, their father had died of heart failure and "was carried home dead from his morning pint". (Military Records: 1946)

In his memoirs, August Kubizek, related what he heard about it in his book, The Young Hitler I Knew, (1953): "He [Alois Sr.] went, as usual, punctually at ten o'clock in the morning to have his drink. Without warning, he collapsed in his chair. Before a doctor or a priest could be called, he was dead. When his fourteen-year-old son saw his dead father, he burst out into uncontrollable weeping." [Kubizek did not meet Hitler until the end of October 1904 almost two years after Alois' death.]

On January 5, 1903, Alois Sr.'s obituary, written by one of his Leonding acquaintances, was published in the Linz Tagepost and hinted at his often argumentative and aggressive nature.

"We have buried a good man: this we can rightly say about Alois Hitler, Higher Official of the Imperial Customs, retired, who was carried to his final resting place today. On the third of this month his life came to a sudden end as a result of an apoplectic stroke in the Gasthaus Stiefler, where he had gone because he was feeling unwell, hoping to revive himself with a glass of wine.

Alois Hitler was in his 65th year, and had experienced a full measure of joy and sorrow. Having only an elementary school education, he had first learned the trade of a cobbler, but later taught himself the knowledge needed for a civil service career, which he served with distinction, and in addition he achieved success in husbandry. Salzburg, Braunau, Simbach, Linz, were among the places where he saw service."

"Alois Hitler was a progressively minded man through and through and, as such, he was a warm friend of free education. In company he was always cheerful, not to say boisterous. The harsh words that sometimes fell from his lips could not belie the warm heart that beat under the rough exterior.

He was always an energetic champion of law and order. Well-informed on all kinds of matters, he could always be counted on to pronounce authoritatively on any subject. Fond of singing, he was never happier than when in a joyful company of fellow enthusiasts. In the sphere of bee-keeping he was an authority."

"Not the least of his characteristics was his great frugality and sense of economy and thrift. All in all, Hitler's passing has left a great gap, not only in his family: he leaves a widow and four children not well provided for; but also in the circle of his friends and acquaintances who will preserve pleasant memories of him."

By contrast, Hitler said in Mein Kampf that his father attacked everyone in authority: State, religion, morality and society during his rages.

He also described his father as having the "nastiest manner" and "a depraved mentality".

"Not a single good shred is left for humanity, not a single institution is left un-attacked; starting with the teacher, up to the head of the State, be it religion, or morality as such, be it the State or society. No matter which, everything is pulled down in the nastiest manner into the filth of a depraved mentality." (Mein Kampf: 1925)

When he was nearing the end of his life, Hitler told Christa Schroeder [one of his Berlin bunker secretaries]: "I never loved my father, but feared him. He was prone to rages and would resort to violence. My poor mother would then always be afraid for me." (spartacus-educational.com: 2015)

However, he did tell his childhood friend August Kubizek, proudly and more than once, that his father had reached the rank of Captain in the civil service, but apart from the few derogatory paragraphs he afforded him in Mein Kampf, he rarely if ever spoke about his father to anyone.

Cravings for a strong male

After his father's death, Hitler searched for strong male role models to act as father figures he could try to emulate. He did not want to be like his violent and abusive father who he both feared and rejected.

There is some evidence that he attempted to regard some of his teachers as role models but his attempts to admire them always miscarried.

Later, he attempted to find great men in history who could fill this need. Caesar, Napoleon and Frederick the Great were only a few of the many to whom he became attached. Also, during his early political career, "he was very submissive to a succession of important men to whom he looked for guidance, Gustav Ritter von Kahr [politician], Erich Ludendorff [army general] and Paul von Hindenburg [German President until 1934], to name only a few.

Several of his Nazi colleagues noticed that Hitler lost his self-confidence when brought face-to-face with an accepted authority figure. He had almost groveled when he first met President von Hindenburg and in some photos of them, it looks as though he is about to kiss the older man's hand.

"His deep craving for guidance from an older man grew with the years. He could only submit to a person who was perfect in every respect, literally a super-man".

BOWING TO HINDENBURG: Hitler in 1932, a year before he became German Chancellor

"But with neurotic types like Hitler, no sooner do they discover a single weakness or shortcoming than they depose him from the pedestal on which they have placed him. They then treat their fallen heroes badly for having failed to live up to their expectations. And so Hitler has spent his life looking for a competent guide but always ends up with the discovery that the person he has chosen falls short of his requirements and is fundamentally no more capable than himself." (Nizkor Project: 1943)

"In the end, he turned on them one after another and treated them in a despicable fashion when he discovered their personal shortcomings and inadequacies." (Ibid.)

Perverse satisfaction
The psychiatrists and psychoanalysts who compiled the Nizkor Project suggested that throughout his childhood, Adolf Hitler derived a perverse satisfaction, perhaps even sexual excitement, from antagonizing his father and the beatings which followed.

They also believed that by the time he was on the verge of adolescence [when his younger brother Edmund died], it brought "many dormant attitudes nearer the surface of his consciousness".

These attitudes included "a rejection of the father as a role model; anal tendencies which found an outlet in smearing [his feces], his passive, feminine tendencies; his masochistic tendencies and his desire to be dominated by a strong masculine figure".

Nazi defector, Ernst Hanfstaengl (The Missing Years: 1957) attempted to put Hitler's strange sexuality into context.

He believed that his former boss was neither "fish, flesh nor fowl" and neither "fully homosexual nor fully heterosexual".

He said: "I had formed the firm conviction that he was impotent, the repressed masturbating type."

Years later, Hitler's Nazi propaganda minister, Joseph Goebbels simply said: "The Fuhrer does not change. He is the same now as he was when he was a boy".

After his father's death
Hitler's mother Klara, who was then aged 42, moved the family to a modest apartment where she tried to keep herself and her two surviving children on the savings and pensions left by her husband.

Number 31 Humboldtstrasse was a three-story, tenement building. (The Young Hitler I Knew: 1953) "The Hitlers lived on the third floor. The small kitchen, with green painted furniture, had only one window, which looked out onto the courtyard. The living room, with the two beds of his mother and little Paula, overlooked the street. Adolf lived and studied in the closet, off the bedroom. The preoccupation with the well-being of her only surviving son depressed her increasingly."

Like her husband, she was keen for Adolf to do well at school but her attempts at persuasion achieved no more success than her husband's threats and he continued to obtain poor grades.

Professor Huemer at the Linz Realschule explained to Klara Hitler that her son's promotion to the fourth form would only be possible if he re-sat his French exam and then attended another school. Klara decided to send her son to the Realschule at Steyr, a small industrial town 25 miles east of Linz.

When he began his schooling in Steyr, in September 1904, he was obliged to board with another pupil at the home of 31-year-old Petronella Cichini and her elderly husband.

While he was there, Mrs. Cichini apparently opened his letters and she and Adolf had frequent arguments about his "right to privacy".

The Hitler family's Jewish physician, Dr. Eduard Bloch said Hitler was sent to Steyr because it had the reputation of being easier. But his performance there was very mediocre. The only subjects he did well in were free-hand drawing, in which he was marked "praise-worthy" and gymnastics, for which he received the mark of "excellent". In the first semester "German Language" was "unsatisfactory" and in "History" he was only "adequate". (Nizkor Project: 1943)

His sister Paula said: "Of those last years, we lived together with my mother, I especially remember the cheerfulness of my brother and his extraordinary interest for history, geography, architecture, painting and music.

At school he was nothing less than a show boy, and came home with bad school reports and admonitions." (Military Records: 1946)

At the end of the school year, he discovered he had failed once again.

His friend, August Kubizek said: "In those gloomy days of autumn, 1905, Adolf was on the razor's edge. Superficially, the decision the sixteen-year-old had to take was whether to repeat the fourth form in the technical school at Steyr, or leave school forever. Should he, for his mother's sake, continue on a path which he knew was mistaken and hopeless for him; or should he ignore the grief that he would cause his mother and choose the other way, the path towards art which didn't offer much comfort to her. But he knew how upset his mother was by this decision and this, caused him immeasurable grief."

Kubizek continued : "What did he care about bad reports? But to his mother they meant that Adolf would not reach his goal [of becoming a civil servant like his father] and it was impossible to convince her that his future lay elsewhere. So she took this, her greatest worry, the future of her son, with her to the grave." (The Young Hitler I Knew: 1953)

Manipulating his mother

In summer 1905, Klara brought her family to Spital to spend time with her relatives. While there, Adolf began to suffer from a respiratory illness and Klara sent for a doctor.

Dr. Karl Keiss traveled to Spital from nearby Weitra to examine him, and gave a diagnosis of Consumption.

Kubizek said: "Adolf passed through a grave crisis. It manifested itself by his falling seriously ill. He described it in his book Mein Kampf as 'lung trouble'. Others assert that it was some gastric trouble brought on by auto-suggestion."

"For a long time afterward, he was plagued by coughs and nasty catarrhs, especially on damp, foggy days. Also, in his mother's eyes, he was released by this illness from continuing school. Thus, it just suited his decision." (Ibid.)

Years later, Hitler wrote in Mein Kampf (1925): "My mother, felt obliged to continue my education in accordance with my father's wish; in other words, to have me study for the civil servant's career. I, for my part, was more than ever determined absolutely not to undertake this career. Then suddenly an illness came to my help and in a few weeks decided my future and the eternal domestic quarrel."

He left school the same year (1905) aged 16, without a school leaving certificate which would have consequences later in his life.

Sending his feces to the school principal

Hitler's poor academic results would also have consequences for the Steyr school principal. The first mention of Hitler's unusual attitude to feces (his own on this occasion) is mentioned in Donald Hook's book, The Madmen of History (1976) which detailed some of Hitler's disturbing malevolence toward the outside world even when he was young.

Here are a few summarized paragraphs from the book:

At the age of 16, Hitler did so badly in his school exams that he would have to repeat the entire year.

When the principal wrote to his mother Klara to inform her, she read the letter and then handed it to her son. Young Adolf apparently went to the toilet, defecated and then used the letter to wipe his bottom; he then put the letter back in the envelope, re-addressed it to the principal and posted it back to the school.

This episode involving what psychiatrists call "fecal smearing" is important as it was the first indication that Adolf Hitler had an unusual attitude toward his own body waste.

In his adult life, he became both a coprophile (someone who derives sexual pleasure from feces) and a urophile (the same thing only with urine) particularly during his relationship with his niece, Geli Raubal.

Hitler celebrated his release from further schooling by getting drunk. However, he found the experience so humiliating that he vowed never to get drunk again.

August Kubizek said when Hitler finished his schooling (Ibid.):"From that moment, I remember Adolf surrounded by books, especially by the volumes of his favorite work, with which he never parted, the German Mythology. He said he had 'beaten the school at its own game'."

He spent the next two years at home with his mother, painting, going for long walks and generally being spoiled.

"The years that followed were without any visible aim. He described it as 'the hollowness of the life of leisure' in Mein Kampf. He did not go to school, he did not bother about any practical training, he lived with his mother and let her keep him." (Ibid.)

THE REST OF HITLER'S FAMILY

His sister Paula

Paula Hitler (b.1896-d.1960) was seven years younger than her brother Adolf. Her personal diary, only discovered in 2005, confirmed the dysfunctional nature of the Hitler household.

Paula confessed that her older brother Adolf turned his inner rage against her and regularly beat her. When she was eight years old, she wrote: "Once again I feel my brother's loose hand across my face."

Her typewritten journal was discovered among an assortment of documents unearthed by historians Dr. Timothy Ryback and Florian Beierl.

Dr. Ryback told The Guardian newspaper (in 2005): "Adolf was the older brother and became the father figure. He was very strict with Paula and regularly slapped her around. She justified it in a starry-eyed way, because she believed it was 'for the good of her education.'"

One excerpt described the violence exercised by Hitler's father, and how their mother Klara tried to protect her son.

"Fearing that the father could no longer control himself in his unbridled rage, she [Adolf's mother] decides to put an end to the beating. She goes up to the attic, covers Adolf who is lying on the floor, but cannot deflect the father's final blow. Without a sound she absorbs it."

Beierl said: "This is a picture of a completely dysfunctional family that the public has never seen before. The terror of the Third Reich was cultivated in Hitler's own home."

Paula Hitler said she did not see her brother between 1908 and 1921 – she assumed he had died during WW1 – and when they finally met again in Vienna, she was delighted to see him.

Nazi researchers believe Hitler never mentioned her in his autobiography because he was embarrassed by her "weak mental state". In fact, in conversations, whenever he referred to either Paula or his older half-sister Angela, he called them the "stupid geese".

Paula worked between the wars as a secretary in a Viennese attic addressing envelopes and spent most of WW2 working as a secretary in a military hospital. She was interviewed by US Intelligence officers in May, 1945 and said tearfully, "Please remember, he was my brother."

She said it was a pity he had not become the architect he always wanted to be. During her second interview with US intelligence on June 5, 1946, she claimed she had seen her brother once a year throughout the 1930s and early 1940s and met Eva Braun only once. (Military Records: 1946)

She had changed her name from Hitler to "Wolf" in 1938 to protect herself from public interest and also said she had lost her job because of her brother's political activity.

"When my brother became more and more active and the name 'Hitler' was known in Vienna, I was eventually dismissed from my position. I went to Munich and described my difficult situation to my brother. He assured me that he would provide for me in future. He did so until his death." This included a gift of 3,000 marks every Christmas. (Ibid.)

In mid April 1945, she said she had been taken by two SS officers to the safety of a Berchtesgaden hotel.

During her interview, she pleaded ignorance of the Holocaust and claimed though her brother was anti-Jewish, it was a throwback to his time in Vienna when he believed the art business was controlled by Jews.

"I don't believe my brother ordered the crime committed to innumerable human beings in the concentration camps or that he even knew of these crimes." (Ibid.) She also said she had never been a member of the Nazi Party but would have joined if her brother had asked her to, in order "to please him".

SILLY GOOSE: She was classified as "on the simple side" by US psychiatrists investigating Hitler's early life

But Paula 'Wolf' Hitler was not the innocent she always pretended to be. According to an article in The Guardian newspaper (2005), she was "engaged to one of the Holocaust's most notorious euthanasia doctors."

His name was Dr. Erwin Jekelius and he sent at least 4,000 people, including children to their deaths, either using the gas chamber or by lethal injection. Paula Hitler apparently knew about it.

Hitler disapproved of the relationship and sent the doctor to serve on the Eastern Front where he was taken prisoner by the Soviets. He died in captivity in 1952. In the same year, Paula Hitler moved permanently to Berchtesgaden, reportedly living "in seclusion" in a two-room flat as "Paula Wolf".

During this time, it is understood she was looked after financially by former SS officers and others from her older brother's inner circle.

In 1958, she was living alone and surviving on social security payments.

She continued to live, unmarried, in a two-bedroom flat near Berchtesgaden for the rest of her days; her main interest being the Catholic Church.

Of her brother, Adolf Hitler, she said: "His end brought untold misery to me." She died on June 1, 1960 aged 64.

INDUSTRIOUS: Angela was classified as the most "normal" person in Adolf Hitler's family

Angela, his older half-sister

Angela Raubal Hitler (b.1883-d.1949) was Adolf Hitler's older half-sister and the mother of Geli Raubal, who according to his own testimony, was the love of his life. Angela is the only member of the family Hitler ever mentioned to friends and associates.

The Nizkor Project authors described her as "the most normal one in the family and a decent and industrious person".

In 1903, Angela married a civil servant named Leo Raubal in Linz and had three children by him - Geli, Leo and Friedl. Following her husband's death in 1910, she moved to Vienna looking for work. At first, she worked as a domestic but she was a woman who harbored ambitions for herself and her children. After WW1, she became a manager at a well-regarded college called the Mensa Academica Judaica. "Some of our informants knew her during this time and report that during the student riots. Angela defended the Jewish students from attack, and on several occasions beat the Aryan students off the steps of the dining hall with a club. She is a rather large, strong peasant type of person who is well able to take an active part." (Ibid.)

When Adolf Hitler was discharged from the army at the close of WW1, it is alleged that he went to Vienna to visit Angela with whom he had no contact for more than ten years.

While he was imprisoned in Landsberg Castle, she made the trip from Vienna to Munich to visit him with her 17-year-old daughter 'Geli'.

At Hitler's request, in 1925, she moved to Munich with Geli, and for almost a decade, worked as one of his housekeepers. It was during this time that Hitler became obsessed with her daughter, his half-niece.

In 1931, when Geli committed suicide in Hitler's apartment using his gun, Angela stood by her brother, believing at first, that her daughter's death had been a "tragic accident".

Five years later, friction developed between brother and sister, over a property deal that fell through, and she left Berchtesgaden for Dresden where she married Professor Martin Hammitzch [who designed the famous Yenidze cigarette factory in Dresden].

Her brother did not attend her second wedding. Hitler apparently disapproved of the marriage, and referred to his sister sarcastically as "Frau Hammitzch". In turn, she disapproved of his relationship with Eva Braun.

It seems, however, that Hitler re-established contact with Angela during WW2, because she remained his intermediary with the rest of the family with whom he did not want to have any contact.

In 1941, Angela sold her memoirs of her years with Hitler to the Nazi publishers, Eher Verlag [Alternative Publisher] for 20,000 Reichmarks.

Her only son, Leo Raubal, fought for the Nazi's during WW2. He flew with the Luftwaffe and was captured in Stalingrad in 1943. He was imprisoned in Moscow until 1955 but by the time he was released and returned to Austria, his mother was already dead.

Following the destruction of Dresden in the massive bomb attacks of February 13 to14,1945 Hitler moved his sister Angela to Berchtesgaden to prevent her being captured by the Russians. In his last will and testament, he guaranteed her a pension of 1,000 Reichmarks per month but it is not known if she ever received the payments. Her second husband, Professor Hammitzch shot himself when he realized Germany had lost the war.

Angela always spoke highly of her brother after his death, and claimed he had known nothing about the Holocaust. She died in 1949, several days after suffering from a stroke.

Alois Jr., his older half-brother
Alois Hitler Jr. (b.1882-d.1956) was the illegitimate son of his father's second wife,

born during the lifetime of his first wife. He was given the surname "Matzelsberger" until he was recognized by his father, Alois Sr. He was seven years older than his half-brother, Adolf.

Alois Jr. did not get along with his father's third wife, Klara who focused all her attention on her own children.

He suffered terrible beatings at the hands of his drunken father Alois Sr. and in 1896, aged only 15, he left the family home saying he wanted nothing more to do with his family. The side-effect of this was that his father then focused all his ambitions, and violent abuse on his youngest son, Adolf.

After leaving home, Alois Jr. worked as an apprentice waiter for a few years but struggled to stay on the right side of the law. In 1900, he received a five-month jail sentence for theft. Two years later, he was sentenced to eight months in jail for the same offense.

After his release from prison, he went to London and later to Dublin where he met Irish woman Bridget Dowling who he married in 1910. They moved to Liverpool and had a son called William Patrick Hitler. [Bridget Dowling claimed Adolf Hitler stayed with them in Liverpool in 1913 to avoid conscription into the Austrian army.]

In 1911, Alois Jr. worked in the Lyons cafe, a Jewish-owned company in Liverpool. He deserted his wife Bridget and their son in 1914.

The family had never been a happy one and broke up several times in the course of four years. It is alleged that he was very much like his own father and regularly beat his wife and tried to beat his infant son.

In 1914, aged 32, he returned to Germany and sold razor blades for several years.

BIGAMIST & THIEF: Alois Jr. was jailed for theft and charged with bigamy

In 1916, he married a German woman, Hedwig Heidemann without ever divorcing his first wife.

After the war, he tried to make Bridget (via a third party) believe that he was dead. However, the authorities eventually discovered his deception.

In 1924, he appeared before a Hamburg court on charges of bigamy and was threatened with a six month jail sentence, but his first wife did not want to press charges, and he was let off.

In 1934, he opened a cafe-restaurant called "The Alois" located at 3 Wittenbergplatz in Berlin where SA men were regular customers. He was described as a typical "chubby landlord, with little or no resemblance to his famous half-brother, who lived in constant fear that his license to sell alcohol would be revoked [by Hitler]."

The two brothers rarely met and when they did, Adolf "took a very high-handed attitude laying down the law". (Nizkor Project: 1943).

Alois Jr. is not mentioned in Mein Kampf (1925) and only a few people in Germany knew of his relationship to the Fuhrer. Hitler never visited his restaurant which went bankrupt during WW2.

With his second wife Hedwig, Alois Jr. had a son, Heinz Hitler (1920-1942), who fought on the Eastern Front for Nazi Germany. He joined the Wehrmacht in January 1942 but died a few weeks later in Moscow.

His eldest son, William Patrick, fought for the Allies and survived.

After WW2 Alois Jr. was arrested by the British but released as he had never joined the Nazi Party.

He then got involved with a right-wing party in the newly formed Federal Republic of Germany but never played a prominent role.

For the rest of his life, he survived by doing odd jobs and selling his autograph to tourists to make extra cash.

He died in Hamburg aged 74.

William Patrick, his half-nephew

William Patrick Hitler (b.1911-1987), the first son of Alois Hitler Jr., co-operated with the US intelligence agents and psychiatrists who wrote the intimate profile of Hitler, the Nizkor Project (1943) just before he joined the US navy (in 1944).

He is significant in Hitler's life because he increased his uncle's paranoia about his potential Jewish ancestry by sending him regular blackmail letters. He fled Germany in 1938 fearing his uncle might have him murdered.

William Patrick was born in Liverpool and brought up there by his Irish mother Bridget Dowling when his father Alois Jr. abandoned the family.

He returned to Germany in 1933 in the hope of making "easy money" from his uncle when he became German Chancellor.

Hitler organized a job for him at the Reich Credit Bank in Berlin, then at an Opel automobile factory and later as a car salesman.

He did not succeed in any of these jobs.

Unhappy with his lot, he continued to pester his uncle for a better job and issued blackmail threats that he would sell embarrassing stories about the family to newspapers unless his "personal circumstances improved"; he then tried to blackmail him over the family's potential Jewish ancestry.

In 1938, Adolf Hitler asked his nephew to relinquish his British citizenship in exchange for a high-ranking Nazi job. Suspicious of his uncle's real intentions, William Patrick left Germany fearing for his life and returned to London where he wrote an article for Look magazine called "Why I Hate my Uncle".

The story attracted the attention of renowned US publisher, William Randolph Hearst, and he was invited to do a lecture tour in America to talk about his famous uncle. He was 28 years old at the time.

BLACKMAILER: William Patrick Hitler feared his uncle might have him killed

He and his mother were stranded in the USA when WW2 broke out and they lived in Queens, New York for several years.

After writing a letter to President Franklin D. Roosevelt, William Patrick was "cleared" to join the US Navy in 1944. He served as a Pharmacist's Mate until he was discharged from the navy in 1947.

As he had been wounded in action, he was awarded the Purple Heart medal for bravery. When he left the navy, he changed his surname to "Stuart-Houston", married a German woman with whom he had three sons (one of them worked for the CIA).

The family moved to Patchogue, Long Island where he used his medical training to establish a business analyzing blood samples for hospitals.

He died aged 76 in 1987.

MADNESS & DISABILITY

U.S. psychiatrists said Hitler's mother Klara may have had a strain of syphilis in her blood. In their report, they noted that her sister was married and had two sons, one of whom was a hunchback with a speech impediment. And according to Hitler's childhood friend, August Kubizek (The Young Hitler I Knew:1953) there was a "humpbacked" aunt on his mother's side called Johanna.

The Nizkor Project authors also pointed to the fact that at least three of Klara's children died in infancy which they said was a "a poor record" and they suspected "some constitutional weakness; a taint of syphilis is not beyond the realm of possibility."

Indeed, if Hitler knew of this strain of syphilis on his mother's side, it might explain his obsession with the disease in adulthood. The fact that Klara's marriage to Alois Sr. was also incestuous did not improve the prospects of health and well-being for her offspring.

The Hitler's family physician, Dr. Eduard Bloch said he was certain that there was another daughter, slightly older than Adolf, who he described as "an imbecile". This daughter has never been officially mentioned in the history of the family.

"He [Dr. Bloch] is absolutely certain [of the existence of this child] because he noticed that the family always tried to hide the child and keep her out of the way when he came to attend the mother, perhaps feeling ashamed."

The doctor also said of Hitler's younger sister, Paula, that she too was "a little on the stupid side, perhaps a high-grade moron". (Nizkor Project: 1943)

If Klara Hitler's side of the family had a taint of syphilis, his father Alois's side experienced serious mental problems. The susceptibility of Hitler's extended family to mental illness was known within the higher reaches of the Nazi party, almost from the very beginning but the details were covered up once he became German Chancellor.

A string of idiots

A 1944 secret Gestapo report typed on the special "Fuhrer typewriter" said that his father's line had "idiot progeny" and they in turn "produced a string of idiots". (The Independent: 2005)

In fact, mental problems were rife in Hitler's family, with at least one relative committing suicide and several living in mental asylums.

Nazi researcher, Dr. Timothy Ryback said among them was a tax official called Joseph Veit.

"One of his sons had committed suicide; a daughter had died in an asylum, a

surviving daughter was half mad, and a third daughter was feeble-minded.
The Gestapo established that a family in Graz had a dossier of photographs and certificates on all this but SS-chief Heinrich Himmler had them seized to prevent their misuse." (Ibid.)
Ryback concluded: "Hitler's secrecy about his own family was legendary. This man really did have something to hide."

Insane cousin gassed to death
One of Adolf Hitler's second cousins was gassed to death under the Nazi policy of eliminating mental health patients. The woman, Aloisia Veit (b.1891-d.1940), daughter of Joseph Veit was from his father's side of the family.
She spent nine years sectioned at the Am Steinhof Psychiatric Institution in Vienna which was run by euthanasia doctor, Erwin Jekelius, who was Paula Hitler's fiance before his death in 1952.

HORRIBLE END: Aloisia Veit slept with a skull in her bed and wanted doctors to kill her; she was gassed to death under the Nazi regime

Under the Nazi regime, anyone with a mental or physical defect, even something as minor as a harelip, could be wiped out in pursuit of a pure and flawless Aryan race. Hitler had decreed that the mentally disabled were "useless mouths" and "unworthy of life". As a result of these policies, his cousin Aloisia Veit, who suffered from a severe form of schizophrenia, died in a room pumped full of carbon monoxide on December 6, 1940 at Hartheim Castle which was also a training ground for SS killers, near Linz.

She became one of thousands of mentally ill people exterminated as part of a systematic campaign to eliminate or sterilize those deemed socially undesirable. When her medical files were discovered, they revealed that Nazi doctors diagnosed her as suffering from "mental instability, helplessness, depression, distraction, hallucinations and delusions".

During her incarceration, she liked to sleep with a human skull in her bed and her treatment included confinement in a caged room where she was chained to an iron bed. She had told her doctors that she was "haunted by ghosts". (The Independent: 2005)

At one point, she pleaded in a letter to be provided with poison so that she could kill herself. "I'm sure it would only require a small amount to free me from my appalling torture," she wrote.

Aged 49 at the time of her death, a stamp on Aloisia Veit's medical file, discovered in 2005 called "The Hitler Collection" gave researchers "proof of her extermination".

Wolfgang Eisenmenger, a forensic medical specialist involved in the research, concluded:

"Given the basis of the Nazi ideology and Hitler's own world view, the very notion that congenital insanity existed in Hitler's family is interesting, to say the very least." (Ibid.)

Hitler's Jewish relatives

When he was working as a customs official in Braunau, in 1889, Alois Sr. chose a Jewish man from Vienna to act as his son Adolf's godfather. Historians have suggested that the teenage Hitler went to live with this Jewish godfather when he first attempted to gain entry into the Viennese Art Academy.

According to historian and author Brigitte Hamann (Hitler's Vienna: 2010) Hitler's Jewish godfather was a man called Johann Prinz.

In a census document from 1885, Mr. and Mrs. Prinz were mentioned as "a married couple, the husband being a swimming pool attendant at the Sofienbad, Vienna," living in the Third District, 28 Lowengasse. Whether they were still at this address ten years later [next census] is not documented.

The Nizkor Project authors said that Nazi Party officials made efforts to cover up something which happened in the two years following his mother's death. They suggested Hitler may well have lived with his Jewish godparents who supported him while he was preparing work for the Art Academy,.

But "when he failed to be admitted at the end of a year, they put him out and made him go to work."

One of his male companions in Vienna, Reinhold Hanisch, mentioned that when they were particularly destitute, they went to visit a well-to-do Jew that Hitler said was "his father". (I was Hitler's Buddy: 1939)

The wealthy Jew would have nothing to do with him and sent him [Hitler] packing. "This would certainly make much more sense and would indicate that Hitler had contact with his godparents before the visit and that they were fed up with him and would help him no further." (Ibid.)

Indeed, Adolf Hitler worried all his adult life about whether he had Jewish ancestry. He had denounced "thousands of years of inbreeding among Jews" in his speeches and sent millions to their deaths during the Nazi Party's "Final Solution" which began in 1942. The last thing he needed was a revelation that he himself was of Jewish origin.

Secret paranoia

According to Rittmeister von Schuh, a physician who had known Hitler since 1917, he "suffered from painful doubts; did he or did he not have Jewish blood?"

Ronald Hayman (Hitler & Geli: 1997) said: "What worried him most was the mystery surrounding his paternal grandfather".

In Munich, during the early 1920s, his political opponents had put forward the idea that he was of Jewish descent, and the rumors had not died down by the beginning of the 1930s.

Historian Ian Kershaw (Hitler 1889-1936: 1998) who is credited with creating the term "Nazi" said anti-Nazi journalists suggested that the name 'Huttler' was Jewish and "revealed" that he could be traced to a Jewish family called Hitler in Bucharest. They also claimed that his father had been "sired by Baron Rothschild, in whose house in Vienna his grandmother had allegedly spent some time as a servant." Hitler grew increasingly alarmed by these rumors.

After briefing his personal lawyer, Hans Frank, to find out the facts, Hitler was told that his grandmother, Maria Anna Schicklgruber, who became pregnant in 1836 when she was aged 41 and still unmarried, had been working as maid or cook for a Jewish family." (Hitler & Geli: 1997)

According to Ian Kershaw, [Hans] Frank discovered that Maria Anna Schicklgruber had given birth to her child in the home of a Jewish family called Frankenberger in Graz.

Not only that - Frankenberger senior had reputedly paid regular installments to support the child on behalf of his son, until the child's fourteenth birthday.

Letters were allegedly exchanged for years between Maria Anna Schicklgruber and the Frankenbergers and Hitler feared that the truth about his grandmother's secret lover might become known to the German public.

He carried his paranoia with him even as he instigated the Holocaust.

While awaiting the hangman's rope at Nuremberg in 1946, Hans Frank told the court that at the end of 1930, he was summoned by Hitler and shown a letter written by William Patrick Hitler (his half-nephew) which threatened to expose the Fuhrer's purported Jewish origins. His nephew had threatened to go to newspapers to tell them the rumors about his uncle were true.

Ronald Hayman (Hitler & Geli: 1997) said: "Subsequent research has revealed that there were no Jewish families in Graz [where his grandmother had worked], but Hitler did not know this during his lifetime, and never found out who his grandfather was."

This meant his secret paranoia about his Jewish ancestry remained with him his entire life.

Blackmail list

Having to fend off blackmailers became a recurring theme in Adolf Hitler's life and not just over his alleged Jewish ancestry. The Nazi propaganda machine and "Party fixers" had their hands full keeping what really went on in Hitler's private life private.

There was so much he needed to hide: the insanity in the family background, the incestuous marriage of his parents, his years as a vagrant in Vienna, his sexual orientation during WW1, his arrests for sodomy in Munich in the early 1920s and rumors he had sex with a minor in the late 1920s.

There were more blackmail threats over the pornographic images he had drawn of his niece Geli and the sexually explicit letter he had written to her. Also, after her death by suicide, rumors began to circulate that he had a perverted sexual relationship with her which involved both coprophilia [feces] and urophilia [urine]. There were also rumors that he had murdered his niece to keep her silent for good.

Then the beautiful actress, Renate Mueller claimed Hitler was a sadomasochist who enjoyed being kicked and beaten while he lay on the ground. Shortly before her death, she contacted German newspapers to let them know. The list went on and on.

Throughout his political career, he was also blackmailed for having had so many casual gay relationships. Sometimes Nazi party fixers paid off the blackmailers; sometimes Hitler ordered the murders of his tormentors.

It is little wonder that when he became Fuhrer, his doctors revealed that he had a very poor sleeping pattern, suffered from terrifying nightmares and took sleeping potions to help get him through the night.

Dr. Walter C. Langer et al said there was unanimous agreement among the psychoanalysts and psychiatrists [examining his personality and character] that Hitler was a hysteric bordering on schizophrenia.

In 1943, they wrote: "He has not lost complete contact with the world about him and is still striving to make some kind of psychological adjustment which will give him a feeling of security in his social group. It also means that there is a definite moral component in his character no matter how deeply it may be buried or how seriously it has been distorted."

These doctors also predicted that Adolf Hitler would die by committing suicide.

CHAPTER 2: HITLER'S MOTHER FIXATION

"I appeal to those who, severed from the Motherland and who now in painful emotion long for the hour that will allow them to return to the arms of the beloved mother," Adolf Hitler, as Fuhrer, speaking about Germany.

HITLER BECAME SO dependent on his mother's love that he never really got over her death from breast cancer in December 1907. From that time onward, until his own death, he carried a picture of her with him wherever he went; he also had a picture of her hanging over his bed and another on his work desk. He compared other women to her – unfavorably - and never allowed himself to become emotionally or sexually honest with any woman with the exception of his tragic half-niece, Geli Raubal.

His childhood friend, August Kubizek (The Young Hitler I Knew: 1953) said Hitler's inflexibility was responsible for causing his mother innumerable sorrows, yet he really loved her. "I remember many occasions when he showed his love most deeply and movingly during her illness; he never spoke of her but with deep affection. He was a good son."

As the Nizkor Project (1943) authors pointed out, when his mother died, "he cut himself off from the world in which love played any part for fear of being hurt and what love he could experience was fixated on the abstract entity, Germany."

Konrad Heiden, (Der Fuhrer: Hitler's Rise to Power: 1944) a journalist working in Munich was one of the first people to investigate Hitler's early life. He said: "Adolf Hitler was a model case for psychoanalysis, one of whose main theories is that every man wants to murder his father and marry his mother. Hitler hated his father, and not only in his subconscious."

"Constantly humiliated and corrected by him, receiving no protection against the mistreatment of outsiders, never recognized or appreciated, driven into a lurking silence, thus, as a child, early sharpened by hard treatment, he seems to have grown accustomed to the idea that right is always on the side of the stronger."

The more he grew to despise and fear his father, the more dependent he became on his mother's love. Indeed, Hitler admitted that one of his happiest childhood memories was "sleeping alone with his mother in the big bed when his father was away".

The Hitler family's physician, Dr. Eduard Bloch, said:

"Outwardly, his love for his mother was his most striking feature. She was a very sweet and affectionate woman. I have never seen a closer attachment between mother and son."

Mother's darling

Klara Hitler was extremely conscientious and hard-working, an exemplary housekeeper who never allowed a spot or speck of dust to be found in the family home. A devout Catholic, she accepted the trials and tribulations that fell upon her with Christian resignation. Even her last illness, which extended over many months and caused her great pain, she endured without a single complaint. "She probably accepted her violent husband's behavior with the same spirit of abnegation." (Nizkor Project: 1943)

She had lost three children in the course of three or four years. Then Adolf arrived. Under these circumstances, it is almost inevitable that he became the focal point in her life and that she left no stone unturned to keep him alive.

As a young boy, he was often ill and his mother became even more protective of him - the last thing she wanted was to lose another child. She doted on him and tried to fulfill his every need.

She described him as "moonstruck" and he described himself as his "mother's darling".

ADORED: Hitler loved his gentle mother Klara; as an adult, he had a picture of her hanging over his bed

Paula Hitler said their mother was "a very soft and tender person".

"If there were ever quarrels or differences of opinion between my parents, it was always on account of the children. It was especially my brother Adolf who challenged my father to extreme harshness and who got his sound thrashings every day. He was a scrubby little rogue, and all attempts of his father to thrash him for his rudeness and to cause him to love the profession of the civil service were in vain. How often on the other hand my mother would caress him and try to obtain with her kindness what father could not succeed in obtaining with harshness!" (spartacus-educational.com: 2015)

A heavy price

As early as 1932, Dr. Louis L. Snyder (Hitler and Nazism: 1932) predicted the world would pay a heavy price for Klara Hitler's excessive love for her son. "Hitler's mother was a quiet, hardworking woman with a solemn, pale face and large, staring eyes who labored diligently to please her husband. Hitler loved his indulgent mother, and she in turn considered him her favorite child. She told him how different he was from other children but despite her love, he developed into a discontented and resentful child, psychologically, through him the world would pay for her own unhappiness with her husband."

For his part, young Adolf found it very distressing to see his mother suffering from his father's "drunken beatings".

In his autobiography Mein Kampf, he referred to himself as "the little one", the victim. "There is a boy, let us say, of three when the parents fight almost daily, their brutality leaves nothing to the imagination; then the results of such visual education must slowly but inevitably become apparent to the little one."

"Those who are not familiar with such conditions can hardly imagine the results, especially when the mutual differences express themselves in the form of brutal attacks on the part of the father towards the mother or to assaults due to drunkenness. The poor little boy at the age of six, senses things which would make even a grown-up person shudder. The other things the little fellow hears at home do not tend to further his respect for his surroundings".

Oedipus complex

As the authors of the Nizkor Project revealed: "It is during these early years, when the child's acquaintanceship with the world is still meager and his capacities are still immature, that the chances of misinterpreting the nature of the world about him are the greatest."

"It is almost certain that when he was young, Adolf Hitler had temper tantrums. [He became notorious in later life for his rages]. Their purpose was to get his own way with his mother, a technique by which he could dominate her whenever he wished. Life with his mother during these early years must have been a veritable paradise except for the fact that his father would intrude and disrupt the happy relationship. Even when his father did not make a scene or lift his whip, he would demand attention from his wife."

"There is every reason to suppose that during his early years, instead of identifying himself with his father as most boys do, Hitler identified himself with his mother. This was perhaps easier for him than for most boys since there is a large feminine component in his physical makeup." (Ibid.)

Hitler's psychiatric researchers said infantile sexual feelings were probably quite prominent in this relationship as well as fantasies [about his mother] of a childish nature. The more he loved his mother, the more afraid he became of his father's vengeance should his secret be discovered. They said: "Little boys frequently fantasize about ways and means of ridding the environment of the intruder. As his libidinal attachment to his mother became stronger, both the resentment and fear [of his father] undoubtedly increased."

When his father Alois died in 1903, this left the door open for more fantasies about his mother: "Perhaps the situation aroused desires in him which he could no longer face on a conscious level and he could only keep these in check by either remaining in bed and playing the part of a helpless child or absenting himself from the situation entirely".

Seeing his parents having sex
These psychiatrists also said Adolf Hitler must have seen his parents having sexual intercourse, an event which took "a significant psychological toll on him and something he would never forget".
"He viewed this as a brutal assault on his mother and was indignant toward his father for this, and toward his mother for not resisting him. He also experienced feelings of helplessness for not being able to intervene. Adolf felt betrayed by his mother and this affected his relationships with women for the rest of his life."
The feeling of betrayal became accentuated still further when his baby brother Edmund was born. Because he felt his mother had first "seduced him" with her love and then betrayed him by submitting to his father (even though he beat her regularly) and he lost his respect for the female sex.
"His younger brother became a new rival and the newcomer no doubt became the victim of Adolf's animosity; he may have fantasized about getting rid of him as he had earlier contemplated getting rid of his father. "There is nothing abnormal in this except the intensity of the emotions involved." (Ibid.)
In the end, the consequences of his intense emotions restricted his sexuality as an adult: "Outside of the single exception of his niece [Geli Raubal], Hitler lived a loveless life. His distrust of both men and women was so deep. He hated his father, distrusted his mother [for submitting to sex with his father], and despised himself for his weakness [perversions]. The immature child finds such a state of mind almost unendurable for any length of time and in order to gain peace and security in his environment, these feelings are gradually repressed from his memory."
In his later years, Hitler counted "absolute loyalty to me" as one of the most important aspects of his relationships with both sexes.

Rewarding bad behavior
When he was thrown out of school for refusing to repeat the year in 1905, Hitler loafed around his mother's house for two years, daubing at paints, going for long walks in the countryside, either alone or with August Kubizek, where he could be seen wandering the hills giving speeches to nobody in particular.
He made no effort to find work or to increase the family income. He admitted later that he had been "a milk sop" during these years.
According to Arthur H. Mitchell (Hitler's Mountain: 2010) his soft-hearted mother Klara rewarded her son's laziness by buying him a grand piano and then paid for private tuition to encourage his interest in music.
Brigitte Hamann (Hitler's Vienna: 2010) said that from October 1906 onward Hitler took piano lessons with August Kubizek's teacher.
These lessons cost five kronen per month, though he did not progress well with the classes. In 1938, his teacher visibly cringed when he was required to tell the Nazi Party's archive about the young Hitler's prowess as a piano player. He said:

"As far as the lessons are concerned, he was never distracted, and, as for other conversations, before or after the lessons, rather reserved. In short, at the time, I wouldn't have had the slightest idea as to what a great statesman was taking lessons with me." (Ibid.)

Hitler's sister, Paula told US intelligence officers about this time.

"At home every day he was sitting for hours on the beautiful Heitzmann grand piano my mother had given him. This extraordinary interest for music, especially for Wagner and Liszt, remained with him for all his life. Particularly strong was his interest for the theater and especially for the opera. I can remember that he was visiting the opera house 13 times to hear Die Gotterdammerung [In Norse mythology it prophesied war among various gods that ultimately results in burning, drowning and renewal of the world.]". (Military Records: 1946)

She said his Christmas present to their mother had always been a theater ticket.

"Very often, he used to give lectures on themes concerning history and policy to my mother and to me in a rhetorical way." (Ibid.)

Meanwhile, the household was surviving on Alois Sr.'s meager civil service pension and in early 1907, Hitler decided to discontinue his piano lessons as he could not master a single tune. In his autobiography Mein Kampf, he admitted the family was living in virtual poverty at the time.

Racked with guilt

His friend August Kubizek said young Adolf was racked with guilt because of his own indolence: "The idea that he, a young man of eighteen, should continue to be kept by his mother had become unbearable to him. It was a painful dilemma which made him almost physically ill. On the one hand, he loved his mother above everything; she was the only person on earth to whom he felt really close, and she reciprocated his feeling to the same extent, although she was deeply disturbed by her son's unusual nature, however proud she was at times of him." (The Young Hitler I Knew: 1953)

Klara Hitler became seriously ill in late 1906 and on January 14, 1907, she was in such excruciating pain that she consulted with the family physician, Dr. Bloch. "She complained of a pain in her chest. She spoke in a quiet, hushed voice; almost a whisper. The pain she said, had been great; enough to keep her awake nights on end. She had been busy with her household so had neglected to seek medical aid. Besides, she thought the pain would pass away." (spartacus-educational.com: 2015)

Dr. Bloch proposed using gauze soaked in iodoform, packed onto the suppurating wound, the best treatment for cancer at the time, and her condition improved enough for her to get back on her feet.

But another examination showed Klara Hitler had an extensive tumor of the breast. Dr. Bloch recommended a hospital stay for extensive tests.

Historian Brigitte Hamann (Hitler's Vienna: 2010) said Klara believed that a hospital stay might leave the household in penury and she was reluctant to go. "Because she had no health insurance, such a hospital stay posed an enormous financial burden, particularly because the daily rate, was set at five kronen. In addition, there were various other invoices, such as the surgeon's bill. For the twenty-day stay (January 17 to February 5), the hospital charged one hundred kronen, which, according to the bill, was paid by 'the son'."

During Klara's stay at the Catholic Hospital in Herrenstrasse, Hitler visited her every day.

After a brief recuperation period, she had difficulty climbing the stairs and in early May 1907 the family moved to the small town of Urfahr across the Danube, to 46 Hauptstrasse.

HITLER'S ONLY CHILDHOOD FRIEND: August Kubizek and Adolf Hitler had an "exclusive" friendship for five years; Hitler would not allow him to have other friends

Financial difficulties may have been a factor. Urfahr was particularly cheap because of its agrarian markets, but also because it was free of the consumption tax that made all goods more expensive in Linz. Even before the move, Hitler had done the family's major shopping in Urfahr. (Ibid.)

Brigitte Hamann said that after only two weeks, the family moved again, this time to nearby 9 Bluetenstrasse in Urfahr. At 50 kronen, the rent was very high, amounting to almost half of Klara's widow's pension, which was certainly more than the family could afford.

"Thus it continued to be necessary to tap the small capital acquired from the sale of the family home. Klara, who was seriously ill, lived another few comfortable months there."

According to Dr. Bloch, the apartment had three small rooms. The windows offered a magnificent view of Mount Postling. "My predominant impression of the simple furnished-apartment was its cleanliness. It glistened; even though she was seriously ill, Frau Hitler was a superb housekeeper." (Ibid.)

COUNTRYSIDE: Another early painting by Hitler, location unknown

Leaving his mother

Despite his mother's worries about his future, "He succeeded in convincing her that it was essential for him to go to the Academy in Vienna to study painting. Adolf had also settled with his mother the financial side of his plan."

His living expenses and the Academy fees were to be paid out of the small legacy left to him by his father and now administered by his guardian [the Mayor of Leonding].

He hoped that, with great economy, he would be able to manage on this for a year. 'What would happen afterward remained to be seen', he said. Perhaps he would earn something by the sale of some drawings and pictures." (The Young Hitler I Knew: 1953)

Kubizek said he "felt lonely and miserable" after Hitler's departure [in autumn 1907]. "For several weeks, I had no news at all from him. And it was during those days that I felt most deeply how much he meant to me. Now I felt very lonely and miserable."

The reason he had not heard from Hitler was that he had failed the entrance exam to study Art in Vienna; he never told his friend or his mother Klara, and until she died from breast cancer in December 1907, she believed her son was studying a combination of Art and Architecture in Vienna.

When Kubizek went to visit Klara at the family home, he said she "seemed more careworn than ever. Her face was deeply lined. Her eyes were lifeless, her voice sounded tired and resigned. I had the impression that, now that Adolf was no longer there, she had let herself go, Now, on her own, she seemed to me an old,

sick woman." (Ibid.)
Klara Hitler told Kubizek: "He's as pigheaded as his father. Why this crazy journey
to Vienna? Instead of holding on to his little legacy, it's just being frittered away.
And after that? Nothing will come of his painting. And story-writing doesn't earn
anything either. Adolf doesn't give it a thought; he goes his way, just as if he were
alone in the world. I shall not live to see him making an independent position for
himself. If only I knew what on earth he is studying! Unfortunately, he does not
mention that at all. However, I imagine that he is very busy."

Incurable
Hitler returned to Urfahr when he heard his mother was close to death in
November 1907. Klara had delayed telling him she was terminally ill as she did not
want to disturb "his studies in Vienna", but finally she sent word for him to come
home
Kubizek remembered that when doctors told Hitler the cancer was incurable, his
eyes blazed and his temper flared. "Incurable, what do they mean by that?" he
screamed. Then he declared that he would "run the family household for his
mother" until her death. (The Young Hitler I Knew:1953)
Dr. Bloch said: "With an illness such as that suffered by Frau Hitler, there is usually
a great amount of pain. She bore her burden well; unflinching and uncomplaining.
But it seemed to torture her son. An anguished grimace would come over him
when he saw pain contract her face. There was little that could be done. An
injection of morphine from time to time would give temporary relief; but nothing
lasting." (spartacus-educational.com: 2015)
Yet Adolf seemed enormously grateful even for these short periods of release. The
doctor said he would never forget Klara Hitler during those final days. "She was
tall, slender and rather handsome, yet wasted by disease. She was soft-spoken,
patient; more concerned about what would happen to her family than she was
about her approaching death."
Her great concern in dying, he said, was: "What would become of poor Adolf, he is
still so young." Adolf was almost 19 years old.
He recalled that Hitler "slept in the tiny bedroom adjoining his mother so that he
could be summoned at any time during the night. During the day, he hovered
about the large bed in which she lay." (Ibid.)
Paula Hitler remembered: "During this time, my brother Adolf spoiled my mother
with overflowing tenderness. He was indefatigable in his care for her, wanted to
comply with any desire she could possibly have and did all to demonstrate his
great love for her." (Military Records: 1946)

Love and tenderness
August Kubizek said his friend changed into somebody he hardly recognized: "He
was transformed. I knew Adolf's low opinion of such monotonous chores [house
work]. I had not realized that his unbounded love for his mother would enable him
to carry out this unaccustomed domestic work so efficiently that she could not
praise him enough for it. One day, I found Adolf kneeling on the floor. He was
wearing a blue apron and scrubbing out the kitchen, which had not been cleaned

for a long time. I was really surprised and I must have shown it, for Frau Klara smiled in spite of her pain." (The Young Hitler I Knew: 1953)

"There, you see, Adolf can do anything," she said proudly.

Kubizek said: "His mother's bed now stood in the kitchen because that was heated during the day. The kitchen cupboard had been moved into the living room, and in its place was the couch, on which Adolf slept, so that he could be near her during the night. Frau Klara told me that every morning she discussed the dinner with Adolf. He always chose her favorite dishes, and prepared them so well that she herself couldn't have done better."

"The pleasure of having her son back and his devotion to her had transformed the serious, worn face. Adolf, who was always so punctilious about his neat dress, certainly looked comical in his old clothes with the apron tied around him, so touched was I by his changed attitude, knowing how much self-restraint this work was costing him." (Ibid.)

"I didn't trust my own eyes and ears. Not a cross word, not an impatient remark, no violent insistence on having his own way. He forgot himself entirely in those weeks, and lived only for his mother."

"Certainly this was partly due to the fact that he had spent the last four years of his life alone with her. There was a peculiar spiritual harmony between mother and son which I have never since come across. An atmosphere of relaxed, almost serene contentment surrounded the dying woman."

The last time Kubizek saw Hitler's mother, she was sitting up in bed.

"Adolf had his arm around her shoulders to support her, as, while she was sitting up, the terrible pain was less severe. 'Gustl,' she said 'go on being a good friend to my son when I'm no longer here. He has no one else.'" (Ibid.)

His mother's death

Klara Hitler died on December 21, 1907 and was buried on Christmas Eve. To preserve a last impression of her, Hitler sketched her on her deathbed.

Dr. Bloch said Adolf was completely broken by her passing: "In all my career I have never seen anyone so prostrate with grief, never seen a young man as broken with grief as Adolf Hitler was at the death of his mother ".

Paula Hitler (Military Records: 1946) said their mother's last wish was granted. "Her last desire was accomplished; she was buried beside the father. We accompanied her on her last journey from Linz to Leonding, where she was buried on December 23, 1907."

Hitler wore a black top hat and morning coat as he led the small funeral procession to his mother's resting place.

Dr. Bloch said: "After the funeral, he [Hitler] stood at her grave for a long time when the sisters had left. The bottom had obviously fallen out of his world. His mother would turn over in her grave if she knew what he turned out to be."

Hitler and his sisters [Angela and Paula] came to speak to the doctor after the funeral but Adolf remained silent.

Dr. Bloch remembered: "As the little group left, Hitler said: 'I shall be grateful to you forever.'" [Decades later, in 1939, Hitler allowed Bloch, who was Jewish, to emigrate with his wife from Austria to the United States.]

Hitler said in Mein Kampf (1925):
"It was the conclusion of a long and painful illness which from the beginning left little hope of recovery. Yet it was a dreadful blow, particularly for me. I had honored my father, but my mother I had loved."
He would never enjoy Christmas again. Every year for the rest of his life, he usually spent this time in a state of isolation and brooding and he never allowed his associates [in the Nazi party] to have a Christmas tree or other festive props to celebrate the season.
August Kubizek said: (The Young Hitler I Knew: 1953): "Not only had he now lost both his parents, but with his mother he had lost the only creature on earth on whom he had concentrated his love, and who had loved him in return. All he ever told me of that Christmas Eve was that he had wandered around for hours. Only towards morning had he returned home and gone to sleep."

Haunted by her image
Hitler's mother fixation lasted until his own death in 1945. He was haunted by her memory and carried a picture of her with him even in his last days in the Berlin bunker.
Rudolph Binion, author of Hitler Among the Germans (1976) suggested that the dictator was asexual throughout his life because "his tie to his mother unsuited Hitler for any normal erotic relationship."
The author pointed to a statement made by Hitler in the early 1920s "My only bride is my motherland" and concluded that any sexual relations he attempted were badly affected by his mother's picture hanging over his bed in each one of his bedrooms.
Dr. Langer and his team said unconsciously, all the emotions Hitler had once felt for his mother now became transferred to Germany. Germany became a symbol of his ideal mother. He showed no sexual interest in women until his late thirties, but even so, he always believed in an idealistic form of love if "a loyal woman could be found".
In later life, Hitler said: 'the longing grew stronger to go there, where, since my early youth I had been drawn by secret wishes and secret love'."
The authors said it was significant that although Germans invariably refer to Germany as the "Fatherland", Hitler almost always referred to it as the "Motherland". They said: "We can understand why Hitler fell on his knees and thanked God when WW1 broke out. To him it did not mean simply a war but an opportunity of fighting for his symbolic mother, Germany, of proving his manhood and of being accepted by her."

POEM TO MY MOTHER BY ADOLF HITLER
When your mother has grown older,
When her dear, faithful eyes
no longer see life as they once did,
When her feet, grown tired,
No longer want to carry her as she walks -
Then lend her your arm in support,

Escort her with happy pleasure.
The hour will come when, weeping, you
Must accompany her on her final walk.
And if she asks you something,
Then give her an answer.
And if she asks again, then speak!
And if she asks yet again, respond to her,
Not impatiently, but with gentle calm.
And if she cannot understand you properly
Explain all to her happily.
The hour will come, the bitter hour,
When her mouth asks for nothing more. (Adolf Hitler, 1923)

*FAMILY BREAK UP: Paula (front left) went to live with
their older half-sister, Angela (front right) and her
daughter Geli Raubal (center) pictured here circa 1916*

In his autobiography Mein Kampf (1925) Hitler described the years leading up to
his mother's death and mentioned an unnamed immorality: "It is difficult to say
which is worse; his unbelievable ignorance as far as knowledge and ability are
concerned, or the biting impudence of his behavior combined with an immorality
which makes one's hair stand on end, a youth who despises all authority, now he
loiters about, and God knows when he comes home."
Could this immorality have referred to the young man who had become his
"exclusive friend"? August Kubizek said: "The memory of what really did happen

is naturally influenced by my deep emotional feelings at the time." (The young Hitler I Knew: 1953).

A few days after his mother's funeral, Hitler left for Vienna and about six months later, he persuaded his special friend Kubizek to join him there.

Paula Hitler told US officials that for a short while her brother remained in contact (by letter) but then suddenly all communication stopped. For the next 12 years, he chose to completely avoid the rest of his family.

Paula said: "In the few letters I got from my brother, he was recommending certain books to me and gave well-meaning advice." (Military Records: 1946)

"I remember that he once sent me the book Don Quixote which he thought I would particularly enjoy. I submitted to his authority only with inner resistance. In fact, we did quarrel frequently, but we were fond of each other." "

"A last attempt by my aunt [Klara's sister] in 1908 to persuade him to take up the career of a civil servant was in vain. From that time onward, he ceased to write letters to us." (Ibid.)

Paula Hitler would not see her brother again until 1921, by which time he had become the leader of a fledgling political grouping in Germany called the Nazi Party.

PART TWO: HITLER THE HOMOSEXUAL

CHAPTER 3: HITLER'S FIRST BOYFRIEND, AUGUST KUBIZEK

"Throughout his early adult life [up to the age of 37], in Vienna, in the Army, in Munich, in Landsberg Prison, the informants of all these periods make a point that Hitler had absolutely no interest in women or any contact with them." (Nizkor Project: 1943)

In his autobiography (The Young Hitler I Knew: 1953) August Kubizek wrote about Hitler's sexuality and what he said spoke volumes.
"I lived side by side with Adolf when he grew from a boy of fifteen to a young man. He confided to me things that he had told to no one, not even his mother. As far back as the days in Linz, our friendship was so intimate that I should have noticed if he had actually made the acquaintance of a girl. He would have had less time for me, his interests would have taken a different direction. I think I can say, with certainty, Adolf never met a girl, either in Linz or in Vienna, who actually gave herself to him."
Dr. Robert G. L. Waite (Psychopathic God: 1977) said, even so, Hitler enjoyed talking about sex in general and "was particularly interested in deviant sexual behavior".
And Kubizek confessed in a private letter to a friend that Hitler "chattered by the hour about depraved [sexual] customs". But he also remembered that Hitler had a tender side: "He was full of deep understanding and sympathy. Without telling him, he knew exactly how I felt. He always knew what I needed and what I wanted."
In 1908, when they left Linz, the two young men lived together in a small room on Stumpergasse, a run-down area of Vienna. Jewish reporter, H.R. Trevor-Roper said: "A love of music and a romantic friendship kept them together but Hitler was always the dominant one, with Kubizek the recessive partner."
When their "exclusive friendship" ended suddenly in November 1908, a heartbroken Kubizek said that during their turbulent time together, Hitler often "tormented himself" and "wallowed deeper and deeper in self-criticism and self-accusation". He also said that for several years after they split up, he felt completely desolate at the loss of their relationship.
The two men would not meet again for almost 30 years.

ADOLF HITLER FIRST MET August 'Gustl' Kubizek (b.1888-d.1956) when they competed for standing room at the opera house in Linz in 1904. Kubizek was 16 and almost nine months older than his new friend Adolf.
"I can still see myself rushing into the theater, undecided whether to choose the left or right hand pillar. The right-hand one, was already taken; somebody was even more enthusiastic than I was. Half annoyed, half surprised, I glanced at my

rival. He was a remarkably pale, skinny youth, about my own age, who was following the performance with glistening eyes. I surmised that he came from a better-class home, for he was dressed with meticulous care. The black ebony cane, topped by an elegant ivory shoe, was essentially a student's attribute. We took note of each other without exchanging a word. I am sure it was around All Saints' Day in 1904."

SUBMISSIVE PARTNER: August Kubizek, pictured here
aged 18, was devoted to his friend

Some time later, during the interval of a performance, the two teenagers began talking about the casting and "rejoiced" in their common adverse criticism. At first, Hitler revealed little of his life to Kubizek. "He seemed to be very sensitive about questions that did not suit him and spoke but rarely of his family. I could only conclude that Adolf's relations must have been rather peculiar. Apparently among all the grown-ups he accepted only one person, his mother. It was this very fact that he was out of the ordinary attracted me even more." (The Young Hitler I Knew: 1953)

Hitler's manner of speaking, Kubizek noted, was "very choice". Contrary to those around him, he did not speak Austrian dialect but High German. In addition, he had a "well-developed sense of performing".

"He displayed his desire to be the center of attention by being given to talking much and persistently, always in the form of monologues. He did not permit anyone to contradict him." (Hitler's Vienna: 2010)

Despite Hitler's penchant for giving monologues, the two teenagers became inseparable. According to Kubizek, "Adolf made much of polite conduct and strict, proper form. With his only salt-and-pepper colored suit, with perfect creases, he wore white shirts ironed by his mother and black kid gloves, as well as a special touch, a little black ebony cane and sometimes even a top hat, an outfit like a college student's. Since Linz didn't have a university, the young people of all classes and strata of society all the more eagerly emulated students' customs." (Ibid.)

I can't bear it
Kubizek noticed immediately that patience was not one of Adolf's outstanding virtues. When he brought the conversation to the subject of school it was the first outburst of temper that he experienced with his new friend. In fact, whenever the subject of school came up, Hitler flew into a rage. "As he emancipated himself from the hated atmosphere of school, so did our friendship gain in value and importance. His classmates, mostly from rich homes, did not accept as an equal the queer youngster who came daily to town 'from the peasants'." (The Young Hitler I Knew: 1953)
"One day, a young man, about our age, came around the corner, a plump, rather dandified young gentleman. He recognized Adolf as a former classmate, stopped, and grinning all over his face, called out, 'Hello, Hitler!' He took him familiarly by the arm and asked him quite sincerely how he was getting on. But my friend went red with rage. I knew from former experience that this change of expression boded ill. 'What the devil has that to do with you?' he threw at him excitedly, and pushed him sharply away. Then he took my arm and went with me without bothering about the young man whose flushed and baffled face I can still see before me. 'All future civil servants', said Adolf, still furious, 'and with this lot I had to sit in the same class'. It was a long time before he calmed down." (Ibid.)

Exclusive friendship
Kubizek explained: "Adolf was exceedingly violent and high-strung. There was no end to the things, even trivial ones that could upset him. A few thoughtless words could produce in him outbursts of temper which I thought were quite out of proportion to the significance of the matter. But he lost his temper most of all when it was suggested that he should become a civil servant."
Almost immediately, Hitler expected Kubizek to be at his beck and call whenever he wanted which meant his work as an upholsterer in his father's business became a hindrance to their friendship.
"Impatiently he would twirl the small black cane which he always carried. I was surprised that he had so much spare time and asked innocently whether he had a job. 'Of course not,' was his gruff reply. He did not consider a 'bread-and-butter job' as he called it, was necessary for him. In his mouth that expression sounded full of contempt." (Ibid.)
Also, Hitler did not like it when his friend associated with other people and soon warned Kubizek that their friendship had to be exclusive. Kubizek remembered when his violin teacher Heinrich Dessauer died. "Adolf went to the funeral with me, which surprised me as he did not know the teacher. When I expressed my surprise Hitler said, 'I can't bear it that you should mix with other young people

and talk to them'."

Kubizek soon discovered his new friend's peculiar preference for nocturnal excursions and "staying overnight in some unfamiliar district" and together they explored all the outposts of Linz in all directions.

On fine days, Hitler would frequent a bench on the Turmleitenweg where he established a kind of open air study to write poetry or to paint landscapes.

"He would read his books, sketch and paint in water colors. Here were born his first poems. Another spot, which later became a favorite, was even more lonely and secluded. We would sit on a high, overhanging rock looking down on the Danube. The sight of the gently flowing river always moved Adolf. 'This is the ideal setting for my sonnet!' And on our way home, he confessed that he was going to try to extend the material into a play." (Ibid.)

Kubizek realized that their relationship endured mainly because he was a very patient listener and he was not unhappy with his "passive" role because it made him realize how much his friend needed him.

"His claims on me were boundless and took up all my spare time. He demanded everything from me, but was also prepared to do everything for me. Adolf was as much to me as a dozen other ordinary friends. He who could stick so obstinately to his point of view could also be so considerate that sometimes he made me feel quite ashamed."

"Adolf was by nature very reserved. There was always a certain element in his personality into which he would allow nobody to penetrate. He had his inscrutable secrets, and in many respects always remained a riddle to me. All that separated us disappeared when we stood in front of a magnificent work of art such as the Monastery of St. Florian. Then, fired by enthusiasm, Adolf would lower all his defenses and I felt the full joy of our friendship." (Ibid.)

Kubizek remembered his "grim and sour humor was often mixed with irony, but always an irony with friendly intent".

"Once, he saw me at a concert where I was playing the trumpet. He got enormous amusement out of imitating me and insisted that with my blown-out cheeks I looked like one of Rubens' angels."

Welded together

The two young men saw each other at every opera performance and met outside the theater afterward. On most evenings, they went for a stroll, arm-in-arm, along the Landstrasse.

They discovered they had a lot in common. August Kubizek was the first born and only surviving child of Michael and Maria Kubizek. His sisters Maria, Therese and Karoline all died in early childhood and as the surviving sons of grief-stricken mothers, it helped them to forge a special bond.

"The first time I went to visit him at home, his room was littered with sketches, drawings, blueprints. Here was The New Theater, there the Mountain Hotel on the Lichtenberg. It was like an architect's office. He gave his whole self to his imaginary building and was completely carried away by it. Once he had conceived an idea he was like one possessed. Nothing else existed for him, he was oblivious to time, sleep and hunger."(Ibid.)

"Like him, I considered art to be the greatest thing in man's life. I had nothing in common with his former classmates, I had nothing to do with the civil service and I lived entirely for art. In addition I knew a lot about music."

When they were short of money, they walked the streets of Linz, admiring the architecture and historical buildings. In the evenings, if they did have money, they attended whatever concert happened to be playing in the town.

On May 26, 1906, the "Buffalo Bill Circus Show" performed a Wild West spectacle involving 800 performers in costumes, among them a hundred American Indians and as many horses. And on June 7, Kubizek and Hitler marveled at 150 luxury cars and their noble "gentlemen drivers" who were making a stop in Linz during their tour. (Hitler's Vienna: 2010)

Then, on October 13, 1906, the State Theater performed the greatest musical hit of the era, Franz Lehar's The Merry Widow for the first time and the two young men attended.

Hitler's trance

In his memoirs (The Young Hitler I knew: 1953), the unworldly Kubizek described the outstanding impression Rienzi, der letzte der Tribunen [Rienzi, the Last of the Tribunes] had for both of them; with the end of each act "overpowering" and full of roaring shouts of "Heil!"

"Now we were in the theater, burning with enthusiasm, and living breathlessly through Rienzi's rise and subsequent downfall. When at last it was over, it was past midnight. As if propelled by an invisible force, Adolf climbed up to the top of the Freinberg [cliff]. We were no longer in solitude and darkness, for the stars shone brilliantly above us." (Ibid.)

Hitler stood in front of him and grasped his hands in a trance-like state. He was deeply moved. "His eyes were feverish with excitement. He spoke for an hour without stopping. The words did not come smoothly from his mouth as they usually did, but rather erupted, hoarse and raucous. From his voice, I could tell how much this experience had shaken him. Never before and never again have I heard Adolf Hitler speak as he did in that hour, as we stood there alone under the stars, as though we were the only creatures in the world."

Like Rienzi had become the savior of Italy in the opera, he would one day become the "savior of Germany".

Kubizek said it was as if "another being spoke out of his body, it was a state of complete ecstasy and rapture, in which he transferred the character of Rienzi to the plane of his own ambitions. Like flood waters breaking their dikes, his words burst forth from him. He conjured up in grandiose, inspiring pictures of his own future and that of his people."

"Such rapture I had only witnessed so far in the theater, when an actor had to express some violent emotions, and at first, confronted by such eruptions, I could only stand gaping and passive, forgetting to applaud. I had never imagined that a man could produce such an effect with mere words."

Up to that point, Hitler had wanted to become an artist, a painter, or perhaps an architect. "Now this was no longer the case; he was talking of a mandate, a special mission which one day would be entrusted to him. Many years had to pass before I realized the significance of this enraptured hour for my friend. His words were followed by silence. We descended into the town. The clock struck three. We parted in front of my house and I was astonished to see that he did not go in the direction of his home, but turned again towards the mountains."

When he became Fuhrer, the spirited Rienzi became the secret anthem of the Third Reich, well known as the introduction to the Nuremberg Nazi Party conventions.

Historian Brigitte Hamann (Ibid.) said: "Hitler remained faithful to his favorite operetta until the end of his life. In 1943-44, at the so-called 'Wolf Entrenchment' in East Prussia, he never listened to anything but the Merry Widow, as an ear witness reported with a moan." (Hitler's Vienna: 2010)

As Fuhrer, he also watched as many "pornographic versions" of the Merry Widow as he could when he got the opportunity.

Hitler's first girl crush

Before they moved to Vienna to live together, Hitler developed a crush on a local Linz girl "from a family of high social status" called Stefanie Isak who was two years older than him.

FANTASY GIRLFRIEND: Stephanie Isak, who was Jewish, became part of his model for the ideal Aryan woman

In his short book, Reminiscences, which Kubizek wrote for the Nazi Party archive in 1938, he said: "One evening in the spring of 1905, as we were taking our usual stroll, Adolf gripped my arm and asked me excitedly what I thought of the slim blonde girl walking along the Landstrasse arm-in-arm with her mother. 'You must know, I'm in love with her', he said resolutely'."

Kubizek described her as "a distinguished-looking girl, tall and slim with thick fair hair, which she mostly wore swept back in a bun." [Unknown to Kubizek, Hitler and the Nazi Party, Stefanie Isak was of Jewish descent.]

He said "her eyes were very beautiful". And Hitler loathed the men who flirted with her, especially "the military officers, who he called conceited blockheads. It annoyed him that Stefanie mixed with such idlers who, Hitler insisted wore corsets and used scent".

"He [Hitler] imagined Stefanie as his wife, building the house in which they lived and surrounded it with a magnificent garden. But he never spoke to her, always saying he would do so 'tomorrow'." (The Young Hitler I Knew: 1953)

Kubizek said that Hitler's "strange timidity" was prompted by the fear that any closer acquaintance might destroy this ideal.

"Love was a field where the unforeseeable might happen, and which might become dangerous. Stefanie was the most fertile and purest dream of his life, a beautiful illusion as he himself avoided any personal meeting [with her], this girl, she remained a creature of his dream world."

Kubizek noticed that his friend often mixed his dream world with reality: "Stephanie and Adolf had an affair in which nothing happens," he said.

But it appeared to be real to Hitler and after his mother's funeral, he "lacerated himself with the most awful punishment he could devise and said that he would give up Stefanie, that is, he would give up his fantasies about her."

Hitler also threatened to throw himself into the Danube because he claimed his unrequited feelings were so strong. His fantasy relationship with her lasted for several years and when he left Linz for Vienna, an idealized image of her became his "moral touchstone".

Years later, she became part of Hitler's model for the ideal Aryan woman. After WW2, Stefanie Isak said she had always been completely unaware of Hitler's feelings for her: "I once received a letter from someone who said they were to attend the Academy of Arts, and that I should wait for him; he would come back and marry me! I had no idea who the letter might have been from." (spartacus-educational.com: 2015)

Kubizek (who remained behind in Linz for a few months) was "commissioned" to find out more about her so that he could report the details to Hitler in Vienna.

Vienna calling

Hitler went to Vienna for the first time in May 1906 [when he spent two months with his half-sister Angela Raubal], and when he returned home, he was no longer satisfied with friendly and familiar but "philistine" Linz. Kubizek said his mind turned more and more frequently toward the capital. "It would be a great adventure for him to move from this absolute calm into the center of the storm." Kubizek had visited him while he was there and they were both impressed by the cultural life and the splendor of its buildings.

"He [Hitler] had stayed long enough to grow enthusiastic about everything that had specially attracted him, the Hof Museum, the Hof Opera, the Burg Theater, the magnificent buildings on the Ring but not long enough to observe the distress and misery which were concealed by the magnificent facade." (Bloch/Kubizek: 2013) This deceptive picture, largely "produced by his artistic imagination, held a powerful attraction for him".

Hitler became morose in Linz because of his constant yearning for new experiences and Kubizek noticed that "Outwardly, this seeking for a new path showed itself in dangerous fits of depression. At such times, he was inaccessible, uncommunicative and distant. But when I asked him what was wrong, his only answer would be, 'Leave me alone', or a brusque, 'I don't know myself'." (Ibid.)

Money woes
One day, Hitler told his friend that he had found a solution to their financial woes. He would buy a lottery ticket and they would win the top prize. Hitler was convinced it would happen. While they waited for the draw, they imagined what they would do together with all the money.

"The first and foremost destination was Bayreuth, where we were to enjoy the perfect performances of the great master's [Richard Wagner] musical dramas. After Bayreuth, we were to visit famous cities, magnificent cathedrals, palaces and castles, but also industrial centers, shipyards and ports. The time that elapsed before the draw was for me the happiest period of our friendship. Love and enthusiasm, great thoughts, lofty ideas, all that we had already. The only thing lacking was money. When we got that too, what more could we want?"

When the numbers for the lottery were published, Hitler rushed off to buy the local newspaper. When it finally sank in that they had not won, he raged and fumed and accused the organizers of being "crooks". But it had been a romantic gesture and much appreciated by Kubizek.

Then Hitler found another way to achieve his dream of adventure which included living in Vienna. He persuaded his guardian, the Mayor of Leonding, Josef Mayroher to release his inheritance. If he lived frugally, he could remain in Vienna for a year; the only problem was he did not want to be alone.

Now Kubizek said Hitler's frequent "Come with me, Gustl" took on a definite goal. "He had a horror of going alone, because this journey to Vienna was quite a different proposition from his earlier visits. Then, he still had his mother; his home still existed and his mother was waiting to welcome him with open arms. Now going to Vienna would be the last and final decision from which there was no turning back, a jump into the dark." (The Young Hitler I Knew: 1953)

Kubizek was expected to take over his father's upholstery business, but secretly harbored dreams of becoming a musical conductor. With Hitler's encouragement, he had devoted more and more time to his passion, eventually completing all the musical training available to him in Linz. But to achieve his goal of becoming a conductor, he would require higher education in music which was only offered in Vienna.

"Having put this idea into my head, he [Hitler] never gave up his efforts to persuade me. He comforted me when I despaired, he bolstered up my self-confidence when I was in danger of losing it, he praised, he criticized, he was occasionally rude and violent and railed at me furiously, but he never lost sight of the goal which he had set for me; and if sometimes we had such furious rows that I believed it was the end of everything, we would enthusiastically renew our friendship after a concert performance." (Ibid.)

DAUBING THE BRUSH: Hitler became obsessed with the idea of living in Vienna but he wanted Kubizek to join him

What the gullible Kubizek did not know and would later discover is that Hitler had already been rejected by the Academy of Art in Vienna; so he, Kubizek, would be going to Vienna having been completely hoodwinked but even when he found out about Hitler's deception he was all forgiving.

He wrote many years later: "He had been refused by the Academy, he had failed even before he had got a footing in Vienna. Nothing more terrible could have happened to him. But he was too proud to talk about it, and so he concealed from me what had happened. He concealed it from his mother, too. Not until the next year, when we were living together in Vienna, did all these circumstances gradually become clear to me." (Ibid.)

Convincing Kubizek's father
Historian Brigitte Hamann (Hitler's Vienna:2010) said it was impressive how Hitler, not yet aged 19, was able to persuade Kubizek's father to let his only son leave his upholstery workshop so he could attend the Vienna Conservatory of Music. Kubizek later admitted the decision changed the course of his life. "Adolf had already prepared the ground work. Without my knowledge, he had succeeded in convincing my mother of my musical vocation. He had made detailed inquiries

about the study of music and now he gave me exact information on the subject, telling me, in his tempting way, how much he enjoyed attending operas and concerts." (The Young Hitler I Knew: 1953)

Kubizek's father was quite fond of Adolf but saw him as "a young man who had failed at school and thought too highly of himself to learn a trade".

"My father had tolerated our friendship, but would have preferred a more sound companion for me, nevertheless he managed to win over my father to our plan in so comparatively short a time. I should go to Vienna for a trial period only to look around for a while. If the facilities for training came up to my expectations, I could then make a final decision, but failing this, I could return home and return to the upholstery business." (Ibid.)

It was all the more surprising, Kubizek said because Hitler, who "was inflexible and hated compromise", had done exactly that to get what he wanted.

He had already set himself up in a one-room flat on the second floor at No. 29 Stumpergasse, Vienna and a beseeching postcard arrived for Kubizek, dated February 18, 1908. The card showed a view of the Armour Collection at the Vienna Museum of the History of Art.

"Dear Friend, am anxiously expecting news of your arrival. Write soon so that I can prepare everything for your festive welcome. The whole of Vienna is awaiting you, therefore come soon. I will, of course, come and meet you." [On the back of the postcard he wrote:] "Well, as I said before, at first you will stay with me. Later we shall see. One can get a piano here in the so-called 'Dorotheum' for as little as 50/60 Fls. Well, many regards to you and your esteemed parents, from your friend, Adolf Hitler. Beg you again, come soon."

29 Stumper Alley

Hitler's room in Stumpergasse was located in one of the poorest back alleys in Vienna. He had failed to mention this in his postcard.

"I found myself in the Station Hall looking around for my friend. In his dark, good-quality overcoat, dark hat and the walking stick with the ivory handle, he appeared almost elegant. He was obviously delighted to see me and greeted me warmly and, as was then the custom, kissed me lightly on the cheek." (The Young Hitler I Knew: 1953)

At first, the two young men agreed that he would find his own accommodation (with Hitler's help) with enough space for a grand piano which was a requirement of the Conservatory.

Kubizek said: "In our hunt for lodgings which heralded my entry into Vienna, I had a foretaste of the misery, distress and filth that awaited us. Through dark, foul-smelling backyards, up and down stairs, through sordid and filthy hallways, past doors behind which adults and children huddled together in a small sunless room, the human beings as decayed and miserable as their surroundings, this impression has remained unforgettably with me."

One potential landlady turned out to be a prostitute who took a shine to Hitler and deliberately let her robe fall open in front of him. He was furious and went as "red as a peony" before they managed to scramble to the exit. "All I remember is Adolf

furiously exclaiming as we got into the street again, 'What a Mrs. Potiphar!." (Ibid.)
After this episode, Hitler suggested that they move in together and Kubizek
agreed. They would share a room in Hitler's tenement building in the
Stumpergasse where the landlady had no objection to Kubizek having a piano and
provided them with a slightly larger room to accommodate two people.

They had no view of the sky; the smell of kerosene was ever present and once the
piano and two beds were inserted in the room, there was little or no space to walk
about. "The space between the beds and the piano, as well as that between the
beds and the table, was hardly more than one foot wide. And for Adolf, room to
stride up and down was every bit as important as playing the piano was for me."
This lack of space caused Hitler many ill-tempered tantrums.

Their circumstances were modest in the extreme. Hitler lived on bread, butter and
milk for weeks at a time. For lunch he often bought a piece of poppy seed cake or
nut cake to add to it. Every fortnight, Kubizek's mother sent a food parcel, and
then they feasted like kings.

But in money matters, Kubizek said "Adolf was very precise. I never knew how
much, or rather, how little, money he had."

Dog's life
Almost immediately after moving into the room, Kubizek worried that Hitler had
become mentally unbalanced.

"He would fly into a temper at the slightest thing. There were days when nothing I
did seemed right to him, and he made our life together very hard to bear. I had
gone through terrible days with him after the wreck of his school career, and also
after his mother's death. I did not know to what this present mood of deep
depression was due to, but I thought that sooner or later it would improve."

Hitler began to call his poverty stricken existence "a dog's life".

"It was largely his own fault that he was in this position; but this he would never
admit. Even more than from hunger, he suffered from the lack of cleanliness, as he
was almost pathologically sensitive about anything concerning the body. At all
costs, he would keep his linen and clothing clean. No one, meeting this carefully
dressed young man in the street, would have thought that he went hungry every
day, and lived in a hopelessly bug-infested back room in the Sixth District."
(Bloch/Kubizek: 2013)

"Every evening he would put his trousers carefully under the mattress so that the
next morning he could rejoice in a faultless crease. Adolf realized the value of a
good appearance, and, in spite of his lack of vanity, knew how to make the best of
himself." (Ibid.)

The high spots of their social life included visits to the Hof Opera and listening to
Wagner. "This was not a simple visit to the theater, but the opportunity of being
transported into that extraordinary state which Wagner's music produced in him;
that trance, that escape into a mystical dream world which he needed in order to
endure the tensions of his turbulent nature."

In Vienna, Hitler went to see Lohengrin (which he knew by heart) and the
Meistersinger at least ten times. In fact, Kubizek noticed that sometimes, only
music could cheer him up.

"When we went on Sundays to the performances of sacred music in the Burgkapelle, we could hear at no expense soloists from the Vienna Opera House and the Vienna Boys' Choir. Adolf was particularly fond of this famous boys' choir, and he told me again and again how grateful he was for that early musical training he had received at Lambach [monastery from where he had been expelled for smoking]." (Ibid.)

In his dream world, Hitler wanted to create "a mobile Reich orchestra" so that "the masses" could experience the joys of the opera and of course, Kubizek would be its chief conductor.

Physically repugnant

As time passed in Vienna, Hitler became more and more interested in political affairs although he never lost sight of his artistic aspirations. "The years in Linz were dominated by art; the following years in Vienna, by politics. I was fully aware that it was only in artistic matters I counted for him."

Hitler often told him: "In politics, Gustl, you are nothing but a fool."

Even so, he regularly compelled his friend to go to the Viennese parliament even though he knew politics bored him to tears.

Hitler told him that if he was a true friend, then he would share, and take part in, all of his interests.

"He made up for the utter insignificance of his own existence by taking an interest in all public affairs, and he saw everywhere only obstacles and hostility. With his undoubted gifts, what a happy life he could have led; and how difficult he made things for himself! With the same fanaticism with which he loved the German people, and this 'Reich' did he reject everything foreign. He had no desire to know other countries. He was always up against something and at odds with the world." (The Young Hitler I Knew: 1953)

Hitler spent many hours worrying about, and speaking at length about "the masses" but he did not want to have any physical contact with them.

"All his thoughts and ambitions were directed towards the problem of how to help the simple, decent, but underprivileged people, with whom he himself identified; they were ever-present in his thoughts. But in actual fact he always avoided any contact with such people."

For example, the motley crowd at the Prater [open air theater] was "physically repugnant to him" and " he disliked any physical contact with people." This aversion included refusing to shake hands with strangers and sometimes even with people he knew.

Incest incarnate

Hitler also hated the babel [of foreigners] in the streets of Vienna, and called them the "incest incarnate". He hated the Austrian state, which ruined "Germanism", and the pillars which supported this State: the reigning royal house, the Church, the nobility, the capitalists and the Jews.

Kubizek said Hitler's "accumulated hatred" of all forces which threatened the Germans was mainly concentrated upon the Jews. (Bloch/Kubizek: 2013)

As an extramural student at the university, the aspiring conductor was allowed to eat in the canteen and to procure cheap meal tickets for friends but Hitler refused to join him there. Eventually, probably due to hunger, he consented to go. "I knew how much he liked sweets, so as well as the main dish, I got some cakes I thought he would enjoy; you could see from his face how hungry he was, but as he sulkily gulped it down, he venomously hissed at me, 'I don't understand how you can enjoy anything among such people!'" Hitler was referring to the Jewish students in the canteen. That was reason enough for him to stop going there."

But Hitler soon let his hunger get the better of him. "He squeezed himself in next to me in the canteen, turned his back on the rest and greedily wolfed down his favorite nut cake. Many a time, in my political indifference, I was secretly amused to see him swinging between his anti-Semitism and his passion for nut cake." (Ibid.)

On another occasion, when Kubizek tried to help Hitler out of his poverty, he found himself, yet again, at the mercy of Hitler's ferocious temper. One of his fellow students at the Music Conservatory worked as a journalist on the Wiener Tagblatt [Daily News], and when Kubizek mentioned Hitler's dire situation, the journalist suggested Hitler could do drawings for the paper.

"But when we went to see my fellow student, there was a terrific row. As soon as Adolf saw him, he turned about, even before he had entered the room, and going down the stairs shouted at me, 'You idiot! Didn't you see that he is a Jew?' Actually, I had not. But in future I took care not to burn my fingers."

Then one day, while Kubizek prepared for his exams [June 1908], Hitler stormed into their room, full of excitement. He had just come from the local police station after an incident in the Mariahilferstrasse connected with a "Handelee" Jew. [The word Handelee was used to designate eastern Jews who dressed in caftans and sold trinkets on the streets.]

The Mariahilferstrasse was part of the hidden red light district in Vienna.

Hitler said a Handelee had been standing in front of the Gerngross store begging which was banned by the State; the police had been looking for witnesses to the begging offense and Hitler had volunteered to testify against him. The Jewish man was then taken into custody.

Shortly after this incident, the two young men attended a Jewish wedding at Hitler's suggestion. Kubizek thought his friend's views might have mellowed but he was mistaken, as a few days later, Hitler came back to their little apartment and announced: "Today, I joined the anti-Semite Union and have put down your name as well". (Ibid.)

Jealousy and arguments

Hitler was convinced he was destined to become an architect though Kubizek started to have his doubts. When he told Hitler that he had successfully passed the entrance exam at the Music Conservatory, Hitler said: "I had no idea I had such a clever friend." (The Young Hitler I Knew: 1953)

In fact, whenever Kubizek talked about his studies, Hitler became "irritable".

When Kubizek offered to give him piano lessons, he snarled at him: "You can keep your scales and such rubbish. I'll get on by myself." When he had calmed down, he said, "Why should I become a musician, Gustl? After all, I have you!" "Soon our life together in Vienna showed its drawbacks because of the different subjects Adolf and I were studying. In the morning, when I was at the Conservatory, my friend was still asleep; and in the afternoon when Adolf wanted to work, my practicing disturbed him. This led to frequent friction. When I occasionally became impatient, he shouted at me rudely,."

"Even if I had managed to persuade Adolf to submit his drawings or his literary work to a newspaper editor or a publisher, he would soon have quarreled with his employer, for he could never tolerate any interference with his work. He simply could not bear taking orders from people, for he received enough orders from himself." (Ibid.)

The lack of space in their room and Kubizek's practicing the piano "at all hours" continued to cause arguments though they usually managed to resolve them with good humor.

A card from Hitler during one of Kubizek's trips to see his parents.
April 20, 1908 [Hitler's birthday].

"Dear Gustl, You write that you are having such lovely weather, which almost upsets me as, if it were not raining here, we too should be having lovely weather. I am very pleased that you are bringing a viola. On Tuesday I shall buy myself 2 crowns' worth of cotton wool and 20 kreuzers' worth of paste, for my ears naturally. That on top of this you are going blind affects me very deeply; you will play more wrong notes than ever. Then you will become blind and I gradually mad. Oh, dear! Your friend, Adolf Hitler."

Lonely bench
Kubizek noticed that Hitler never showed any desire to mix with people who shared his own professional interests. But he read voraciously and frequented the local libraries almost daily, reading politics, art, architecture, philosophy and history.

"The book he always returned to was called Legends of Gods and Heroes: the Treasures of Germanic Mythology and he always had his Schopenhauer by him and later Nietzsche, too." (The Young Hitler I Knew: 1953)

He also noticed that Hitler's pursuits and study were not directed towards any particular goal.

"Wherever he looked, he saw injustice, hate and enmity. Nothing was free from his criticism; nothing found favor in his eyes. All this time he was ceaselessly busy. I had no idea what a student at the Academy of Arts was supposed to do. One day he would be sitting for hours over books, then again he would sit writing till the small hours, or on another day the piano, the table, his bed and mine, and even the floor, were completely covered with designs. Woe betide me if I disturbed him on these occasions!" (Ibid.)

Sometimes, when Kubizek opened the piano to play, Hitler would shuffle his sheets of drawings together, put them in a cupboard, grab his coat and make off to Schonbrunn. He had found a quiet bench there among the lawns and trees, where no one ever disturbed him.

Kubizek said that he too was fond of this spot and often visited the lonely bench to reminisce when their relationship ended.

Flying Valkyries

During his "study of architecture", Hitler also attempted to write plays and dramas but these works were never finished. He then decided to write an opera. Kubizek remembered the change in him: "The weeks of dark visions and grave depressions were past; he was again full of hope and courage."

All Kubizek had to do was to write down Hitler's musical thoughts and ideas which tested their relationship to the limit. "His attempt to make use of me made the whole thing even more complicated, for my theoretical knowledge only hindered his intuition. It reduced him to utter despair that he had a musical idea which he considered bold and important, without being able to pin it down."
(Bloch/Kubizek: 2013))

"Why, then, did I not go? I knew the normal interests of young people of my age: flirtations, shallow pleasures, idle play and a lot of meaningless thoughts. Adolf was the exact opposite."

Kubizek realized there was an incredible earnestness in Hitler, a passionate interest in everything that happened and, most important, an unfailing devotion to the beauty, majesty and grandeur of art.

"It was this that attracted me especially to him and restored my equilibrium after hours of exhaustion. All this was well worth a few sleepless nights and those more or less heated quarrels to which I had become accustomed."

Hitler's settings and imagined scenery for his opera included both heaven and hell with flying "Valkyries", a "Wolf Lake", a priest in robes slaughtering a bull and monsters with metal wings.

Kubizek said: "I do not know what became of our opera. One day new, pressing problems confronted my friend, which required his immediate attention."

Choking with a catalog of hates

Eventually, the innocent Kubizek grew suspicious of Hitler's studies. "I wanted to ask Adolf how his studies in the Academy left him so much free time that he could write dramas, but I knew how sensitive he was about everything connected with his chosen profession." (Bloch/Kubizek: 2013)

As the days passed, Hitler's mood swings worried him more and more.

"I had never known him torment himself in this way before. He wallowed deeper and deeper in self-criticism and t it only needed the slightest touch for his self-accusation to become an accusation against the times, against the whole world; choking with his catalog of hates, he would pour his fury over everything, against mankind in general who did not understand him, who did not appreciate him and by whom he was persecuted. I see him before me, striding up and down the small space in boundless anger, shaken to his very depths. I sat at the piano with my fingers motionless on the keyboard and listened to him, upset by his hymn of hate." (Ibid.)

One day, Kubizek had to practice but Hitler wanted to read. As it was raining, he could not go off to Schonbrunn.

"This eternal strumming," Hitler shouted, "One's never safe from it."

"It's quite simple," Kubizek answered, and getting up took his timetable out of his music case, and with a drawing pin fixed it on the cupboard door. Now Hitler could see exactly when he was out, when not, and just when his hours for practicing took place.

"And now hang your timetable under it," he said.

Apparently Hitler did not need any such thing. He kept his timetable in his head. So now, the sight of the timetable stuck on the wall, which must have seemed to him like an officially accredited guarantee for Kubizek's future, brought about an explosion.

"This Academy!" Hitler screamed, "a lot of old-fashioned fossilized civil servants, bureaucrats, devoid of understanding, stupid lumps of officials. The whole Academy ought to be blown up!"

Kubizek said his friend's face was livid, the mouth quite small, the lips almost white.

"They rejected me, they threw me out, they turned me down," Hitler said.

Kubizek was shocked. Foolishly, he asked if he had told his mother Klara about his rejection before her death.

"What are you thinking of?" he replied. "How could I burden my dying mother with such a worry?"

For a while they were both silent.

"And what now?" Kubizek asked him which produced yet another one of Hitler's outbursts.

"What now, what now," Hitler repeated irritably. "Are you starting too, what now?" He sat himself down at the table and surrounded himself with his books and repeated: "What now?"

Kubizek made to take down his timetable but Hitler raised his head, saw it and said calmly, "Never mind." (Ibid.)

A drop of bitterness

Hitler later recalled his first rejection from the Art Academy in autumn 1907 (Mein Kampf: 1925): "I had set out with a pile of drawings, convinced that it would be child's play to pass the examination. At the Realschule I had been by far the best in my class at drawing, and since then my ability had developed amazingly; my own satisfaction caused me to take a joyful pride in hoping for the best. Yet a drop of bitterness put in its appearance: my talent for painting seemed to be excelled by my talent for drawing, especially in almost all fields of architecture."

But Hitler was told his test drawing for the Academy was "unsatisfactory" and this rejection left him feeling depressed and humiliated.

He later said (Ibid.): "When I presented myself to the rector, requesting an explanation for my non-acceptance that gentleman assured me that the drawings I had submitted incontrovertibly showed my unfitness for painting, and that my ability obviously lay in the field of architecture; for me, he said, the Academy's school of painting was out of the question, the place for me was the School of Architecture."

Hitler was then filled with optimism: "In a few days, I knew myself that I would become an architect. Yet this was an incredibly difficult path, for what I had missed, out of obstinacy, in the technical school, now took its bitter revenge. The attendance at the school of architecture of the academy was dependent on the attendance at a technical school for building, and entrance to the latter required one to have passed the matriculation examination at a secondary school. I didn't fulfill any one of these conditions." (Ibid.)

MOCK UP: Hitler's earliest vision of the Brandenburg Gate

Hitler did apply to the School of Architecture, but he was rejected again, on this occasion, because he did not have a School Leaving Certificate. In fact, he was not allowed to sit the entrance exam.
Kubizek reflected on his friend's behavior: "What did he have his books for? He wanted to prove to me that, even without the Conservatory he could equal my achievements in the musical field. For it was not the Professor's wisdom that counted, he said, but genius." (The Young Hitler I Knew: 1953)
Hitler believed that after a "Storm of Revolution" formal qualifications would no longer be necessary.
"He cursed the old-fashioned Academy where there was no understanding for true artistry. He spoke of the trip-wires which had been cunningly laid for the sole purpose of ruining his career. But he would show these incompetent, senile fools that he could go ahead without them!" (Ibid.)

YOUNG HITLER'S SEXUALITY

Sexually normal
August Kubizek said that in terms of sexuality, Adolf Hitler was "normal" even though he showed no interest in the opposite sex. "I must categorically assert that Adolf, in physical as well as sexual respects, was absolutely normal. What was

extraordinary in him was not to be found in the erotic or sexual spheres, but in quite other realms of his being. When he used to describe to me in vivid terms the necessity of early marriage, which alone was capable of ensuring the future of the people; when he used to set forth measures for increasing the number of children per family and described how, in his ideal state, the problems of love, sexual relations, of marriage, of family, of children would all be solved, I would think of Stefanie [Isak].

For, after all, what Adolf was laying down here in such a convincing manner was really only the dreamed-of, ideal life with her, transported to a political and social plane." (The Young Hitler I Knew: 1953)

"His conceptions of love and marriage were definitely not those of his father, and while his mother loved him dearly, she certainly had not influenced him much in this respect. His ideas of morality were based not upon experience, but on abstract, logical conclusions. He still looked upon Stefanie, who he had never spoken to, as the ideal model of German womanhood, unrivaled by anything he saw in Vienna." (Ibid.)

Women flocked to Adolf

Despite his friend's strict views on morality, Kubizek noticed that Hitler found favor with the opposite sex but never took advantage of it.

"When we used to walk up and down the foyer during the intervals at the Opera, I was struck by how much attention the girls and women paid to us. Adolf appealed so much to the passing ladies, in spite of his modest clothing and his cold, reserved manner in public, that occasionally one or the other of them would turn round to look at him, which, according to the strict etiquette prevailing at the Opera, was considered highly improper." (Bloch/Kubizek: 2013) Some of the women even gave him notes with their contact details.

Apparently, Hitler did nothing to provoke this behavior: "On the contrary, he hardly noticed the ladies' encouraging glances, or, at most, would make an annoyed comment about them to me. All Adolf said, contemptuously, was, 'Another one' and passed the note to me. Then, with a semi-mocking glance, he asked me whether perhaps I would like to keep the suggested appointment."

Kubizek concluded: "As far as girls were concerned, he was doubtless quite pleased about my shyness, if only for the reason that it left me with more free time to spend with him." (Ibid.)

He said, even in the street, Hitler was shown preferential treatment. "When, at night, we came home from the Opera or the Burg Theater, now and again one of the streetwalkers would approach us, in spite of our poor appearance, and ask us to come home with her. But here again it was only Adolf who got the invitation. I used to ask myself what the girls found so attractive in him. He was not at all what is understood as a handsome man. Perhaps it was the extraordinarily bright eyes that attracted them. Perhaps it was just his obvious indifference to the opposite sex that invited them to test his resistance."

Whatever the reason, women sensed something "exceptional" about him.

But Kubizek said that ultimately they did not make any female acquaintances as Hitler had "too high an opinion of himself for a superficial flirtation or for a merely physical relationship with a girl."

Also, Hitler would never have allowed him to indulge in such affairs [with women] as "any step in this direction would have meant the inevitable end of our friendship; he would never have tolerated my having any interest in other people. As always, our friendship had to be utterly exclusive". (Ibid.)

Woman hater

When Kubizek was given the opportunity to earn extra money teaching music, Hitler was furious. Most of his students were women who came from wealthy homes, including "two daughters of a brewer in Kolomea, the daughter of a landowner in Radautz, and also the daughter of a businessman in Spalato".

One evening, a wealthy female student called unexpectedly at 29 Stumpergasse to ask him about a musical assignment, and during their innocent discussion, Hitler returned to the flat.

Kubizek said: "When I introduced him to my pupil, Adolf said nothing, but hardly had the girl got outside when he went for me wildly, for since his unfortunate experience with Stefanie [Isak], he was a woman hater. Was our room, already spoiled by that monster, that grand piano, to become the rendezvous for this crew of musical women? I had a job to convince him that the poor girl was not suffering from love pangs but from examination pains." (Bloch/Kubizek: 2013)

Hitler then gave his innocent friend a lecture about "the senselessness of women studying". Like blows, Hitler's words fell on him, "as though I was the cloth manufacturer or brewer who had sent his daughter to study at the Conservatory".

Celibacy and Prostitution

Hitler described married love between a man and woman "who had kept themselves pure in body and soul" until their wedding night as the "Flame of Light". Whenever the questions of love, marriage or sexual relations were raised, this magical formula cropped up. (The Young Hitler I Knew: 1953)

"To keep the 'Flame of Life' pure and unsullied would be the most important task of the 'Ideal State' with which my friend occupied himself in his lonely hours. The 'Flame of Life' was the symbol of sacred love and these couples would produce healthy children for the nation." (Ibid.)

On the other hand, he called the prostitution which was rife in Vienna as the "Sink of Iniquity".

Kubizek said they came across this prostitution in its "most varied forms" both in the elegant streets of the center and in the slums of the suburbs. Hitler described this prostitution as "A Monument to the Shame of our Times". Of course, in his ideal State, there was no longer any "Sink of Iniquity". or "Monuments of Shame".

One evening, much to Kubizek's surprise, Hitler took his arm and said: "Come, Gustl! We must see the 'Sink of Iniquity' once."

Hitler already knew the way and the two young men turned into the small, ill-lit, Spittelberggasse to look for prostitutes.

Kubizek remembered: "So there we were. The girls sat there, some behind the window pane, some at the open window; a few of them were still remarkably young, others prematurely aged and faded. In their scanty and slovenly attire they sat there, making up their faces or combing their hair or looking at themselves in the mirror, without, however, for one moment losing sight of the men strolling by." (Ibid.)

Hitler insisted they walk up and down the street several times, much to Kubizek's embarrassment. "One of these girls seized just the moment when we were passing her window to take off her chemise while another busied herself with her stockings, showing her naked legs. Adolf grew angry at the prostitutes' tricks of seduction. Now he said he had learned the customs of the market for commercial love, and thus the purpose of his visit was fulfilled."

And the two young men returned to their apartment.

Homosexual encounter

Another evening, at the corner of Mariahilferstrasse, a well-dressed, prosperous-looking man spoke to them and asked them about themselves. When they told him that they were students: "My friend studies music," explained Hitler, "and I architecture", he invited them to supper at the Hotel Kummer.

Kubizek recalled: "He allowed us to order anything we pleased and for once Adolf could eat as many tarts and pastries as he could manage. Meanwhile, he told us that he was a manufacturer from Vocklabruck and did not like anything to do with women, as they were only gold diggers. We thanked him; he came out of the restaurant with us, and we went home." (Bloch/Kubizek: 2013)

Later that night, Hitler asked his naive friend if he had liked the man.

"Very much.," Kubizek said. "A very cultured man, with pronounced artistic leanings."

"And what else?" continued Adolf with an enigmatic expression. "As apparently you don't understand, Gustl, what it's all about, look at this little card!"

The man had slipped Hitler a card without Kubizek noticing, on which he had scribbled an invitation to visit him alone at the Hotel Kummer.

Hitler said in a matter-of-fact manner: "He's a homosexual."

"Naturally this, too, had long been one of his problems and, as an abnormal practice, he wished to see it fought against relentlessly, and he himself scrupulously avoided all personal contact with such men. The visiting card of the famous manufacturer from Vocklabruck disappeared into our stove."

Kubizek concluded: "It seemed to me quite natural that Adolf should turn with disgust and repugnance from these and other sexual aberrations of the big city, that he refrained from masturbation and that in all matters of sex he obeyed those strict rules that he laid down for himself and for the future State."

Brokeback Mountain?

At weekends, Hitler and Kubizek often enjoyed overnight excursions in the Viennese countryside but getting Hitler out of bed was always a problem.

"To try to shake him awake was a risky undertaking, he was likely to become utterly impossible. 'Why do you wake me so early?' he would shout at me. If I succeeded in getting him out of bed and on the move, I had to consider the first few hours lost, because after having been awakened so early, he would be silent and sullen for a long time, replying to questions only with reluctant grunts." (The

Young Hitler I Knew: 1953)
He only stopped sulking when they were far away from Vienna in the bright green countryside.

Most vivid in Kubizek's memory was one mountain excursion to Semmering they made in the summer of 1908.

"It was a wonderful moment, perhaps the most beautiful that I have ever experienced with my friend."

They climbed a small mountain in the sunshine in their city clothes but on the way back down, they were caught in a rain storm.

He remembered their thin city trousers fluttered around their legs as they hurried down the valley. "And what rain! Actual streams of water poured down on us from the clouds that seemed to hang just above the treetops. We ran and ran, as hard as we could. Soon there was not a single dry spot on us and our shoes too were full of water." (Ibid.)

To Kubizek's surprise, Hitler was not at all put out by the thunder and lightning, the storm or the rain.

"He was in a splendid mood and, although soaked to the skin, became more and more genial as the rain grew heavier."

For both of them, the adventure could not go on long enough. They skipped along the stony path and suddenly, just off it, spotted a little hut.

In the lower half of the hut lay a pile of hay, dry, and sufficient for them both to sleep in.

"Adolf took off his shoes, jacket and trousers and began to wring out his clothes. I felt very sorry for him, standing there in the doorway in his soaking underclothes, chattering with cold. Sensitive as he was to any kind of chill, how easily he could catch pneumonia." (Ibid.)

Kubizek found a canvas square, stretched it out on the hay and told him to take off his wet underclothes.

"He laid himself naked on the cloth and I took hold of the ends and wrapped it firmly round him. Then I fetched a second square and put that over him. This done, I wrung out all our clothes and hung them up, wrapped myself too, and lay down."

Hitler was enjoying the whole adventure hugely and "its romantic ending especially appealed to him".

The next morning, as usual, he had difficulty getting Hitler to wake up. "When he was finally roused, he worked his feet free of their wrappings and, with the canvas wrapped round him, walked to the door to look at the weather. His slim, straight figure, with the white cloth thrown toga-like across the shoulders, looked like that of an Indian ascetic. This was our last great excursion together. These walks and adventures [were] beautiful."

Hitler the pacifist
August Kubizek said that during their time together in the Stumpergasse flat, Hitler "was utterly averse to anything to do with war or soldiers".

"Even the idea of compulsory military service could infuriate him. No, he would never let himself be forced into being a soldier. If he ever became a soldier, he would do it of his own free will, and certainly never in the Austrian army."

One night Hitler was close to tears and hysterical when he spoke. This was not that unusual. "Sometimes, when his diatribes became too lengthy, I fell asleep. As soon as he noticed it, he shook me awake and shouted at me to ask whether I was no longer interested in his words; if so, I should go on sleeping, like all those who had no national conscience. So I made an effort and forced myself to keep my eyes open." (The Young Hitler I Knew: 1953)

BASHING THE BISHOP: Karlskirche Church in Vienna by Hitler; a religious skeptic but he would mimic the Catholic Church's slogans to win followers for the Nazi Party

Another night, he spoke of the Wright brothers' airplane. "He quoted from a newspaper that these famous aviators had built a small, comparatively lightweight gun into their aircraft and had made experiments in the effect that shooting from the air would be likely to have. Adolf, who was a pronounced pacifist, was outraged. 'As soon as a new invention is made,' he said, 'it is immediately put to the service of war. Who wants war?' he asked. Certainly not the little man, far from it'." Hitler said wars were arranged by crowned and uncrowned rulers guided by the armament industry. "While these gentlemen earned gigantic sums and remained far from the firing line, the little man has to risk his life without knowing to what purpose." (Ibid.)

Then when Kubizek received his call-up papers for military service, Hitler naturally exploded. "I can still see how his face changed color, how his eyes took on that extraordinary glitter which used to herald an outburst of rage. Then he started raving. 'You are not to register, on any account, Gustl!' he screamed. 'You're a fool if you go there. The best thing to do is to tear up this stupid bit of paper!' This moribund Hapsburg Empire did not deserve a single soldier." (Bloch/Kubizek: 2013)

As Hitler was nine months younger than him, he did expect his own call-up until the following year.

Having passed his medical examination, the obedient Kubizek went to Linz and signed up to do eight weeks training with the Austrian reserves. When he returned after a few days, he said Hitler was no longer furious with him.

"Adolf greeted me very warmly, because, in spite of everything, he was glad that I would continue to live with him. Of course, he made great fun of the 'Reservist'. He could not possibly imagine how they would make a soldier out of me. At home, Adolf sketched my head and drew a cocked hat with a plume on top of it. He said: 'There you are, Gustl, you look like a veteran even before you're a recruit'." (The Young Hitler I Knew: 1953)

I don't want to be alone

Shortly afterward, Hitler went to Kubizek's end of semester graduation, where "Adolf became more and more depressed". Kubizek was expected to visit his parents in Linz and then go on to do his military training which would mean over two months living apart. Hitler had no home in Linz to go back to so they decided he would stay in the flat in Stumpergasse and Kubizek would send his share of the rent while he was gone.

He tried to reassure Hitler that whatever happened they would stay together. "I told him that I would try to get an engagement as a viola player with the Vienna Symphony Orchestra during the next school year. Then I would be so much better off that I would be able to help him substantially." (Ibid.)

But Hitler was very irritable and made no response to his suggestion. Kubizek remembered: "Neither did he tell me a word of his future plans, but in view of my own success, I did not take offense at this. He promised to write often and keep me informed of everything of interest to me that went on in Vienna."

At the beginning of July 1908, Kubizek left for Linz. The parting was difficult for them both.

"Adolf assured me, for the hundredth time, how little he wanted to be left alone. He accompanied me to the West Bahnhof [station]. He hated sentimentality of any kind. The more anything touched him, the cooler he became. So now, he just took both my hands and pressed them firmly. Then he turned and made for the exit, without once turning around."

Unknown to Kubizek, in October 1908, Hitler had failed the entrance test at the Academy of Fine Arts yet again. This third rejection must have been the final humiliation for him.

In his book, Mein Kampf (1925) he said: "I owe it to that period that I grew hard and am still capable of being hard. And even more, I exalt it for tearing me away from the hollowness of comfortable life; for drawing the mother's darling out of his soft downy bed; for hurling me, despite all resistance, into a world of misery and poverty, thus making me acquainted with those for whom I was later to fight."

Biographer, Alan Bullock (Hitler: A Study in Tyranny: 1962) summed up Hitler's first year in Vienna perfectly:

"Apart from Kubizek, he lived a solitary life. He had no other friends. Women were attracted to him, but he showed complete indifference to them. Much of the time he spent dreaming or brooding. His moods alternated between abstracted preoccupation and outbursts of excited talk. He wandered for hours through the streets and parks, staring at buildings which he admired, or suddenly disappearing into the public library in pursuit of some new enthusiasm. Again and again, the two young men visited the Opera and the Burgtheater. But while Kubizek pursued his studies at the Conservatory, Hitler was incapable of any disciplined or systematic work. He had the artist's temperament without either talent, training, or creative energy."

Finding him gone

On November 20, August Kubizek, having completed his military service, returned to Vienna expecting to restart his life with Hitler in their room in Stumpergasse. But the landlady, Frau Zakrey told him his friend had paid his share of the rent and then left without giving her a forwarding address.

Kubizek was devastated.

"In my thoughts, I went over again the last weeks we had spent together. Of course there had been differences of opinion and rows, but with Adolf this was quite normal. In these four years, our friendship had become so close that it was taken for granted, and so was our resolve to stay together in the future. I felt deserted and alone, and with the constant memory of our friendship in my mind, I just could not decide to turn elsewhere for companionship. Perhaps he would be standing at the exit at the end of the performance, waiting for me, and I should again hear his familiar, impatient voice saying, 'Oh, come on, Gustl!' But all my hopes of seeing Adolf again proved vain, and meanwhile something became clear: he did not want to come back to me."

Kubizek learned decades later that Hitler had moved out of their Stumpergasse flat because the rent was too high. At first, he had taken furnished rooms in Simon Denk Gasse but he could not afford the rent there either and soon found himself homeless.

Kubizek said: "Adolf had disappeared into the shadowy depths of the metropolis. He did not wish to have a friend because he was ashamed of his own poverty. He wanted to go his way alone, and bear alone whatever destiny brought him. It was the road into the wilderness. Then began for him those years of bitterest misery of which he himself says little and of which there is no reliable witness." (Ibid.)

Indeed, for the next four years, "Hitler chose to bury himself in obscurity" and lived among the city's vagrants. (Nizkor Project: 1943)

Best years of my life
Fifteen years later, when Kubizek saw Hitler on the front page of the Munich Illustrated [circa 1923] the caption read "The well-known National Socialist orator, Adolf Hitler".

He remembered: "Small pale features, he had hardly changed at all. The face seemed to have become sterner, more mature, more manly, but hardly any older. Immediately, I thought back to the night on the Freinberg when Adolf had described to me how he, like Rienzi, would rise to be the Tribune of the people. What the sixteen-year-old had seen then in a visionary's trance had really come to pass." (The Young Hitler I Knew: 1953)

From that time onward, Kubizek, followed Hitler's political career with interest. "When I read his speeches, I could actually see him in front of me, striding up and down in the gloomy back room in the Stumpergasse between the door and the piano. I reread his cards and letters. Perhaps he had long since forgotten the lanky, music-mad carpenter's apprentice he had met in the Linz Theater." (Ibid.)

Kubizek did not attempt to contact him until February 1933 when he wrote to congratulate him on becoming Chancellor of Germany. Six months later he received a card from Munich HQ.

Munich, August 4, 1933, The Brown House

"My dear Kubizek,
I have only just been shown your letter of February 2. In view of the hundreds of thousands of letters I have received since January, this is not to be wondered at. So much the greater was my pleasure to receive news of you after so many years and to have your address. I should be very glad, once the period of my hardest struggles are past to revive once more with you those memories of the best years of my life.

Perhaps you could come to visit me. With all good wishes to you and your mother, I remain, in memory of our old friendship. Yours, Adolf Hitler"

Kubizek was delighted: "So be had not forgotten me. That in spite of all the strain of his work, he remembered me made me very happy. He called the years we had spent together the 'best years' of his life. So he had already forgotten the misery that went with them."

But the end of Hitler's letter caused him embarrassment. "Perhaps you could come to visit me," Hitler had written. He knew he could not simply go up to his house on the Obersalzberg in Germany and say "Here I am". (Ibid.)

He felt his life was unimportant and uninteresting and "to tell him about Eferding would only bore him". Besides, Kubizek had given up music to become a civil servant and knew how Hitler felt about civil servants.

Five years later
On March 12, 1938, on the very spot where his father had once served as a customs official, Adolf Hitler and the German army crossed the border into

Austria. On the same evening, he addressed the assembled from the balcony of the Linz Town Hall, still "as modest and shabby" as it had always been.

As a civil servant, Kubizek was too busy "billeting German troops" to leave his home town, Eferding to hear the speech.

But when Hitler came again to Linz, on April 8, and stayed at the Hotel Weinzinger [after a political demonstration at the Kraus locomotive works], Kubizek resolved to see him. It had been 30 years since they had last met. (Bloch/Kubizek: 2013)

"The Square in front of the hotel was crammed with people, but I made my way through to the cordon of SA men. I became quite giddy and realized that it had been foolish of me to come. I had to accept that my erstwhile friend had become Reich Chancellor and this highest position in the State had created an unbridgeable gulf between us. The days when he had confided to me the most intimate affairs of his heart, were definitely over." (Ibid.)

Albert Bormann [brother of Martin Bormann] approached him to say Hitler was unwell and would not be receiving anybody else that day. Would he come again tomorrow at lunchtime?

Bormann then invited Kubizek to sit down and immediately plugged him for information about his boss. He complained about Hitler's outbursts of temper which he said "nobody could cope with"; he also complained that Hitler stayed up late and slept late but only his entourage were obliged to get up early.

Then he wanted to know about his boss's "queer diet".

"Had the Chancellor always eaten the same way?"

Kubizek told him that when he was young, "Hitler had been fond of meat". [He did not become a vegetarian until 1931, after his niece, Geli Raubal's death.]

For you alone

The next day, the eve of the plebiscite [election] in Austria. Kubizek waited nervously in the Hotel Weinzinger at the appointed hour. He said: "As Hitler suddenly came out of one of the hotel rooms, he recognized me immediately and with the joyful cry, 'Gustl!' he left his entourage standing there and came and took me by the arm. I still remember how he took my outstretched right hand in both of his and held it firmly and how his eyes, which were still as bright and as piercing as ever, gazed into mine. He was obviously moved, just as I was. I could hear it in his voice." (The Young Hitler I Knew: 1953)

"The Chancellor preceded me to the lift. We went up to the second floor where he had his rooms. We were alone. Once more Hitler took my hand, gazed at me for a long time and said, 'You are just the same as you always were, Kubizek. I should have recognized you immediately anywhere." (Ibid.)

Hitler said it was not the right time for a heart-to-heart.

"I no longer have a private life as in the old days, and can't do just what I want like other people. I'd like to stroll across the old [Danube] bridge with you once again. But that's no longer possible. Wherever I go I'm surrounded. Of course, I will come to see you [in Eferding], Kubizek but my visit will be for you alone. Then we will go strolling along the Danube. I can't manage it here, they don't leave me alone."

Kubizek told him that since 1920 he had been a municipal employee, a civil servant, and was working as a town clerk.

"Town clerk," Hitler said, "what's that? So you've become a civil servant, a pen-

pusher! That's not the right thing for you. What has happened to your music?"
Kubizek explained that the outbreak of WW1 had ruined his career.
Hitler offered to help him with his musical career saying "You won't end your days
as a pen pusher!" He asked him to "write out a report" detailing everything he
wanted from him, but when Kubizek said he had no personal request save for the
Fuhrer to sign a few postcards, Hitler was astonished.
It was obviously something new to him.

STILL HANDSOME: Kubizek and Hitler held hands
at Richard Wagner's grave

The conversation moved on to Kubizek's family.
"Three sons!" Hitler shouted, impressed. "So you've got three sons. I have no
family. I am alone. But I should like to look after your sons." (Ibid.) He was pleased
that they were all musically gifted and that two of them were also clever
draftsmen. [Hitler arranged for the musical studies of Kubizek's three sons at the
Bruckner Conservatory in Linz and his son Rudolf's drawings were examined by a
Professor at Munich's Academy].
They sat reminiscing for a good hour. A dewy-eyed Kubizek spread the letters,
postcards and drawings Hitler had given him on the table. He was surprised to see
the number of mementos and paid particular attention to the water color of the
Postlingberg. He said there were certain clever painters who could copy his water

colors so precisely that they could not be distinguished from the original.
As there had already been attempts by the Nazi Party to confiscate Kubizek's mementos of Hitler, he asked what he should do. "These documents are your own personal property," Hitler answered, "No one can claim them from you."

Reminiscences

Shortly after their meeting in Linz, the Nazi Party approached Kubizek to see if he would write the story of his friendship with their boss. He agreed and in 1938, he wrote two short propaganda booklets called Reminiscences about his teenage years with Hitler. His writing was heavily edited by the Nazi Party to show the Fuhrer in a "normal" light.

During the writing period, Kubizek became familiar with several of Hitler's Nazi cronies. Martin Bormann, Hitler's personal secretary, got in contact to demand Kubizek hand over all his documents on Hitler which he refused to do.

He had developed a formula to keep Nazi officials off his back. If they demanded something of him he did not like, he would say "I need to speak to Hitler personally about this matter", and they would immediately back off.

Kubizek remembered meeting Deputy Fuhrer, Rudolf Hess with pleasure. When he arrived in Linz to help him with his memoir of Hitler, he sent a Mercedes to fetch him for a rendezvous at the Bergbahn Hotel.

"Rudolf Hess and Frau Winifred Wagner were the most fully informed about Hitler's youth and, consequently, about me. The Minister [Hess] invited me to lunch which was served on the hotel's terrace. After the meal, I had to recount to him all my memories in great detail. I had the feeling that, in a real, human way, Rudolf Hess was much closer to Hitler than many others." (The Young Hitler I Knew: 1953)

Hitler's deputy asked him if the Fuhrer had any sense of humor when he was young.

Hess said: "One feels the lack of it. He was capable of loving and admiring, hating and despising, all with the greatest seriousness. One thing he could not do was to pass over something with a smile," Hess said. (Ibid.)

[Rudolf Hess had been one of Hitler's regular lovers since their imprisonment together in Landsberg prison].

Heart thudding

Kubizek's "greatest desire" was fulfilled in July 1939 when he made his first pilgrimage to Bayreuth music festival, an annual favorite of Hitler's. As young men in Linz and Vienna they dreamt of going to the opera there.

"My heart was thudding as I opened the envelope. By the command of the Reich Chancellor, I was invited to the Richard Wagner Festival in Bayreuth. I was to report to Herr Kannenberg in Haus Wahnfried on July 25, 1939." (Bloch/Kubizek: 2013)

The Festival opened with The Flying Dutchman followed by Gotterdammerung on August 2, but as he prepared for his journey home to Eferding, he was disappointed that he had not met Hitler. Then one of the Nazi officials in Bayreuth suggested it would be a good idea for him to stay on another day and Kubizek understood the hint.

The following day, an SS officer came to fetch him for a trip to see Hitler at Haus Wahnfried.

"There stood Frau Winifred Wagner [Richard Wagner's daughter] in lively conversation with Reich Minister Hess. Indeed there was a preponderance of military personalities present and it struck me that the general situation was very strained. I felt very out of place in this tense atmosphere and the same sinking feeling, like stage fright, that I had experienced in the Hotel Weinzinger in Linz came back to me." (Ibid.)

With his heart "beating wildly" a starry-eyed Kubizek prepared a few words of thanks for the Fuhrer.

"His bright eyes shine with the pleasure of seeing me again and he comes towards me with a beaming face. Now he takes my right hand in both of his and wishes me welcome. This heartfelt greeting moves me so much that I can hardly speak." (The Young Hitler I Knew: 1953)

"Now we are talking in just the same way as we had done in our youth about all that enchanted us. Hitler then spoke of his plans to make Richard Wagner's work available to the greatest possible number of the German people."

Holding hands

Hitler reproached him for not coming to Germany sooner and Kubizek explained that as an "Austrian subject", prior to 1938, he would have needed a passport to come to Germany.

Apparently Hitler laughed heartily and said: "Yes, politically you were always a child, Gustl!" They walked through French doors and down steps to Richard Wagner's tomb.

"Hitler took my hand and I could feel how moved he was. It was quite still; nothing disturbed the solemn peace."(The Young Hitler I Knew: 1953)

Hitler broke the silence: "I am happy that we have met once more on this spot which always was the most venerable place for us both."

Kubizek reflected on the difference in their circumstances. "Whoever had known us both in those days in Vienna must have been certain that my future was predictable. After finishing at the Conservatory, I would start my career as an opera conductor, a career to which my early successes pointed. It must have seemed equally certain that Adolf, with his purposeless studies and his disdain for all professional training, would turn out a failure. Now fate had given its verdict. Here at Richard Wagner's tomb stood, hand-in-hand, the two poor unknown students from the dark back room of the Stumpergasse. And what were they now?" (Ibid.)

"The 'dead cert' was a little insignificant clerk in a small Austrian town who also dabbled in music, and the other had risen to be the Chancellor of the Reich. And what did the future have in store for us? Only one thing could be safely predicted: while the one would remain in his obscurity, whatever might happen, the other would go down in history."

Kubizek reminded Hitler of "his prophetic trance" in Linz where he saw his own future for the first time after they had watched a performance of Rienzi. Hitler

remembered it well and said: 'In that hour it began'."
He then said it would be a bad idea for them to meet at his home on the
Obersalzberg [the Berghof], so he had given orders that Kubizek should always be
able to come to Bayreuth when he was there. "I should like you to be always here
with me," he said. (Ibid.)
"He stood at the garden gate and waved to me as I went. Soon I heard the cheers of
the crowds greeting him in the Richard Wagnerstrasse, the Chancellor was leaving
Bayreuth to fly to Berlin."

Stay with me always
The two men met for the last time in July 1940 in Bayreuth. "He came towards me
with both hands outstretched. He wore a simple gray-green tunic and his face was
fresh and sunburnt. His delight seemed to be even deeper, more heartfelt. Hitler
took me aside and we stood alone while the other guests continued their
conversations at a distance." (Bloch/Kubizek: 2013)
Hitler said: "This year, this is the only performance I can see. But it can't be helped,
there's a war on. This war is holding up our work of reconstruction for many
years. It is a shame. After all I have not become the Chancellor of the Greater
German Reich to make war."
By this time, Germany had already invaded both Austria and Poland.
Hitler continued: "This war is robbing me of my best years. You know my plans,
Kubizek, you know how much I still want to build. And here I have to stand by and
watch the war robbing me of my best years. It's a shame. Time doesn't stand still.
We are growing older, Kubizek. Not many more years and it will be too late to do
what remains to be done."
Hitler said finally: "When that moment comes, I shall call you and then you must
stay with me always." (Ibid.)
When the Gotterdammerung came to an end; Kubizek walked slowly down the
drive leading from the theater and noticed the street was roped off. A few minutes
later, a motor column approached along the street and he saw Hitler standing
erect in his car. The column halted and the car approached him. "Hitler smiled at
me, leaned out of his car and, taking my hand, shook it heartily, saying, 'Auf
Wiedersehen'." It would be the last time they ever met.
During the war, Kubizek continued to use "his formula" of demanding to speak to
Hitler personally to keep the SS and other Nazi officials off his back for a further
two years.
In 1942, the man who had always claimed to have no interest in politics, became a
member of the Nazi Party. He said later it was a "gesture of loyalty" to his old
friend. By that time, both the tide and WW2 had turned against Hitler.
In December 1945, he gathered his collection of postcards and other keepsakes
and concealed them carefully in the basement of his Eferding home. He was
arrested by the Allies, but when his house was searched, his Hitler documents and
paintings were never discovered. He had built a false wall in the basement of his
house to protect them.
Kubizek was held at Glasenbach prisoner camp, where he was interrogated by the
US Army Criminal Investigation Command, then imprisoned for 16 months

(released April 8, 1947) without ever being charged with breaking the law.

KUBIZEK'S INTERROGATION

In Glasenbach, he recalled some of the interrogations he was subjected to which usually ran along the the same lines (Bloch/ Kubizek: 2013)):
"You are a friend of Adolf Hitler's?"
"Yes."
"Since when?"
"Since 1904."
"What do you mean by that? At that time he was a nobody. How could you be his friend when he was still a nobody? What did you get out of it?"
"Nothing."
"But you admit that you were his friend. Did he give you money?"
"No."
"A car, a house?"
"Not that either."
"Did he introduce you to beautiful women?"
"Nor that."
"Did you see him often?"
"Occasionally."
"How did you manage to see him?"
"I just went to him."
"So you were with him. Really? Quite close?'
"Yes, quite close."
"Alone?"
"Alone."
"Without any guard?"
"Without any guard."
"So you could have killed him?"
"Yes, I could have."
"And why didn't you kill him?"
"Because he was my friend."

Most of Adolf Hitler's personal friends and acquaintances, who survived WW2, attempted to make money out of knowing him and August Kubizek was no exception.
His book The Young Hitler I knew (1953) was translated into several languages and became a bestseller. It included a selection of pictures, postcards and sketches given to him by the young Hitler between the years 1904 and 1909. He wrote in the book's epilogue: "Even though I, a fundamentally un-political individual, had always kept aloof from the political events of the period which ended forever in 1945, nevertheless no power on earth could compel me to deny my friendship with Adolf Hitler."
August Kubizek died aged 68 in Eferding, Austria in 1956.

CHAPTER 4: HITLER'S NEXT MALE COMPANION, REINHOLD HANISCH

THE YEARS FROM 1909 to 1913 are the least documented time of Adolf Hitler's life. It is assumed that like so many other vagrants in Vienna, he succumbed to a life of casual male prostitution in order to survive.

In November 1908, he was evicted from his room for non-payment of rent and found himself homeless.

In his book Mein Kampf (1925), he described this time in harrowing terms: "As the Goddess of Misery took me in her arms and so often threatened to break me, the Will to Resist grew, and in the end, the Will triumphed."

In early 1909, when he was 20 years old, Hitler picked up occasional work on building sites around Vienna. Records show that his employment usually ended in disaster.

He was run off one building site for antagonizing other workmen with his political speeches and bizarre behavior. He was run off another job with the threat that "if he appeared again he would be thrown off the scaffold". (Nizkor Project: 1943)

Without work, he sank lower and lower in the social scale and at times must have been on the verge of starvation. At other times, he found odd jobs carrying luggage, shoveling snow or running errands, but a large part of his time was spent in breadlines or begging on the streets. (Ibid.)

From 1909 to early 1913, Hitler lived in men-only homeless shelters run by charitable organizations. According to Jewish war reporter, H.R. Trevor Roper, "He appears to have used various addresses, including a flop house in the Meidling area and rooms in Simon Denk Gasse, but No. 27 Meldemannstrasse Men's Home remained his base until 1913, when he left Vienna for Munich, apparently to avoid military service in the Austro-Hungarian army."

Former Nazi, Ernst Hanfstaengl (The Missing Years: 1957) said many of these shelters were places where gay men went to find casual companions and male prostitutes went to make extra cash.

In December 1909, Hitler found a bed in a doss-house behind Meidling Station in Vienna. It was here that he met fellow vagrant, Reinhold Hanisch (b.1884-d.1937), a drifter from Bohemia, who became his occasional lover and business partner for the next seven months. Apart from August Kubizek, Hanisch remains one of the few witnesses to Adolf Hitler's five-year sojourn in the Austrian capital.

Thirty years after they first met [they met on December 21, 1909 Reinhold Hanisch's book, I was Hitler's buddy (1939) was published.

In it, he described his first impressions of the down-at-heel vagrant, who would one day become German dictator:

"On the very first day, there sat next to the bed allotted to me a man who had nothing on except an old torn pair of trousers, Hitler. His clothes were being cleaned of lice, since for days he had been wandering about without a roof and was in a terribly neglected condition."

"The neighbor on my right looked sad and so we asked him questions. For several days, he had been living on benches in the parks where his sleep was often disturbed by policemen. He had landed here [Meidling Men's Home] dead tired, hungry, with sore feet. His blue checked suit was turned lilac from the rain and the burning in the Asylum bleached it. We gave him our bread because he had nothing to eat. An old beggar standing nearby advised him to go to the convent in the Gumpenderferstrasse, where every morning between nine and ten, soup was given to the poor. We said this was 'calling on Kathie' because the name of the Mother Superior was Katherine."

DIPPING THE WICK: Hitler's portrait of his friend Hanisch

Hanisch said: "My neighbor's name was Adolf Hitler. He was awkward. The Asylum meant to him an entirely new world where he could not find his way, but we all advised him as best we could and our good humor raised his spirits a little. I was also calling on Kathie daily and we became close friends. He told us that he was a painter, an artist and had read quite a lot, that his father was a small custom's official in Braunau-am-Inn and that he had attended the Realschule in Linz. Now he had come to Vienna in the hope of earning a living here. His landlady had dispossessed him and he had found himself on the street without shelter."
"After he was forced out of his room, he had spent several evenings in a cheap coffee house in the Kaiserstrasse but now was entirely without money. For days, he hadn't eaten anything. One night, in his great distress he begged a drunk gentleman for a few pennies but the drunk man raised his cane and insulted him. Hitler was very bitter about this but I made fun of him saying. 'Look here, don't you know you should never approach a drunk?'"

Ian Kershaw (Hitler 1889-1936: 1998) said the men's home they stayed in was far from luxury: "The hostel was a night shelter offering short-term accommodation. A bath or shower, disinfection of clothes, soup and bread, and a bed in the dormitory were provided. But during the day, the inmates were turned out to fend for themselves. Hitler went in the mornings along with other destitutes to a nearby convent where the nuns doled out soup. Their time was otherwise spent visiting public warming-rooms, or trying to earn a bit of money."

"On one occasion, Hanisch took Hitler off to shovel snow, but without an overcoat, Hitler was in no condition to stick at it for long. Instead, he offered to carry bags for passengers at the Westbahnhof. But his appearance probably did not win him many customers." (Ibid.)

Life on the breadline continued to be very hard indeed and Hanisch described how, when the winter cold set in, their living conditions became even more difficult. Hitler and Hanisch continued the process of daily "calling on Kathie" to receive their welcome bowl of soup and afterward strolled to the Western Railway Station where they tried to find casual work.

Historian Bob Carruthers said: "All too frequently however, Hitler found no employment at all and he was lucky to receive a share of bread from his friend." (Hitler's violent youth: 2015)

Hanisch recalled how Hitler used to go with others to the shelter in Erdberg, which was endowed to Vienna by the Jewish Baron Koenigswarter, and the Asylum too, where Hitler occasionally lived was also a Jewish foundation.

From Erdberg, the two men sometimes went to Favoriten and then to Meidling, a two and a half hour round trip, just to get some bread and soup. That winter, Hitler had no overcoat and with only his thin jacket to warm him, he shivered with cold, was often blue and frostbitten and developed a constant cough. (I was Hitler's buddy: 1939)

When Hanisch heard Hitler had signed over his share of his orphan's pension to his older half-sister, Angela (so she would take care of Paula who was still aged only 13), he encouraged him to write to Angela in Linz to get some badly needed money. At least then he could buy himself an overcoat and he could buy some materials to begin painting.

Under Austrian legislation at the time, orphans of under twenty-four years of age, with no means of their own, were entitled to claim an orphan's pension amounting to one half of the widow's pension. Klara had received a pension of 100 crowns monthly after her husband's death; therefore, Adolf and Paula were entitled to 25 crowns a month each.

When the 50 kronen note arrived (from Angela), Hanisch advised Hitler to buy a secondhand coat in Vienna's Jewish quarter but Hitler was afraid he would be cheated there. Instead, the pair went together to the Dorotheum, a pawn shop operated by the Austrian government and there Hitler bought a dark winter overcoat for 12 kronen.

With the balance of the funds, he was able to move from the Asylum into Maennerheim men's home at 27 Meldemannstrasse. It was a big step up from living in squalor.

According to police registration files, Adolf Hitler, at the time unemployed and living off the sale of his paintings, lived in the Meldemannstrasse dormitory for 3 years from February 9, 1910 until May 24, 1913 when he finally moved to Munich. (Ibid.)

Bob Carruthers said Hitler's circumstances slowly improved and he was able to leave the world of night shelters behind him and transfer permanently to the comparative luxury of the model men's hostel.

The Meldemannstrasse dormitory built in 1905, was financed by a private charitable foundation and aimed at reducing the number of 'Bettgeher' [homeless people] in Vienna. (Hitler's violent youth: 2015)

"The six-floor dormitory was lit by gas lamps and even some electric light bulbs and in the bitter Viennese winters was heated by a modern steam heater. On the ground floor, there was a large mess hall where inexpensive meals could be had; there was also a reading room with a supply of daily newspapers and a library. The underground floor housed cleaning rooms, a luggage room, a bicycle storage room as well as shoemaker's and tailor's workshops. Moreover, the dormitory included a sick room with resident physician, a disinfection chamber for the de-lousing of new residents, washrooms, a shaving room and a bathroom with 16 showers and four bath tubs."

Each of the 544 residents was allocated a small cabin of his own measuring 5ft by 7ft. The cabins were unlocked each evening at 8pm and had to be vacated by 9am but they had a lockable door, a light bulb, a bed, a small table, a clothes hanger and a mirror. The weekly rent was 2.50 crowns. This made Meldemannstrasse a very attractive and affordable lodging place for unskilled laborers or journeymen artisans with an annual income of 1,000 crowns.

"When the dormitory first opened, the Viennese press praised it as 'fantastical quarters, a paradise on earth' and 'a wonder of elegance and inexpensiveness'. It must have felt like a heaven-sent oasis for Adolf Hitler who was slowly beginning to haul himself up from the lowest rungs of society."

Though Carruthers said: "It is typical of Hitler's ungrateful and hypocritical nature that his own life was revolutionized by the efforts of a charitable trust, yet years later, he himself in the pages of Mein Kampf maintained that charitable relief was 'ridiculous and useless'." (Ibid.)

In February 1910, Hanisch also moved into the Men's Home at Meldemannstrasse and began to act as Hitler's sales agent.

Paralysis of the will

In his book, Hanisch recalled asking Hitler if he had any skills he could use to make some money. Hitler told him he was an artist and, if necessary, he could fake some old masters to get some cash. (I was Hitler's buddy: 1939)

Hanisch suggested it would be better to paint picture postcards instead but Hitler was very reluctant at first because he said "he would need a permit" and without one "he did not want to end up in jail". He also complained that he was "tired and wretched and wanted to rest".

With a little persuasion, Hitler agreed to do some paintings and began to produce little copies of views of Vienna, which Hanisch then sold in taverns, fairs and to art dealers.

"We decided to work together and to share the money we earned," Hanisch said. But the man from Bohemia soon discovered that Hitler "was never an ardent worker, was unable to get up in the morning, had difficulty in getting started and seemed to be suffering from a paralysis of the will".

In fact, he said Hitler was very lazy and as soon as he made a small amount of money, he spent the next couple of days in a cafe eating cream cakes and reading newspapers.

Bob Carruthers noted that "This indolent attitude towards work would later drive his Third Reich subordinates to distraction. It seems for his entire adult life, he liked to sleep late and would constantly find excuses to put off dealing with problems or important work. There were frequent political debates in the men's home and Hitler was always ready to lay down his brush to take up an argument." (Hitler's violent youth: 2015)

Hanisch said the subjects which sparked Hitler's interest could be broadly grouped under the Volkisch [national] movement which had developed during the late 19th century in the German Empire. [Hanisch like Hitler held Austrian citizenship]. And because Hitler seemed to prefer giving lectures to actual work, Hanisch was obliged to nag him to speed up his output as the cards began to sell reasonably well in the Viennese taverns. (Ibid.)

But it seems Hitler preferred hanging around other men's night shelters rather than working.

Hanisch told Rudolf Olden, author of Hitler the Pawn (1936):

"Over and over again there were days on which he simply refused to work. Then he would hang around night shelters, living on the bread and soup that he got there, listening to parliament and discussing politics, often getting involved in heated controversies."

Driven to despair

Hanisch described his frustration: "I often was driven to despair by bringing in orders that he simply wouldn't carry out. At Easter, 1910, we earned forty kronen on a big order and we divided it equally. The next morning, when I came downstairs and asked for Hitler, I was told he had already left with [Josef] Neumann, a Jew. After that I couldn't find him for a week. He was sightseeing in Vienna with Neumann and spent much of the time in the museum. When I asked him what the matter was and whether we were going to keep on working, he answered that he must recuperate now, that he must have leisure, and that he was not a coolie." (I was Hitler's buddy: 1939)

Lothar Machtan (The Hidden Hitler: 2001) has suggested that Hitler's week with Josef Neumann involved more than just sightseeing. Hanisch was angered by Neumann who he described as "competition".

However, what transpired between Neumann and Hitler during this week was carefully guarded. They visited cultural spots in Vienna, museums and theaters, but this could not have occupied their entire week which led Machtan to draw the conclusion that Hitler and Neumann's relationship was more than a "normal friendship" and that Hanisch's frustration with the situation was a mask for his sexual jealousy.

The author also noted that the hostels at that time were breeding grounds for male prostitution, being filled with men desperate for survival.

Machtan said Hanisch himself was at ease among the homosexual community and that Hitler was far from alone among the 500 residents at the home; he made friends easily with the other men who, in turn, said Hanisch and Hitler had been "on very close terms". Hitler too had been very much at ease when he and August Kubizek were entertained (and fed) by a wealthy, gay businessman at the Hotel Kummer in Vienna in 1908; and he behaved as though he was already familiar with the sexual attention of older men.

In fact, the author suggested that Hitler made money as a male prostitute to supplement his paltry salary from the sale of his art; saying simply that "if he earned only a meager sum each year, and his friends at the hostel said he was not strapped for funds, he must have had an alternative income".

Hitler continued to be completely indifferent to women during his three years at the dormitory and continued to spurn their attention.

Reinhold Hanisch confirmed Hitler's peculiar moral code and said his friend "was too shy and awkward to have any success with women." (I was Hitler's buddy: 1939)

He also said that Hitler frequently spoke at length on the topic of love and marriage and had "very austere ideas about relations between men and women". He maintained that "if men only wanted to, they could adopt a strictly moral way of living".

Hanisch summed up Hitler's feelings on women as follows: "He often said it was the woman's fault if a man went astray and he used to lecture us about this, saying 'every woman can be had'." In other words, if every woman could be had, why bother with any of them?

Jewish advisers and friends

Reinhold Hanisch also said that during their time together in the Meldemannstrasse, Hitler "was not a Jew-hater". In fact, there were a number of Jews living in the dormitory with whom he was on excellent terms.

He said most of his paintings were sold to Jewish dealers who paid "just as much for them as the Aryans".

Also, during this time, Hitler sent two postcards to Dr. Bloch in Linz, who was also Jewish. One of these was a picture postcard of Vienna; and the other, a copy of the postcard which he had painted. On both of them he wrote of his deep gratitude to the doctor for caring for his mother Klara when she was dying of breast cancer. (Nizkor Project: 1943)

Hanisch said that during their relationship, Hitler himself looked Jewish. "I often joked with him that he must be of Jewish blood, since such a large beard rarely grows on a Christian's chin. Also he had big feet, as a desert wanderer must have."

Bob Carruthers (Hitler's violent youth: 2015) said that most of the future dictator's friends at Meldemannstrasse were indeed Jewish. These included a one-eyed blacksmith called Simon Robinsohn who often assisted Hitler "and since he was a beneficiary of an accident insurance annuity, he was sometimes able to spare a few pennies" and "Hitler often found a Jewish audience who listened to his political debates".

The author also said the Jewish salesman Josef Neumann with whom he had spent a romantic week in Vienna became a real friend to Hitler.

Neumann worked with another Jew who was buying old clothes and peddling them in the streets and he often gave Hitler the old clothes that he couldn't sell.

"Neumann was a good-hearted man who liked Hitler very much and who, in return, appears to have been highly esteemed by Hitler who said that Neumann was 'a very decent man' and even though he was often very much in want, he paid Hitler's debts if they were small." (Ibid.)

Apparently, the two men had long debates about Zionism.

"Neumann stated his position was that if the Jews should leave Austria, it would be a great misfortune for the country for they would carry with them all the Austrian capital. Hitler countered Neumann with the assertion that the Jews were welcome to leave but the money would obviously be confiscated as it was not Jewish but Austrian."

They were on such good terms that when Neumann eventually went to Germany in 1910, he tried to persuade Hitler to join him but he could not make up his mind and eventually the second-hand clothes salesman stepped out of the pages of history. (Ibid.)

Years later, Hanisch would try to use Hitler's friendships with these Jewish men in Vienna to damage the German dictator's reputation.

But his bid to get revenge on his old partner would have dire consequences and like so many of Hitler's personal enemies who had embarrassing information about him, Hanisch would eventually die in a prison cell.

Lover's quarrel

Both the personal and working relationship between Hanisch and Hitler proved difficult to sustain. As with all of Hitler's relationships, Hitler's "sales agent" discovered that as well as being lazy, his friend did not have a sense of humor and was subject to outbursts of temper when he could not get his own way.

Hanisch recalled that Hitler "worshiped" Richard Wagner, not just as a musician but as a revolutionary who had taken part in the struggles of 1848 and apparently he identified with Wagner's ceaseless struggle to find an "artistic patron" in King Ludwig II [a monarch who was openly gay].

When, as a joke, Hanisch said Mozart was a greater composer than Wagner, it sent Hitler into one of his paroxysms of rage. These rages were then always followed by a lengthy, ill-tempered lecture.

Hitler believed Wagner operas were actually "the best form of the divine" but Hanisch noted sarcastically that "everything about Hitler was somehow exaggerated." (Hitler's violent youth: 2015)

By 1910, Hitler could no longer afford the opera tickets which had once been so important to him and this made him depressed.

In his book (I was Hitler's buddy: 1939), the Bohemian attempted to describe some of Hitler's depressive episodes and said he had never seen "such hopeless letting down in distress".

"It was a miserable life and I once asked him what he was really waiting for. The answer he gave me was: 'I don't know myself'."

He also said that after Hitler blew up in a rage, he often broke down in hysterical tears when he was unable to cope. Hanisch implied that one such episode was due to the end of their relationship:

"Hitler had noticed that I was trying to get rid of him because of his laziness. I knew that he was an irascible person and I was afraid he would find me no matter where I went. If he lost his place in the Night Asylum because of his laziness, I was afraid he would descend on me and be a burden. For these reasons, I had been living under an assumed name."

Breaking up

On August 4, 1910 Reinhold Hanisch was reported to the Vienna police by another dormitory resident, Siegfried Loeffner, who had taken over Hanisch's job as Hitler's sales agent.

Through Loeffner, Hitler accused Hanisch of withholding some of the money he had received for a detailed watercolor painting of the Viennese parliament. [Unknown to Hitler, Hanisch had served seven months in prison for theft in Berlin in 1908. He had moved to Vienna to start a new life.]

On August 5, 1910 Hitler made an official complaint against the man he knew as "Fritz Walter".

ACT OF DARKNESS: One of Hitler's many paintings of the Austrian parliament

When police discovered that Hanisch had been using a false name (which was illegal in Austria), they took more interest in the dispute.

Hitler told police: "Since he was destitute, I gave him the pictures I painted to sell. He regularly received fifty per cent of the proceeds from me. For about two weeks, Hanisch did not return to the Home for Men, and stole from me the picture of

parliament, valued at fifty kronen, and a water color, valued at nine kronen."
(spartacus-educational.com: 2015)
As Hanisch denied the charges, Hitler agreed to testify against him, and on August 11, 1910 the Viennese court sentenced him to seven days in prison.
When he was found guilty, Hanisch shouted: "When and where will we meet again to make a settlement?"
Many years later, Hanisch could not help saying bitchily (I was Hitler's buddy: 1939): "Hitler's paintings were shoddy trash done with very little love for the work".

Continuing feud
The feud between the two men seems to have continued for the next 18 months. In order to secure a new revenue source, Hanisch began painting his own pictures and became Hitler's direct competitor.
He started to supply the Jewish frame dealer, Jakob Altenberg and others with his own pictures and postcards with moderate success.
Hitler also supplied Altenberg with paintings which he used to fill the empty frames in his shop window. [When Hitler came to power in Germany, Altenberg's shop was "Aryan-ized" and he was left with a small pension to live on. He escaped deportation as a Jew from Austria because his wife was Aryan].
In early 1912, Hitler was reported to the police by an "anonymous person" because of his unauthorized use of the title "academic painter" and he was warned by authorities not to use it as it implied that he had a university education.
It is most likely that the painter, Karl Leidenroth, who also lived in the men's dormitory had reported Hitler, at Hanisch's suggestion, as the two men had become friends.

Marriage
Reinhold Hanisch left Vienna shortly afterward but his involvement in Hitler's life was far from finished. He served in the Austro-Hungarian army during WW1, but returned to Vienna in July 1918 with his fiancee, Franziska Bisurek. (spartacus-educational.com: 2015)
They married the same year and lived in Vienna's 20th district. The house they rented belonged to the parents of a railroad conductor, Franz Feiler, who earned money on the side as a picture collector, and for whom Hanisch supplied paintings. The business between the two men was not always legal and in July 1923, Hanisch was sentenced by Vienna's district court to three months' imprisonment for theft. From that point onward, his life seems to have gone downhill and his wife divorced him in 1928.

Jewish associates
When Hitler became a political celebrity in Germany, Hanisch tried to make money from their former relationship. He painted fake "Hitler pictures" and sold them in Vienna with a good deal of success. He was also paid handsomely for the interviews he gave [about Hitler] to German and international newspapers in which he did his best to belittle his former partner.

With Hitler's appointment as Chancellor in the spring of 1933, Hanisch's value for giving interviews increased.

The Bavarian anti-Nazi Journalist, Konrad Heiden, who was writing a Hitler biography, turned to him for information as he was the only known witness to Hitler's Vienna period. [August Kubizek's story came later with Reminiscences in 1938 and The Young Hitler I Knew in 1953].

In his interviews, Hanisch said Hitler was both lazy and a liar. "I've never seen him do hard work, yet I heard that he had labored as a construction worker. Contractors employ only strong and powerful people."

Hanisch also maintained that during his many overblown speeches, Hitler had repeatedly opposed the Social Democratic Party and, unlike the other men's home residents, always came down on the side of the Austrian State.

He also stressed that Hitler had good relationships with the Jews in the men's home and the Jewish art dealers in Vienna. In fact, he said "Hitler associated almost exclusively with Jews". He also revealed that along with painting postcards, Hitler had pursued "other money making schemes which were not always legal". Hanisch told Heiden that on one occasion, Hitler and one of his Jewish friends tried to sell ordinary paste as anti-freeze, but only in summer, so the fraud would not be discovered. In effect, Hitler's former intimate did everything he could to damage the Nazi leader.

Hitler fakes

He also tried to take financial advantage of his former partner. In 1930, Hanisch started working as a watercolor painter and often sold the work he produced as pieces from "Hitler's Vienna days". He sometimes painted flowers in the style of Olga Wisinger-Florian which he also sold as Hitler originals.

To cover up the fraud, he asked his friend, Karl Leidenroth to authenticate the forgeries, which he did for a small share of the profits, but this scam only worked for a year or so and in May 1932 Hanisch was sentenced to three days in jail for fraud.

The following year, Franz Feiler, the son of Hanisch's former landlord, (who Hanisch had worked with) began to work as Hitler's Viennese political emissary. Feiler was instructed to buy both genuine and fake Hitler pictures in Vienna. He then brought them to Berchtesgaden where they were examined by Hitler. Then the pictures were either destroyed or transferred to the archives of the Nazi Party HQ in Munich.

During Easter1933, Feiler brought Hitler some of Hanisch's fake paintings and Hitler instructed him to file a complaint for fraud against him which he did on his return to the Austrian capital.

On July 6, 1933, Viennese authorities sentenced Hanisch to several months in prison but he continued to forge Hitler pictures immediately after his release. Three years later, on December 2, 1936, Vienna's regional court sentenced Hanisch for the last time, once again, for fraud.

Bob Carruthers (Hitler's violent youth: 2015) has claimed that the fraudster was arrested in Vienna in 1936 because Hitler had heard about "Hanisch's memoirs", a book about their time together in the Viennese dormitory, and knew that his old adversary was attempting to find a publisher.

In 1937, Reinhold Hanisch was arrested by the SS and sent to Buchenwald concentration camp. The official report relating to his death stated that he died of pleurisy which had developed quickly over three days. Some historians have claimed that he died following a heart attack.

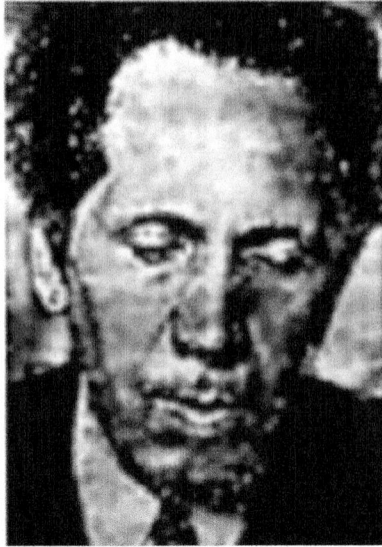

BEATEN MAN: Hanisch discovered it was a very bad idea to make an enemy of Hitler; he died in prison in 1937

Reinhold Hanisch died a broken man on February 2, 1937 after two months incarceration.
Hitler biographer, Joachim Fest (Inside Hitler's Bunker: the Last Days of the Third Reich: 2005) has claimed that Hitler had his old foe murdered to prevent him telling the world what he knew about him.
Hanisch's memoir of Hitler appeared posthumously and was serialized in 1939 in The New Republic. It also appeared as the book, I was Hitler's buddy, in the same year.
Hanisch's fakes continued to occupy Hitler's staff for several years after his death. In October 1942, Hitler ordered Heinrich Himmler to destroy three fake Hitler pictures painted by Hanisch as well as other documents relating to him discovered by the SS.

Cashing in
There is little knowledge of what happened to Hitler over the next two years while he continued to live at the Meldemannstrasse dormitory. In his autobiography Mein Kampf (1925), he provided very few details about his daily life there, though several dormitory residents tried to "cash in" by publishing their recollections of him.

They all reported that he read newspapers each morning in the non-smoking area of the reading room where he also painted, discussed politics and on occasion, gave some of his trademark rambling speeches.

One of the authors cashing in was Josef Greiner, an itinerant worker who published two slim volumes of memoirs in 1938 and 1947. Greiner claimed that at some point, Hitler attempted to rape one of his artist's models but he was very vague on the details; he also claimed that Hitler contracted syphilis from a Leopolstack prostitute but nobody has ever corroborated these lurid claims. (Hitler's violent youth: 2015)

Another author, this time anonymous, fed derogatory stories to a Czech newspaper in the early 1930s accusing Hitler of being a liar and fraud who was deceiving the German people about his true character. These may have been written by a vengeful Reinhold Hanisch before his death.

Pederasty and theft

Psychiatrists Dr. Walter C. Langer et al have attempted to understand why Hitler remained in Vienna for so many years. They concluded that both his laziness and his enjoyment of men only company were most probably the two major factors involved.

"He lived in a flophouse which was known to be inhabited by men who lent themselves to homosexual practices, and it was probably for this reason that he was listed on the Vienna police record as a 'sexual pervert'."

"It is perfectly clear from what Hanisch writes [in his memoirs] that with a very small amount of effort he could have made a fair living and improved his condition by painting water-colors. He refused to make this effort and preferred to live in the filth and poverty which surrounded him. There must have been something in this that he liked, consciously or unconsciously [...] especially as he had such a deep love for Germany and could have gone there at any time. It is also unclear why he left Vienna precisely when he did, unless there is some truth in the rumors that he fled Vienna to avoid arrest for pederasty and theft." (Nizkor Project: 1943)

The psychiatric experts said Hitler's feelings of loss and guilt over his mother's death, the intense hatred he felt for his father, and his confusion over his own sexual identity would eventually lead him into strange forms of sadomasochism and alarming sexual perversions which later displayed themselves as anti-Semitism ... "he probably derived great masochistic satisfaction from his miserable life in Vienna, and it was not until his perversion [coprophilia] became full-blown and he realized its implications that he fled to Munich at the beginning of 1913."

HITLER'S UNKNOWN RELATIONSHIP IN MUNICH

In 1913, while he was still living at the men's home in Meldemannstrasse, Adolf Hitler forged a new relationship with a man four years younger than him called Rudolf Hausler.

The two men became so close that they decided to leave Vienna to set up home together in a Munich apartment which they would share for almost one year.

Only sketchy details are known of Hitler's companion, despite the efforts of

German-Austrian author, Brigitte Hamann (Hitler's Vienna: 2010) who interviewed members of Hausler's family.
She uncovered the existence of the usual postcards and miniature paintings given as gifts by Hitler but Hausler's elderly daughter said she knew little or nothing of her father's relationships before his marriage.

Rudolf Hausler was born in 1893 in Vienna and graduated with a commercial apprenticeship in 1910. Two years later, he became unemployed, and after an argument with his father, was thrown out of the family home.
Though he remained on bad terms with his father, he continued to visit his mother in secret when his father was away at work. For a short time, he became a vagrant and ended up living at the Meldemannstrasse men's home where he stayed from February 4 to May 25, 1913 and where he first met and befriended Adolf Hitler. (Metapedia.de: 2015)

DANDY: Rudolf Hausler poses in his Austro-Hungarian WW1 uniform

By February 1913, Hitler was already an old hand at hostel-living and he seems to have taken the younger man under his wing. By this time, Reinhold Hanisch, Josef Neumann and the other men Hitler spent time with had already left the city, so there were few witnesses to this new and burgeoning relationship.

It seems Hitler was still trying to dodge the military draft and after only a few months together in Meldemannstrasse, Hausler and Hitler decided to move to Munich where they intended to rent a small apartment.

On May 25, 1913 Hitler and Hausler left Vienna and found themselves lodgings in the Schleissheimer district in Munich and between May 1913 and February 1914, they shared a small room in a house owned by a master tailor called Josef Popp. Hitler continued to freelance as a street painter; only working when he needed to pay his rent or needed to eat.

"While Hitler pursued an idle and bohemian lifestyle as a postcard painter, Hausler worked as a casual laborer." (Ibid.)

There is some evidence that Hausler also tried to sell Hitler's paintings but without much success as the market in Munich for such "kitsch" work was not as good as in Vienna. In February 1914, Hausler left the room they shared after a ferocious argument with Hitler.

Years later, their Munich landlord, Josef Popp, told journalists that the younger man moved out because Hitler's late night monologues and constant pacing up and down after dark drove him close to insanity. He could take it no longer.

But Popp also said that Hausler was only absent for about four days, and on his return, rented the room next door to Hitler's. They lived next door to each other for the next six months.

When WW1 began, Hausler returned to Austria [on August 3, 1914] to enlist in the Austro-Hungarian army while Hitler remained behind in Munich in the hope he could serve in the war for Germany.

The two men lost contact during the war years and may well have fallen out over Hausler's decision to fight for Austria.

Hitler remained in contact with their Munich landlord, Josef Popp, sending him regular requests to keep newspaper cuttings relating to his regiment and any mention of awards or commendations he [Hitler] had received.

Meanwhile, Rudolf Hausler served with distinction for the Austro-Hungarian army, becoming a platoon leader while fighting in both Romania and Italy.

He married in post-war Austria and he and his wife had a daughter called Marianne.

By 1921, he was working as an independent merchant in Vienna but from that time onward, seems to have changed his occupation every few years. His wife (of whom little is known) died in 1929.

From 1927 to 1933, Hausler was a bank clerk in Vienna, and from 1933 to 1937, he worked as the managing director of a hotel on the Bishop Koppe in Bohemia. Apparently, in 1933, he attempted to contact Hitler who had become German Chancellor but failed to get any response from him. (Ibid.)

In 1938, during the build-up to WW2, he was working as a manager in a sugar factory and joined the Nazi Party. Soon afterward, he reconnected with Hitler and was quickly promoted to a senior Nazi position.

Between1938 and 1944, he worked as leader of the Viennese branch of the German Labor Front (DAF)and became responsible for allocating working class apartments to trade union members.

Records show that in 1944, Hausler was expelled from the Nazi Party but no official reason was given. He survived the war, after which he went back to living and working in obscurity in Austria.

Unlike so many others who profited from knowing Hitler, he never wrote "memoirs" of his time with the German leader and took his secrets with him to the grave. Rudolf Hausler died in Vienna in 1973.

CHAPTER 5: HITLER'S WWI BOYFRIEND, ERNST SCHMIDT

ADOLF HITLER should have registered for military service by the summer of 1910 but he was unwilling to serve in the Austrian army; and on more than one occasion, he ignored his call-up papers. It took three years for the authorities to catch up with him. Under pressure and fearing a jail sentence, he did attend his third call-up and reported to the army office in Salzburg in the summer of 1913. When he finally did his medical, he was rejected for being: "Unfit for combatant and auxiliary duty, too weak. Unable to bear arms." (spartacus-educational.com: 2015) Hitler felt humiliated.

Later in 1913, he volunteered for the German army and recalled getting his acceptance letter: "I opened the document with trembling hands; no words of mine can describe the satisfaction I felt. Within a few days, I was wearing that uniform which I was not to put off again for nearly six years."

When he heard of the outbreak of war, he remembered his emotions: "falling on my knees, [I] wholeheartedly thanked heaven that I had been granted the happiness to live at this time." (Ibid.)

The Nizkor Project authors said it was inevitable that he would seek enlistment in the German army rather than in the Austrian army and it was also inevitable that he would be a good and obedient soldier.

"Unconsciously, it was as though he was a little boy who was playing the part of a man while his mother stood by and watched him. Her future welfare was his great concern [even though she was already dead] and in order to prove his love, he was willing, if need be, to sacrifice his own life for her."

Hitler joined the 1st Company of the 16th Bavarian Reserve Infantry Regiment and served as a dispatch runner. He soon befriended fellow dispatch runner, Ernst Schmidt, who became his army boyfriend.

Other members of this regiment included Rudolf Hess (but only for a short time as he went off to train as a pilot), Hans Mend who was also a dispatch runner and Max Amann all of whom would play important roles in Hitler's future. Rudolf Hess became Hitler's lover while they were incarcerated in Landsberg Prison in 1924 and a casual lover thereafter.

Army role

During WW1, Hitler carried messages from his regimental headquarters to the front-lines and from the front lines back to HQ. He never spent time in the trenches and he never volunteered for combat duty at the front.

His autobiography, Mein Kampf(1925) makes no mention of his exact duties, probably because most soldiers viewed the job of dispatch runner as a "shirker's post". (spartacus-educational.com: 2015)

But the outbreak of WW1 in 1914 saved Hitler. It gave him something to do; it offered him a meager salary and it provided him with an opportunity to prove that he could succeed at something.

Most important of all, the outbreak of WW1 allowed Hitler to continue the homosexual phase of his life, undisturbed, for a further six years.

"I was very much drawn to Hitler", Ernst Schmidt [during a 1932 newspaper interview about their time together in WW1].

Ernst Schmidt, Hitler's army boyfriend was the son of a miller, born in Wurzbach, southern Germany, on December 16, 1889. After leaving school, he became a painter and decorator. He qualified in 1907 and according to his own account, spent his journeyman's time working "in various parts of Germany, Switzerland, France and Italy". (Ibid.)

On August 6, 1914, he joined the same regiment as Adolf Hitler. In the first few weeks of the war, Schmidt became a dispatch runner with Hitler and from then on, the two men became inseparable.

Lothar Machtan, author of The Hidden Hitler (2001) said: "Employed as regimental runners, they jointly delivered one message with such efficiency, or so we are told, that from November 1914 on, they were permanently assigned to regimental headquarters as so-called combat orderlies. As such, they had more freedom within the military hierarchy than other enlisted men. They were invariably to be seen as a couple, not only when jointly delivering regimental orders to brigade or battalion, but off duty behind the lines."

Hans Mend, a fellow WW1 dispatch runner [interviewed by a member of the German resistance, Friedrich Alfred Schmid-Noerr, in December 1939] said Ernst Schmidt and Adolf Hitler had a sexual relationship which lasted for almost six years between 1914 and 1919.

Glorious meaning of a male community

Even though they had once been army buddies, by 1939, Hans Mend hated Hitler with a passion. In 1931, he had written a pamphlet about Hitler's "brave exploits" during the war called Hitler in the Field of Battle 1914-1918, but he had never received the royalties he felt he was due. To get his revenge, he decided to "come clean with the truth" to damage Hitler's reputation, saying that everything favorable he had previously written was done under duress.

He said this duress had come directly from Nazi Party officials.

Apparently, Mend told Hitler to his face that he would one day "let the world know what he used to be" [implying he would reveal Hitler's homosexuality].

Indeed, Hitler once said that his time with his regiment had taught him "the glorious meaning of a male community".

In his 1939 interview with Schmid-Noerr, Mend said Hitler only joined the army for food and money. "He [Hitler] was unemployed in Munich at the time [outbreak of WW1], and his intention had simply been to get into the army to have a square meal again."

"Private Ernst Schmidt, now a master builder at Garching, near Munich, with whom Hitler had been friendly because he had sometimes worked on building sites with him, was his special pal. The others he was friendliest with were

Privates Tiefenbock, now the owner of a coal merchant's in Munich and Wimmer, now working as a Munich streetcar employee. All three were runners at regimental headquarters."

GLORIOUS TIMES: Ernst Schmidt, Hitler and Karl Lippert

"The only one who had volunteered for combat duty was the Jew, Karl Lippert, a commercial traveler by profession; he later became a clerk at Nazi Party headquarters, where he worked from 1934 on, and still does, so far as I know, not being subject to the Jewish laws. The battalion adjutant was Lieutenant Gutmann, a Jewish typewriter manufacturer from Nuremberg, now emigrated, whom Hitler made up to whenever he wanted preferential treatment of some kind." (Schmid-Noerr: 1939)

Womanish characteristics

As for the subject of Adolf Hitler and women, Hans Mend said: "We noticed that he [Hitler] never looked at a woman. We suspected him of homosexuality right away, because he was known to be abnormal in any case. He was extremely eccentric and displayed womanish characteristics which tended in that direction."

"In 1915, we were billeted in the Le Febre brewery at Fournes. We slept in the hay. Hitler was bedded down at night with Schmidt, his male whore. We heard a rustling in the hay. Then someone switched on his electric flashlight and growled, 'Take a look at those two nancy boys!' I myself took no further interest in the matter."(Ibid.)

Former Nazi, Ernst Hanfstaengl (The Missing Years: 1957) agreed with Mend's assessment and said Hitler was nicknamed "Monk" because of his lack of interest in women. Apparently, when one of his soldier comrades asked him: "Haven't you ever loved a girl?" Hitler replied: "I've never had time for anything like that, and I'll never get around to it."

Crazy Adolf

During the war, Hitler received no packages or letters from anyone. This made him unique. And at Christmas time, when everyone else was receiving gifts and messages, he withdrew from the group and sulked moodily by himself. Christmas was the time of his mother's death and he never enjoyed it for the rest of his life. When his comrades encouraged him to join their group to share their packages, he always refused. (Nizkor Project: 1943)

Though he had his own little circle of friends such as Ernst Schmidt, Max Amann and a few others, he was generally unpopular with the men in his regiment who were wary of him and his odd behavior.

When Hitler did join the general group, he usually harangued other soldiers about political matters. Hans Mend said he was very soon nicknamed "crazy Adolf" by the men he came in contact with. "He struck me as a psychopath from the start. He often flew into a rage when contradicted, throwing himself on the ground and frothing at the mouth." (Schmid-Noerr: 1939)

Subservience

Another peculiarity noticed by his comrades was Hitler's "subservience to his superior officers". It seems that he went out of his way to court their good graces, offering to do their washing and other menial tasks much to the disgust of his comrades.

Hitler's odd behavior in the presence of high-ranking officers has been confirmed by several sources, including those who spoke to US intelligence in 1943. But as soon as these officers were out of earshot, Hitler immediately complained about them. Hans Mend simply said that Hitler had always been two-faced. "He always described himself as a representative of the 'class-conscious proletariat' and whenever he thought he was safe, he referred to his superiors as 'arrogant officers' and called them 'robber knights', 'highwaymen of the nobility', 'a clique of bourgeois exploiters' and 'those swine lie on horsehair mattresses, while we eat horseflesh soup'."

But when senior officers were nearby, apparently Hitler changed his tune and was very respectful.

Mend also said that Hitler was hypocrisy personified. "One of his faces was that of the self-important busybody that he impersonated to his superiors, and, if need be, to his comrades. When Hitler was off duty behind the lines or at headquarters and he heard that some success had been gained at the front, it was quite usual for him to burst in on the other men waving his arms and shouting, 'We've won! We've given the French (or British) another bloody nose!' But with his superiors he always played the ingratiating tell-tale as soon as he saw it might benefit him in some way. That's why his comrades were wary of him." (Schmid-Noerr: 1939)

The OSS report said that this subservience showed Hitler's desire to perform the feminine role in order to please his superiors. It was also part of his desire to find strong male figures he could "submit to".

Sexual bullying (or a small penis)

Nazi defector, Ernst Hanfstaengl (The Missing Years: 1957) claimed that Hitler became the victim of sexual bullying during WW1:: "Old army comrades, who had seen him in the wash-house, had noted that his genital organs were almost freakishly underdeveloped, and he doubtless had some sense of shame about displaying himself."

FOXY FELLAS: Ernst Schmidt, Max Amann (who became Nazi Party publisher in chief), Hitler and their dog Foxl at Fournes in Belgium

For decades, it was alleged that Hitler had lost his testicle at the battle of the Somme during WW1 but this was not the case; having only one testicle had been the case since his childhood. Indeed, one academic researcher who gained access to Hitler's medical files (from his time at Landsberg prison in 1924) revealed that Adolf Hitler suffered from a genital condition called "cryptorchidism" which meant that he only had one testicle, thus confirming the lyrics of one Allied propaganda song which sprang up during WW2.

"The Colonel Bogey March" included the line "Hitler has only got one ball, Goering has two but very small, Himmler has something similar, And poor old Goebbels has no balls at all."

It was originally composed to ridicule Hitler and other Nazi leaders but the comedians who came up with the lyrics had struck much closer to home than perhaps they ever knew. (MailOnline: 2015)

In 2015, German history professor, Peter Fleischmann who investigated Hitler's medical documents said Hitler had an "undescended right testicle" which withered and died when he was an infant. (Bild: 2015)

In fact, Ernst Hanfstaengl (The Missing Years: 1957) said Hitler's lack of endowment which his WW1 comrades had noticed may have resulted in Hitler's peculiar relationships with both men and women.

He said: "This must all be part of the underlying complex in his physical relations, which was compensated for by the terrifying urge for domination expressed in the field of politics."

COMRADES & MORE: Hitler (seated first left) with Ernst Schmidt (standing, first left) and other soldiers

Thigh injury

In October, 1916, Hitler's regiment was engaged at the Battle of the Somme and he was wounded in his left thigh when a shell exploded in the dispatch runners' dug-out, killing and wounding several of the men.

Hitler's lover, Ernst Schmidt was among the injured but did not require long-term medical attention.

By contrast, after treatment in a field hospital, Hitler was obliged to spend several months recovering in the Red Cross hospital at Beelitz, near Berlin.

Hitler missed the "glorious male community" he had enjoyed so much, and in January1917, he wrote to the regiment's adjutant, Captain Fritz Wiedemann, asking permission to return to the 16th Reserve Infantry so he could "serve once again with his former comrades".

He also wrote to his friend, Sergeant Max Amann to see if he could "use his influence" to get him reassigned to his "elective family".

Hitler was allowed to re-join his regiment (and lover Ernst Schmidt) on March 5, 1917. Eighteen months later (October 1918), Hitler was temporarily blinded in a British mustard gas attack and was recovering in hospital when he heard of Germany's surrender.

Hospital witnesses said that he went into a state of deep depression which included periods when he could not stop crying. He spent most of his time turned towards the hospital wall and for several days refused to talk to anyone. (spartacus-educational.com: 2015)

Once again, Hitler's efforts to succeed at something had ended in failure.

Suspicions over Hitler's war record

The Nizkor Project authors said that Hitler's service during WW1 was clouded in mystery like so much else in his life: "There are several things that have never been satisfactorily explained. The first is that Hitler spent four years in the same regiment but was never advanced beyond the rank of Private or Lance Corporal. The second is the Iron Cross First Class which he constantly wears. There is no mention of the award in the history of his regiment."

"It is alleged that his war record has been badly tampered with and that Kurt von Schleicher was eliminated during the Blood Purge [Night of the Long Knives, 1934] because he knew the true facts. [Otto] Strasser who served in the same division says that during the last months of the war, there were so many First Class Crosses being given out that General Headquarters was no longer able to pass on the merits of each individual case." (Ibid.)

Apparently, rank and file soldiers took advantage of the general melee and gave the medals to each other, then they forged the signatures of the commanding officers before sending the documents to the High Command.

"In favor of this explanation is the curious bond which exists between Hitler and his regimental sergeant-major, Max Amann who became the head of the Nazi publishing house Eher Verlag [Alternative Publisher], one of the most lucrative positions in the entire Nazi hierarchy and Amann was called to the position by Hitler." (Ibid.)

Hans Mend told German counter-intelligence that the awarding of Hitler's Second Class medal was also suspicious: "Hitler never had anything to do with guns from the time he joined us. He was never anything other than a runner based behind the lines at regimental headquarters." (Schmid-Noerr: 1939)

"Every two or three days he would have to deliver a message; the rest of the time he spent in the back, painting, talking politics, and having altercations."

Mend said it was Lieutenant Gutmann [who was Jewish] who got Hitler his 2nd Class medal at Christmas 1914. "Colonel Engelhardt was wounded and when he was carried to the rear, Hitler and Bachmann tended him behind the lines. Hitler contrived to make a big fuss about this exploit of his, so he managed to gain Lieutenant Gutmann's backing [to get a medal]."

Mend also hinted that Hitler's sexual activity with other soldiers especially Ernst Schmidt during the war had consequences:

"It was striking, after all, that a man who had served throughout WW1 from October 1914 to the very end should not have received any further promotion."

Once he had obtained political power, Hitler ordered that any embarrassing records concerning his life during WW1 be destroyed or kept under lock and key at Nazi Headquarters in Munich.

Pederastic practices with an officer

When he became Fuhrer, the fact that Adolf Hitler had only managed to rise to the rank of Corporal during WW1 caused him problems gaining the respect of Germany's army generals.

Egon Erwin Kisch, yet another dispatch runner during WW1, said: "Every old soldier knows that the rank of Lance Corporal is only brief and temporary, only a preliminary to more senior non-commissioned rank but a Lance Corporal who never makes sergeant in four years must be a very suspect type. Either he shirks commanding a squad, or he is incompetent to do so."

Historian Lothar Machtan, (Hidden Hitler: 2001) said bluntly that if Hitler had been promoted, he would not have been able to continue his sexual relationship with Ernst Schmidt.

DUBIOUS RECORD: Adolf Hitler wearing his Iron Cross award which was probably a fraud

"Why did Hitler remain a lance corporal throughout the war? His toadying to higher authority, if not his efficiency, should have earned him promotion. We are told that he was offered it but refused. It would probably be more correct to say that he could not bring himself to accept. As a non-com, he would sooner or later have been obliged to give up what had hitherto enabled him to tolerate war service so well, that is, Ernst Schmidt, his other faithful partners, a relatively safe existence in the rear echelon and a toleration of a homosexual lifestyle he could not have pursued as a non-commissioned officer."

His relationship with Schmidt was not exclusive and it seems Hitler enjoyed sexual encounters with other soldiers.

Herman Rauschning (Hitler Speaks: 1939) claimed that Hitler's military record contained a court martial which found him guilty of "pederastic practices with an officer" [perhaps with Rudolf Hess] and that it was for this reason that he was never promoted. Rauschning also claimed that in Munich after the war, Hitler was found guilty of a violation of paragraph 175 which dealt with homosexual activity.

Erich Ebermayer, a gay lawyer and writer who viewed Hitler's military files, confirmed that Hitler's long-term love affair with Schmidt was the reason for his lack of promotion.

In his diary, Ebermayer wrote: "According to the Fuhrer's military record, which was seen by Dr. Kulz, the former Reich Minister of the Interior, homosexual activities precluded Hitler from promotion to sergeant despite his bravery in action." (Ebermayer Diary: 1959)

Ebermayer also said that Hitler preferred the company of "men to whom he was personally attached" and with whom he could "pleasurably converse with shining eyes in humorous, cheerful vein".

Lothar Machtan offered the only "official explanation" for Hitler's lack of promotion which was a comment from one of his commanding officers that "he would never make a non-commissioned officer out of that neurotic fellow, Hitler". (Hidden Hitler: 2001)

Police surveillance

Police reports from Munich after WW1 also suggest that Hitler was pursued by officials because of his sexual orientation.

"According to a Munich police protocol from the early 1920s, a 22-year-old man called Joseph told police: 'I spent the whole night with him.' Another, Michael, who was 18, told them: 'I had been unemployed for months, and my mother and brother were always hungry, so, at his request, I accompanied the man to his home.' Another boy called Franz, said: 'He asked me if I'd like to stay with him and he told me his name was Adolf Hitler.'" (Hidden Hitler: 2001)

Historian, Lothar Machtan said these reports were collected by Otto von Lossow, a German army general who took part in suppressing the Beer Hall Putsch in 1923. He kept the Munich police file for years, as "a form of personal life insurance". If Hitler had attempted to push or intimidate him, he would have blackmailed him with the information. (Ibid.)

Of course, when Hitler became German leader, his school reports, army records and documents relating to his homosexuality were confiscated by the Nazi Party and then destroyed. So too were any family records which might embarrass him or undermine his authority. His medical files were also either destroyed or kept in the Nazi HQ safe in Munich.

Much later, during the Night of the Long Knives in 1934, those who remained a threat because they "knew too much" about his sexual history were imprisoned or murdered.

*GAME OVER: Hitler continued to wear his army uniform
after the war*

Post war era with Schmidt

At the end of WW1, Hitler and Schmidt returned to Munich together. Hitler was now approaching 30 years of age, without education, career or prospects; his only plans were to stay in the German army.

Hitler wrote in Mein Kampf (1925) "I went to the depot of my regiment, which was now in the hands of the Soldier's Councils. With my faithful war comrade, Ernst Schmidt, I came to Traunstein and remained there until the camp was broken up. In March 1919, we were back again in Munich."

Hans Mend told German counter-intelligence that he saw the men together several times immediately after the war. "I met Adolf Hitler again at the end of 1918. I bumped into him on the Marienplatz in Munich, where he was standing with his friend Ernst Schmidt. Hitler was then living in a hostel for the homeless at 29 Lothstrasse, Munich. Soon afterward, having camped at my apartment for several days, he took refuge at Traunstein barracks because he was hungry. He managed to get by as he often did in the future, with the help of his Iron Cross 1st Class and his gift of the gab." (Schmid-Noerr: 1939)

In January 1919, Mend said he ran into Hitler again at the same news stand. "I couldn't help feeling ashamed for 'Red Hitler', he looked so down at heel. Then, one evening, while I was sitting in the Rathaus Cafe with a girl, 'Adi' and his friend Ernst Schmidt came in. 'Hello, Ghost Rider,' Hitler said to me, 'do you know of some lodgings for the two of us?' I offered to put him up for the night out of charity. Afterward my girl told me, 'If you're friendly with people like that [homosexuals], I'm not going out with you any more.'" (Ibid.)

Ernst Schmidt and Hitler continued to spend time together in post-war Munich, mainly in run-down hostels while they lived off the charity of friends and army hand-outs. (spartacus-educational.com: 2015)

According to Schmidt, they attended the city opera when they could afford it: "We only bought the cheapest seats, but that didn't matter. Hitler was lost in the music to the very last note; blind and deaf to all else around him."

He said that Hitler had not yet given up hope of being an artist and during this period, he made contact with the well-known artist, Max Zaeper, to whom he "gave several of his works for expert appraisal" but nothing came of his efforts.

At the time, Hans Mend maintained that Hitler made persistent attempts to join the Communist Party and when they rejected him, he got his revenge by joining the right-wing Freikorps where he met one of his earliest political mentors, Colonel Epp. [Colonel Franz Ritter von Epp, a decorated war hero, supplied the 60,000 Reichmarks to the Nazi Party they needed to found their own propaganda newspaper: Volkischer Beobachter or National Observer which enabled their rise in Germany. Colonel Epp and Hitler later fell out and he died while awaiting trial at Nuremberg in 1947; aged 79.]

NIGHT TIME VISITOR: Ernst Schmidt visited the Berlin
Chancellery for late night suppers, together here in late 1933

Mend said, between 1919 to 1920, Adolf Hitler's political allegiances became fixed. "Next I heard that Hitler was appearing as a public speaker. So as not to run into him, I listened to him in secret at Geislgasteig. That was early in 1920. Later on, I heard him speak at the Circus Krone and in various beer cellars. Aha, I said to myself, Hitler's singing a very different song these days. 'Adi the Red' has changed color! He was soon able to call himself an 'officer instructor'. In that capacity, he visited all kinds of hostelries at night and came across Anton Drexler."

Then Hans Mend said Hitler immediately made use of the "burglar's tactic he later employed with such success" which entailed "sticking his foot in the door and refusing to yield until he was on the inside. That was how he managed to smash Drexler's party. And then he opened his own [political] shop with just seven men." (Schmid-Noerr: 1939)

Smear campaign

Ernst Schmidt shared Hitler's right-wing political opinions and in March 1920, he joined the German Worker's Party (GWP) the forerunner to the Nazi Party.

In 1922, he moved to Garching an der Alz, over sixty miles from Munich, where he became a master builder. He kept in touch with his old boyfriend Hitler and visited him at Landsberg Prison in May 1924, following the Nazi Party's failed coup against the Weimar Republic.

Schmidt also founded a local branch of the GWP in his area.

When Hitler's autobiography was published in 1925, he sent Schmidt a gilt-edged copy inscribed with a personal message.

In 1931, Schmidt joined the Nazi Party's Storm Troopers (SA) as a Staff Sergeant and rose to the rank of Captain. Then in 1932, when Hitler's political opponents distributed smear stories about him and his homosexuality, Schmidt swore several affidavits in his friend's defense, denying that they ever had a gay relationship.

Hitler rewarded him for his loyalty and discretion and soon "Schmidt was able to build himself a large house in Garching and to buy an automobile, the main symbol of social advancement at the time". (spartacus-educational.com: 2015)

DEJA VU: Just like WW1, except it is now Fournes 1940; Ernst Schmidt, Max Amann and Hitler (front row), the lowly Corporal has become their "Fuhrer"

Hitler also awarded Schmidt the Nazi Party's golden badge and used him to promote his own image as a brave soldier during WW1.

In 1937 the Munich Observer published an article called "Adolf Hitler and his front-line comrade" and quoted Schmidt as saying: "If the Fuhrer ever summoned me to perform some special task, I should abandon my job and everything else, and follow him."

In the lead up to WW2, Ernst Schmidt visited Hitler at the Reich Chancellery for late night suppers. He eventually became mayor of Garching, and in 1942, was appointed as district head of the Nazi Party.

After the war, he was arrested by the Allies and imprisoned so that a de-Nazification program could be carried out.

During one interrogation in 1948, Schmidt admitted that he had been the victim of several blackmail attempts concerning his relationship with Hitler. He referred to a man named Philipp Oberbuchner who had written several "anonymous letters of malicious content" but he said he had "refrained from preferring charges against him". (Ibid.) Ernst Schmidt died in1985 aged 96.

But what of Hans Mend, the WW1 dispatch runner who had openly spread smear stories about the German Fuhrer? The Hans Mend who told German counterintelligence: "He [Hitler] has always been a great actor. Not a word he uttered could be trusted. He lied whenever he opened his mouth, always did the opposite of what he said." (Schmid-Noerr: 1939)

Of course, Hitler and his SS thugs would eventually get their revenge on him. More of that later.

CHAPTER 6: LANDSBERG LOVE TRIANGLE

BY 1920, Adolf Hitler had finally discovered something he was actually good at, giving speeches and gaining followers for the fledgling Nazi Party. By this time, his homosexual lifestyle had become well established. The Nazi leadership (many of whom were also gay) had spotted his talent and appointed him as unofficial "education officer" or recruiting agent for the party. As a result, Hitler's over-inflated belief in himself grew and his new status also increased his opportunities to have casual sex with men. (The Surreal Reich: 2010).

Aware of Hitler's increasing political clout, German Chancellor, Engelbert Dollfuss had already compiled police dossiers and affidavits "documenting Hitler's arrests for sodomy" which the Gestapo allegedly seized and destroyed in 1938.

Nazi Party's gay foundations
Scott Lively and Kevin Abrams (Pink Swastika: 1995) noted that the very first meeting of the National Socialist German Workers' Party (Nazi Party) took place in a gay bar. They said: "At the door of the Bratwurstgloeckl, a tavern frequented by homosexual roughnecks and bully-boys, [Ernst] Roehm turned in and joined the handful of sexual deviants and occultists who were celebrating the success of a new campaign of terror."

"Their organization, once known as the German Worker's Party, was now called the 'Nationalsozialistische Deutsche Arbeiterpartei', The National Socialist German Worker's Party - the Nazis. Yes, the Nazis met in a gay bar. It was no coincidence that homosexuals were among those who founded the Nazi Party. In fact, the party grew out of a number of groups in Germany which were centers of homosexual activity and activism." One of these organizations was the Freikorps.

Lively and Abrams said that many of "the characteristic rituals, symbols, activities and philosophies we associate with Nazism came from these organizations or from contemporary homosexuals." (Ibid.)

U.S. investigators (Nizkor Project: 1943) said that as they had nothing to lose to begin with, "they were willing to take risks, and if necessary, take drastic measures to achieve what they wanted".

"They feel themselves to be different and ostracized which usually makes them easy converts to a new philosophy which does not discriminate against them. Being among civilization's discontents, they are always willing to take a chance on something new which holds the promise of improving their lot, even though their chances of success may be small and the risk great." The early Nazi party certainly contained many members who could be regarded in this light." (Ibid.)

Misfits
Konrad Heiden's epic book, Der Fuehrer (1944) described Hitler's Munich circle in the 1920s as a collection of misfits, hunchbacks, sexual outlaws, moral degenerates, decadent aristocrats, ex-cons, and occult con men. He said they were "Fascist libertines" who spent their free time in the Cafe Heck and the Osteria Bavaria, stuffing themselves with pasta and pastries while pimps scoured Munich

schoolyards to supply boys for SA chief, Ernst Roehm's predatory appetites. Heiden said Hitler also attended dissolute gatherings at the home of party photographer, Heinrich Hoffmann, who had a wide acquaintance among artists, models, and other "demi-mondaines".

Adolf Hitler became leader of the fledgling Nazi Party in 1921 by threatening to leave it altogether if he was not given the top job with dictatorial powers. This is a trick he pulled off many times during his political career.

At that time, the over-riding philosophy, towards sexuality, seemed to be that men were for pleasure and women were for breeding children, an idea which derived from ancient Greek thinking. This view of sexuality seems to have continued unabated until the Night of the Long Knives in 1934, when prominent homosexuals in the Nazi Party were murdered.

Casual lovers

According to author, Joseph Howard Tyson (The Surreal Reich: 2010) "Hitler began having gay encounters in Vienna circa 1908 and his one night stands with male strangers continued into the 1920s".

The author said that from the outset, Hitler's earliest bodyguards, Ulrich Graf and Christian Weber, were expected to satisfy their boss's needs as and when required. Former Nazi, Otto Strasser (Gangsters Around Hitler: 1942) also said that from the outset, Hitler's personal bodyguards were almost always one hundred per cent homosexual.

Graf and Weber, who were from working class families, did very well for themselves through their intimacy with their boss and were later rewarded for their discretion and loyalty like so many other Hitler intimates. They benefited from speedy promotion through Nazi ranks and were selected for local and national political jobs. In particular, Christian Weber took advantage of his insider knowledge of Hitler and became known as one of the richest and most corrupt Nazi officials in Munich.

Ulrich Graf (b.1878-d.1950) an amateur wrestler and apprentice butcher was one of the earliest members of the Nazi Party and one of Hitler's first bodyguards and lovers working for him between 1920 to 1923.

During the Beer Hall Putsch [the Nazis attempt to overthrow the Weimar Republic], along with Rudolf Hess, Graf cleared the way to the platform so that Hitler could deliver his speech. During the subsequent march through Munich, when Hitler and General Erich Ludendorff were blocked by about 100 armed police outside the Feldherrnhalle, Graf stepped forward and shouted: "Don't shoot! His excellency, Ludendorff is coming!"

There was immediate gunfire in response and 14 Nazis and four police officers were killed. When Graf shielded Hitler with his own body, he received several non-fatal bullet wounds, and probably saved Hitler's life.

Once he had recovered sufficiently from his wounds, he re-joined the Nazi Party (when Hitler was released from Landsberg prison) in December 1924.

When Hitler came to power in1933, Graf was appointed to the position of Sturmbannfuhrer in Heinrich Himmler's SS, the equivalent of a Major in the

Wehrmacht [army].

In 1936, he was elected to the Reichstag and the following year was promoted to the rank of SS-Oberfuhrer. On April 20, 1943, Hitler's 54th birthday, he was again promoted, this time to SS-Brigadefuhrer.

The same year, on Graf's 65th birthday, [July 1943], Heinrich Himmler sent him a signed copy of the book, Vogt Bartold: The Long Train to the East, thanking him for saving Hitler's life 20 years earlier.

SEXUAL FAVORS FOR HIS BOSS: Ulrich Graf shielded Hitler with his body during the Beer Hall Putsch

At the age of 70, Ulrich Graf was sentenced to five years hard labor for his role in the Nazi Party and the SS during WW2; he died in prison aged 72 in 1950.

One of Hitler's other bodyguards in the early 1920s; Christian Weber (b.1883-d.1945) was also a man of humble origins but unlike Graf who was somewhat of an idealist and fanatic, Weber used his Nazi Party connections and his insider knowledge of Hitler for his own financial gain. Like Graf, he satisfied Hitler's sexual needs while working as his bodyguard and kept his mouth shut until he could get his financial reward.

Weber had started out as a hotel bellboy and bar bouncer, who apparently relished a fist-fight and carried a riding crop with him everywhere; a habit he shared with Hitler.

In late 1921, he was among the marauding group of Nazis that attacked a meeting of the Bavarian League.

Otto Strasser (Gangsters around Hitler: 1942) claimed Weber was a pimp for male prostitutes at this time, and described him as an "ape-like creature" and "the most despicable of Hitler's underlings".

CORRUPT: Christian Weber, satisfying Hitler's sexual needs was part of his job description

Following the Beer Hall Putsch in 1923, Hitler owed Weber, who was by then a horse trader, 1,000 dollars and he insisted the Nazi leader paid the debt in full. The two remained on good terms, so much so, that Ernst Hanfstaengl (The Missing Years: 1957) claimed Weber was one of the few who could make fun of the book Mein Kampf in Hitler's company.

As one of Munich's councilors, Christian Weber became the city's boss and his name became a byword for corruption. Munich citizens often wondered how a former hotel bellboy had become the owner of a number of hotels, villas, petrol stations, a brewery, the city's racecourse and bus service as well as a home in the Munich Residenz district.

On the Night of the Long Knives [1934], he was one of the SS men who traveled to Bad Wiessee to purge the SA leadership of "effeminate" homosexuals. Hitler personally rewarded him for his involvement by promoting him to the rank of SS-Oberfuhrer.

Weber was active during "Kristallnacht" [Night of Broken Glass] on November, 9-10, 1938 and took a group of SS men to Planegg where they ransacked the estate of Jewish nobleman, Baron Rudolf Hirsch. Of course, the estate eventually passed into Weber's own possession.

Christian Weber also took care of security arrangements for Nazi Party functions in Munich but was criticized when Georg Elser's bomb attack on the Burgerbraukeller [in November 1939] missed Hitler and Heinrich Himmler by only ten minutes.

Despite this, he remained important to SS security in Munich and sought and received Hitler's protection on several occasions.

Weber became obese from the trappings of his wealth and over eating. He died in a lorry accident in 1945 on his journey to prison after being arrested by the US military in Berlin.

Party fixers

Historian, Joseph Howard Tyson (The Surreal Reich: 2010) said that in the early 1920s, "Nazi Party fixers", Franz Schwarz and Max Amann were obliged to pay off individuals with knowledge of Hitler's homosexuality" to stop them blowing the whistle on him.

One of Hitler's earliest blackmailers (there would be many over the years) was Kurt Ludecke, a linguist and for a short time Hitler's translator, who was rumored to have sold himself as a prostitute to make money after WW1.

When he first met Hitler, he said "without hesitation, I gave him my soul".

According to Lothar Machtan (Hidden Hitler: 2001), Ludecke and Hitler visited Salzburg and Linz together and went for walks along the same beach where Hitler walked with his first boyfriend, August Kubizek. It is understood that Hitler and Ludecke had a brief gay relationship during which time Hitler confessed that he had casual sex with his bodyguards – including Graf, Weber and Emil Maurice. With this type of intimate knowledge, Ludecke saw the opportunity to make lots of money.

Ernst Hanfstaengl (The Missing Years: 1957), who met Ludecke on several occasions, described him as "an abject rogue, a male prostitute's pimp, a plague on the Party, and a traitor to the Fatherland".

Apparently, Franz Schwarz, eventual Nazi Party treasurer was obliged to pay Ludecke a large sum of money to guarantee his silence.

Beer Hall Putsch

In November, 1923, Hitler and his German Workers' Party comrades tried to overthrow Germany's Weimar Republic in a military coup known as the Beer Hall Putsch. When the effort failed, the ringleaders were convicted and sent to Landsberg Castle, Munich where the ancient Greek views on sexuality and masculine pleasures were prevalent among the prison's new inmates.

During Hitler's trial for treason, Munich's state prosecutor, Ludwig Stenglein had been remarkably tolerant towards the defendant and said ironically: "His private life has always been clean, which deserves special approbation in view of the temptations which naturally came to him as an acclaimed party leader."

In fact, Hitler was allowed to turn the proceedings into a political rally. (spartacus-educational.com: 2015)

William L. Shirer, author of Rise and Fall (1960) said that one important figure was protecting Hitler: "Franz Guertner, the Bavarian Justice Minister and an old friend and protector of the Nazi leader, had seen to it that the judiciary would be complacent and lenient.

Hitler was allowed to interrupt as often as he pleased, cross-examine witnesses at will and speak on his own behalf at any time and at any length; his opening statement consumed four hours, but it was only the first of many long harangues."

Even so, Hitler was found guilty of treason and received a minimum sentence of five years (of which he served only nine months). He was imprisoned along with Rudolf Hess, Emil Maurice, Friedrich Weber, Hermann Kriebel, and Julius Schreck among others.

At the time, Rudolf Hess was openly gay and Emil Maurice, an ex-convict who first met Hitler at the GWP recruitment office in 1919, was unashamedly bisexual. With these two men as his companions, Hitler would be able to continue his homosexual lifestyle with no questions asked for a further nine months. Hitler's Landsberg love triangle had begun.

Julius Schreck would also feature as one of Hitler's regular sex partners but at a later stage. Inevitably, the authorities turned a blind eye to the burgeoning sexual relationships among the Landsberg inmates because male coupling had always been an accepted part of prison life.

Unnatural sexuality

According to the prison warden, Otto Leybold, who wrote about inmate "Adolf Hitler" on September 18, 1924: "He was always reasonable, frugal, modest and polite to everyone, especially the officials at the facility," and said "the prisoner did not smoke or drink and submitted willingly to all restrictions".

But Herman Rauschning, (Hitler Speaks: 1939) described the atmosphere around Hitler as full of "secret lusts" that were far from "normality".

He said: "Most loathsome of all is the reeking miasma of furtive, unnatural sexuality that fills and fouls the whole atmosphere around him, like an evil emanation. Nothing in this environment is straightforward. Surreptitious relationships, substitutes and symbols, false sentiments and secret lusts, nothing in this man's surroundings is natural and genuine, nothing has the openness of a natural instinct."

While at Landsberg, Hitler was examined by Dr. Josef Brinsteiner, who found that the Nazi leader suffered from "right-side cryptorchidism", or an undescended right testicle. Normally men's testicles descend from inside the body into the scrotum during childhood. But in some cases, one or both fail to descend meaning that they atrophy and wither away rather than developing. Dr. Brinsteiner's findings were only revealed in 2015 by University of Erlangen history professor, Peter Fleischmann who discovered the medical documents buried in a Bavarian archive.

But having only one functioning testicle (and one withered one) did not stop Hitler enjoying sex with both Emil Maurice and Rudolf Hess.

Emil Maurice

When Max Amann, Hitler's business manager and later head of Nazi publishing, proposed that he should spend his time in prison writing his autobiography [Mein

Kampf], Hitler, who was poorly educated, was not very keen. (Ibid.)
When Amann suggested that he could dictate his thoughts to a "ghost writer" and suggested this person could be Emil Maurice, Hitler had a change of heart. The only problem with having the dashing Maurice as his ghost writer was that he had been sentenced to only a few weeks in prison and had already been released.

NOT SUCH A HARD LIFE: (left to right) Adolf Hitler, Emil Maurice, Hermann Kriebel, Rudolf Hess, Dr. Friedrich Weber

Hitler had a solution. He asked the prison governor if his friend could "come back to live in the prison to work as his secretary". Surprisingly, prison authorities agreed to the request and Maurice re-joined Hitler and remained with him until his release on parole in December 1924.
Emil Maurice (b.1897 - d.1972), was an early member of the Nazi Party (member No. 19) and helped establish the Gymnastic and Sports Division in August 1921. This group eventually became known as the Sturmabteilung [Storm Detachment]. Hitler's Storm Troopers were often former members of the Freikorps which had a homosexual ethos and had considerable experience in using violence against their rivals.
In the early days of the Nazi Party, Emil Maurice was always in the thick of the action. "The SA wore gray jackets, brown shirts - khaki shirts originally intended for soldiers in Africa but purchased in bulk from the German Army by the Nazi Party - they also wore swastika armbands, ski-caps, knee-breeches, thick woolen socks and combat boots. Accompanied by bands of musicians and carrying swastika flags, they would parade through the streets of Munich.
At the end of the march, Hitler would make one of his passionate speeches that encouraged his supporters to carry out acts of violence against Jews and his left-wing political opponents. The SA was assigned the task of winning the battle of the

streets against the Communists." (spartacus-educational.com: 2015)
Maurice was the son of a watchmaker whose main talent up to 1923 had been as a Nazi street fighter. He was poorly educated like Hitler and therefore struggled to keep up with the feverish delivery of his Nazi boss's life story.
The job of transcribing his words and then editing them was eventually given to Rudolf Hess, who was university educated. Even so, Maurice continued to live at Landsberg prison at Hitler's request.

Kindred spirits
Hitler enjoyed having him around, perhaps believing his dark and handsome friend was a kindred spirit. He had an artistic temperament and played the guitar and mandolin which provided entertainment at Nazi gatherings. And of course, as with Hitler's other bodyguards, Ulrich Graf and Christian Weber, Maurice was happy to satisfy Hitler's sexual needs as and when required.
As a reward for his loyalty and for keeping his mouth shut, Hitler appointed him as his personal Munich bodyguard and chauffeur as soon as they left Landsberg Prison in December 1924.
In Mein Kampf, Hitler unwittingly betrayed his feelings for the much younger man when he described a fracas at a beer hall when Communists tried to break up an event - he marveled at how his "Storm Troopers, although bloodied, swept the enemy literally out of the hall and at their head, my splendid Maurice".

QUALITY TIME TOGETHER: Maurice and Hitler in Landsberg, they kept each others secrets

In 1925, Hitler ordered the formation of a new bodyguard unit which eventually became the SS. He became SS member No. 1 and Emil Maurice became SS member No. 2.

But unknown to Hitler, Maurice successfully blackmailed him in 1927 when he discovered the Nazi leader was attempting to have a sexual relationship with a 16 year old girl.

Then in 1928, Maurice began a steamy affair with Hitler's niece, Geli Raubal while the man she called "Uncle Alf" was also attempting to conduct a relationship with her.

When Hitler discovered the affair, he sacked his "splendid Maurice" as his Munich chauffeur in 1931.

But the two men remained loyal to each other in the years that followed. Maurice became one of the Nazi Party's most notable henchmen who carried out murders on Hitler's orders - at least three during the Night of the Long Knives in 1934.

And when Heinrich Himmler discovered Maurice had a Jewish great-grandfather, and recommended he be "expelled immediately from the SS", Hitler stood by him. In 1935, he ordered Himmler to "make an exception" for his former chauffeur and his wider family who were given the status of "honorary Aryans".

Hitler also protected him against Party members who were resentful of "accepting orders from a Jew" and Maurice eventually became both an elected deputy in Germany's Reichstag and a distinguished Luftwaffe pilot during WW2.

Sex with Hess (or "Black Emma")

The other man in the Landsberg love triangle was Rudolf Hess (b.1894-d.1987) described politely by some scholars as "a somewhat neurotic member of the Nazi party".

Gay lawyer, Erich Ebermayer (Ebermayer Diary: 1959) said: "In view of all who have an intimate knowledge of the circumstances, Hess, known in Party circles as 'Black Emma,' was for many years the Fuhrer's partner, especially during their joint detention in Landsberg."

Ebermayer also pointed out that after his release from prison in early 1925, Hess served for several years as Hitler's personal secretary in spite of having "no official rank in the Nazi Party".

Hess was born in Alexandria, Egypt on April 26, 1894, the son of a prosperous wholesaler and did not live in Germany until he was 14 years old.

He volunteered to join the German Army in 1914 at the outbreak of WW1, partly to escape the control of his domineering father who had refused to let him go to university and tried to force him to work in the family business.

This dysfunctional relationship with his father was something he had in common with Hitler. Again, like Hitler, Rudolf Hess was wounded twice during WW1 and for a short time, he had been part of Hitler's regiment.

Hess joined the Luftwaffe and became an expert aviator, and like so many disaffected German soldiers at the end of the war, he joined the Freikorps where he thrived in the militia's homosexual ethos. (History Learning: 2015)

At the University of Munich, he studied political science and came under the influence of the Thule Society, a secret anti-Semitic political organization devoted to Nordic supremacy.

After hearing Adolf Hitler speak in a small Munich beer hall, Hess joined the Nazi Party on July 1, 1920, becoming member No. 16. When he spoke to Hitler afterward, he said he felt "as though overcome by a vision". (Ibid.)

During their time in Landsberg, Hess made a valiant attempt to convert Hitler's spoken ideas into prose.

He made some editorial suggestions regarding "Lebensraum", the so-called desire for increased living space for Germany and also contributed several paragraphs on the historical role of the British Empire and the organization of the Nazi Party. (spartacus-educational.com: 2015)

In the end, the book Mein Kampf (1925) detailing Hitler's formative years was repetitive, turgid and extremely difficult to read. At Hitler's suggestion, it was originally called Four Years of Struggle against Lies, Stupidity, and Cowardice but the publisher, perhaps eager to make a profit, reduced the title to My Struggle (Mein Kampf). In it, the details of Hitler's early family life, his years in Vienna and his participation in WW1 are either inaccurate, embellished or completely false.

TOTALLY DEVOTED TO YOU: Rudolf Hess said even when Hitler was wrong, he was right; in Landsberg, he suggested Hitler call himself the "Fuhrer"

High-living and luxury

It is ironic that it was while he was incarcerated in Landsberg Castle that Hitler's taste for high-living and luxury first developed.

His wing on the second floor was nicknamed "Feldherrenhuegel", the General's Hill. (Hitler's Time in Jail: 2010) Prison documents show that he and his pals "wanted for nothing" during their time in jail.

According to one Spiegel International (2010) article: "Flowers for the Fuhrer", Hitler was allowed to wear his own clothes, to walk the castle grounds and to receive visitors and gifts without restrictions.

"A steady flow of, party members and journalists spent long spells with him. He was even allowed to have visits from his pet Alsatian dog."

The documents revealed that Hitler's guests included "Captain Roehm, Munich,

Councilor Dr. Frick, Munich, and Alfred Rosenberg, certified architect and writer, Munich".

During the Nazi regime, Roehm became Storm Trooper chief, Frick became Interior Minister of the German Reich and Rosenberg became the Nazi's chief ideologue. (Hitler's Time in Jail: 2010)

One of Hitler's early confidants, Ernst Hanfstaengl said that during his own visit with Hitler, he felt like he had "walked into a delicatessen".

"There was fruit and there were flowers, wine and other alcoholic beverages, ham, sausage, cake, boxes of chocolates and much more," he said.

Then there is the transcript of a letter to Jakob Werlin, a Munich car dealer, which revealed Hitler's increasing aspirations.

The future German dictator was already thinking about what type of car to buy: a Benz 11/40, which "would meet my current requirements," or a 16/50 with a more powerful engine. His preferred color was gray, and he wanted "wire wheels". (Ibid.)

LINING UP FOR IT: Hitler with (from left) Himmler, Weber, Hess and Maurice

The German Savior

More important still, after his release from Landsberg, Hitler was no longer content with the role of a "drummer" heralding the coming of a real savior. With the encouragement of his fellow inmates and prison visitors, he began to believe he was "the Savior".

"Occasionally, he would describe himself in the words of Saint Matthew, 'as a voice crying in the wilderness', or as Saint John the Baptist whose duty was to come and lead the nation to power and glory. More frequently, however, he referred to himself as 'the Fuhrer', a name suggested by Rudolf Hess during their imprisonment." (Nizkor Project: 1943)

Loyalty to intimates
In his later career, Hitler remained loyal to many of his "male companions", particularly those who formed part of the "glorious male community" from WW1 and his sexually discreet fellow inmates at Landsberg Prison.

BUMPING UGLIES: The shared "a beautiful relationship"

Rudolf Hess continued to work as Hitler's personal secretary once they had served their time in prison. In 1932, Hitler appointed him as Chairman of the Nazi's Central Political Commission and gave him the rank of SS General.
On April 21, 1933, Hess was also appointed as Deputy Fuhrer, a figurehead position with mostly ceremonial duties.
One of his most important tasks was to announce the Fuhrer at mass meetings, usually with bellowing, wide eyed fanaticism, as seen in the Nazi propaganda documentary, Triumph Of The Will (1934).
In 1934, Hess gave a bizarre speech which stated that even when Hitler was wrong, he was always right:
"With pride, we see that one man remains beyond all criticism; that is the Fuhrer. This is because everyone feels and knows: he is always right, and he will always be right. Our National Socialism is anchored in uncritical loyalty, in the surrender to the Fuhrer that does not ask for the why in individual cases, in the silent execution of his orders. We believe that the Fuhrer is obeying a higher call to fashion German history. There can be no criticism of this belief." (Ibid.)
Hess was granted other titles such as Reich Minister without Portfolio, member of the Secret Cabinet Council, and member of the Ministerial Council for Reich Defense; all of which had no executive power.

POST PORRIDGE: Adolf Hitler photographed as he exits Landsberg prison in December 1924, after having served only 9 months of a five year sentence

Over the years, Adolf Hitler gradually distanced himself from the increasingly eccentric, fanatical and openly effeminate Hess, who in turn, was devastated by Hitler's loss of personal and sexual interest in him. Hess, would later say "they had shared a beautiful human experience to the very end".

LET'S GET ONE THING STRAIGHT: I'm not, Hitler and Hess chat shortly after their release

CHAPTER 7: "BROTHERHOOD OF POOFS"

BEFORE HITLER BECAME FUHRER, "his peculiar relationships with women, or lack of them, became noticeable and many commentators secretly believed that he was either asexual or homosexual. This belief was based largely on the fact that during the early days of the Nazi Party, many of his inner circle were well-known homosexuals." (Nizkor Report: 1943)

It was also widely known that Hitler preferred to have either gay or bisexual men as his personal bodyguards and chauffeurs. Former Nazi, Hermann Rauschning (Voice of Destruction: 1939) said the general attitude in the Party was: "Do anything you like but don't get caught."

He said he and others were disgusted by Hitler's attitude.

Historian Louis P. Lochner (What about Germany?: 1942) noted: "The only criterion for membership in the Party was that the applicant be 'unconditionally obedient and faithfully devoted to Hitler'. When someone asked if that applied to thieves and criminals, Hitler said, 'Their private lives don't concern me'."

BOYS, BOYS, BOYS: (l to r) Wilhelm Frick, Hermann Kriebel, Erich Ludendorff, Hitler, Wilhelm Bruckner and Ernst Roehm, 1923

Until the Blood Purge in 1934, he never restricted gay Nazi Party membership or promotion within its ranks. "In view of Hitler's pretense at 'purity' in the German media, it is extraordinary that he would be so careless about his homosexual associates." (Nizkor Report: 1943)

But Ernst Roehm had powerful enemies who warned Hitler of the danger of employing "morally objectionable persons in positions of authority"; Goebbels and Himmler were the ringleaders.

Lothar Machtan (Hidden Hitler: 2001) said "homo-eroticism and homosexuality were cornerstones of fascist male-bonding culture prior to 1933." By this time, Munich newspapers had begun to call the Nazi Party's Storm Troopers the "Brotherhood of Poofs" because their leader, Ernst Roehm, and most of the provincial leaders he appointed, were openly gay.

By mid 1933, the media's continuous ridicule began to cause alarm within the Nazi Party hierarchy and both Heinrich Himmler (SS chief) and Joseph Goebbels (propaganda chief) advised Hitler to do something to change the negative perceptions of the German electorate.

They started to work on a strategy and the eventual solution they came up with was fourfold. In a bid to make Nazi Party members "more electable" beginning in 1933 and on into 1934, documents revealing the truth about the rampant homosexuality within the Nazi Party would be seized and then destroyed; "Queen" Ernst Roehm, who had become very powerful as head of the Storm Troopers would be eliminated; new anti-gay laws would be introduced and gay men in the higher echelons of the party would either be married off, imprisoned or murdered.

Much later, Hitler authorized an edict (in 1941) prescribing the death penalty for SS and police members found guilty of "gay activity." (Holocaust Memorial Museum: 2015) The extermination of homosexuals as "sub-humans" and "aberrants" would happen later still.

SEXUAL PERVERSION RECORDS DESTROYED

On May 6, 1933, Storm Troopers, under the command of Ernst Roehm, ransacked the "Sex Research Institute" [also known as the Institute of Sexology] in Berlin. The institute had been founded in 1919 by Dr. Magnus Hirschfeld to conduct research into marital problems, sexually transmitted diseases, and (laws relating to) sexual offenses, abortion, and homosexuality. The author of many works, Hirschfeld, himself a homosexual, had led efforts for three decades to reform laws criminalizing homosexuality.

In 1933, Hirschfeld happened to be in France, where he remained until his death. (Holocaust Memorial Museum: 2015).

Four days after the sex institute was plundered, these sexual records were destroyed in a bizarre public "book burning" ceremony. At the same time, thousands of books viewed as un-German were also thrown onto the huge bonfire. But these so-called books were really the sexual records of top Nazis, including Hitler, records which related to their homosexuality and any arrests or convictions for sodomy.

According to Scott Lively and Kevin Abrams (Pink Swastika: 1995), "Even the enduring image of Nazi book-burning, familiar in 1930s newsreels was directly related to the homosexuality of Nazi leaders. On May 10, the Nazis burned thousands of books and files taken in that raid. The Institute had extensive records of the sexual perversions of numerous Nazi leaders, many of whom had been under treatment at the clinic prior to the beginning of the Nazi regime."

BURN BABY BURN: Up to 40,000 records of sexual perversion, some involving senior Nazis including Hitler, were destroyed in May 1933

Intimate secrets

Treatment at the Sex Research Institute was required by the German courts for persons convicted of sex crimes. Ludwig L. Lenz, Assistant Director of the Sex Institute at the time of the raid, managed to escape with his life and later wrote of the incident.

"Why was it then, since we were completely non-party, that our purely scientific Institute was the first victim which fell to the new regime? The answer to this is simple. We knew too much. It would be against medical principles to provide a list of the Nazi leaders and their perversions [but] not ten percent of the men who, in 1933, took the fate of Germany into their hands, were sexually normal. Our knowledge of such intimate secrets regarding members of the Nazi Party and other documentary material, we possessed about forty thousand confessions and biographical letters, was the cause of the complete and utter destruction of the Institute of Sexology."

Lenz confirmed that during the Nazi's infamous "book burning", the bulk of the smoldering pile was not made of books, but of the records of Nazi perversions stolen from the Sex Research Institute four days earlier. (Pink Swastika: 1995)

Lothar Machtan (Hidden Hitler: 2001) said that even with Hitler's destruction of all literature related to his own homosexuality, some got passed along by people who were either professionally or personally interested.

One of these men was the gay lawyer, Erich Ebermayer. When his diaries were published in 1959, they clearly outlined his own fears as a gay man in 1933. One entry said the Nazi Party was now a movement designed "to eliminate unwelcome initiates from the Fuhrer's own past." (Ebermayer Diary: 1959)

SNUFFING OUT THE TRUTH: Joseph Goebbels on May 10, 1933 during the "book" burning ceremony

Homoerotic orientation

Ebermayer said the Nazi Party had been a homoerotic movement from its earliest days: "The most interesting and shocking thing of all is the slant or, rather, the twist the affair is now taking on, that is, the campaign against homosexuality. It goes without saying that this campaign is spurious and disingenuous. During its time of struggle, the National Socialist movement and not just the Roehm clique was a 'fraternity' such as Blueher portrayed in his [gay] books; its motive force being homo-eroticism."

He said: "My exceedingly trustworthy sources of information about these confidential matters have proudly stressed the homo-erotic orientation of the Fuhrer and his inner circle, and have stated that the Fuhrer still views this problem with the greatest sympathy and understanding, for witness his toleration, indeed, his advancement, of Roehm and his associates."

GETTING RID OF QUEEN ERNST ROEHM

"If you try to tell him anything, he knows everything already," Ernst Roehm (about his boss Adolf Hitler)

Ernst Julius Roehm (b.1887-d.1934) served as a German officer in the Bavarian Army and was badly wounded in the face and chest during WW1, scars he carried for the rest of his life.

Immediately after the war, he became one of the senior members of the Freikorps (Bavarian Border Patrol East) where he encouraged very young men to take up a life of "male bonding" and homosexuality.

In the inter-war years, he became an early Nazi Party member, met Adolf Hitler, and the two became political allies and close friends.

William L. Shirer, author of The Rise and Fall of the Third Reich (1960) described

Ernst Roehm as a "stocky, bull-necked, piggish-eyed, scar-faced professional soldier with a flair for politics and a natural ability as an organizer.
"Like Hitler, he was possessed of a burning hatred for the democratic [Weimar] republic. A tough, ruthless, driving man, albeit, like so many of the early Nazis, a homosexual."

SCARFACE: Ernst Roehm was a decorated
WW1 veteran

Roehm was co-founder of the Storm Troopers (SA), the Nazi Party's "militia" and proved to be a charismatic leader. After his participation in Munich's Beer Hall Putsch, when he and some of his Storm Troopers occupied the War Ministry, he was sentenced to 15 months in Stadelheim prison, Munich but the sentence was overturned.

"I need you"
In May 1925, Roehm fell out with the Nazi Party and immediately resigned from all political movements and military brigades and sought seclusion from public life.
In 1928, he accepted a post in Bolivia as an adviser to the Bolivian Army. He was given the rank of Lieutenant Colonel and began his work after six months' acclimatization and language training. He got on well in his job but during the revolt against the Bolivian government in 1930, he was forced to seek sanctuary in the German embassy. Shortly afterward, he received a phone call from Hitler who

simply said: "I need you" which paved the way for his return to Germany. (spartacus-educational.com: 2015)

In September 1930, Hitler had assumed supreme command of the Storm Troopers (SA) but wanted his old friend to take on the role of Chief-of-Staff.

Roehm accepted the offer and began his new assignment on January 5, 1931.

ONE TIME FRIENDS: Hitler and Roehm; Hitler did not care about the private lives of his Storm Troopers as long as they were loyal to him

The SA by this time numbered over one million members. Its traditional function of party leader escort had been given to the SS but the Storm Troopers continued their street battles with "Reds" and their attacks on Jews.

They also attacked or intimidated anyone deemed hostile to the Nazi agenda including newspaper editors, journalists, professors, politicians, local officials and businessmen. (Ibid.)

Nazi historian, Dr. Louis L. Snyder (Iron Fist in Germany: 1932) said Roehm recruited homosexuals into the SA because he felt Germany needed "a proud and arrogant lot who could brawl, carouse, smash windows, kill and slaughter for the hell of it. Straights, in Roehm's eyes, were not as adept at such behavior as practicing homosexuals."

Openly gay
Unlike others in the Nazi Party, Ernst Roehm was openly gay and proud of it, admitting to associates that he was "far from unhappy" about his sexual orientation. He frequented gay bars, belonged to a homosexual organization called the League for Human Rights, and publicly advocated the repeal of Paragraph 175 to abolish the state prohibition of sodomy.

Joseph Howard Tyson said (Surreal Reich: 2010) the SA leader "came out" as a homosexual in 1924.
"He embraced the Spartan pederastic tradition which encouraged masculine camaraderie, military teamwork and decisive action, unhampered by middle-class piety. Roehm felt that warrior cults like the Teutonic Knights drew strength from macho homosexual attitudes."
In 1931, the Munich Post, a Social Democratic newspaper procured and then published a string of Roehm's private letters discussing his homosexual affairs.
In a letter to Karl Gunther Heimsroth, his doctor, astrologer and one-time lover

[dated 1929], Roehm wrote: "I fancy I'm a homo. I can recall a series of homosexual feelings and acts extending back to my childhood, but I've also had relations with plenty of women, never with any great pleasure, though. I caught three doses of the clap, which I saw as nature's punishment for unnatural intercourse. I now detest all bitches. On the other hand, I'm absolutely devoted to my mother and sister." (Surreal Reich: 2010)

And an anonymous 1932 article called "National Socialism and Inversion" has also been credited to Roehm; it stated that if Nazi Party members performed their official duties well, they were entitled to private lives of "creative eroticism and loving homosexual relationships".

Gay network

Hitler liked Ernst Roehm on a personal level though it is not known if they ever had a sexual relationship. The two men became so close after Roehm's return from Bolivia, that the SA chief addressed Hitler by his first name "Adolf" rather than "mein Fuhrer" like his other colleagues. He was the only Nazi leader to do so. During their conversations, they also addressed each other as "du" (the German familiar form of "you"). No one else in Hitler's inner circle enjoyed such a privilege. Hitler was of course aware of Roehm's homosexuality but had nothing but praise for "his warrior-in-chief" until the summer of 1934.

In response to the complaints about the sexual activity of the Nazi Storm Troopers, Hitler said (Hitler Speaks: 1939): "They would rather SA men took a woman than some fat-bellied moneybag. Why should I concern myself with the private lives of my followers; apart from Roehm's achievements, I can absolutely depend on him. The SA are a band of warriors and not a moral institution".

Roehm was very good at his job and by 1934 the SA had swollen its ranks to almost 3 million men, dwarfing the Wehrmacht [German Army], which was limited to 100,000 under the Treaty of Versailles.

But Hitler's warrior-in-chief had established a kind of gay network within the SA, assigning prominent posts to gay friends and former lovers.

Among Roehm's "sweethearts" was Edmund Heines, whom he appointed first as his deputy and later as leader of the Munich branch of the SA. Another of his favorites was Karl Ernst, who was nicknamed "Frau Rohrbein" because of his intimate friendship with Paul Rohrbein, Berlin's SA commander.

Roehm's so-called human relations consultant, Peter Granninger specialized in procuring handsome youths, whom his boss took to Carl du Moulin Eckardt's bachelor pad for sexual encounters.

In the early 1930s, Granninger recruited eleven boys from Munich's Gisela High School, whom he "broke in" before passing them on to Roehm.

When Granninger obtained a post with the Silesian SA chapter in March 1934, Roehm's servant Johann Hotsch took over the role of procurer of young boys for him. (Surreal Reich: 2010)

Dossier on Roehm

As Fuhrer, Adolf Hitler appeared to have complete control over Nazi Germany but like most dictators, he constantly feared that he might be ousted by others who wanted his job. To protect himself from a possible coup, Hitler used the tactic of divide and rule and encouraged other leaders such as Hermann Goering, Joseph Goebbels, Heinrich Himmler and Ernst Roehm to compete with each other for senior positions. (spartacus-educational.com: 2015)

CONSPIRATORS: Hitler, Hermann Goering, Joseph Goebbels and Rudolf Hess in 1934 all conspired against Ernst Roehm

One of the consequences of this policy was that these men developed a dislike for each other. Roehm was particularly hated because as leader of the SA, he had tremendous power and the means to remove any one of his competitors. Worried about their own positions within the hierarchy, Goering and Himmler asked Reinhard Heydrich (SS security chief) to assemble a dossier on Roehm with the purpose of ruining his position as SA chief. Heydrich also feared Roehm and he manufactured evidence to suggest that Roehm had been paid 12 million marks by the French to overthrow Hitler.

These reports were passed on to Hitler who initially refused to believe the dossier but he had his own reasons for wanting his friend removed.

Powerful Nazi supporters had been complaining about "Queen" Roehm for some time. Party financiers disapproved of the fact that he and many of the SA leaders were gay. It was bad for the Nazi Party's public image. At the same time, Heinrich Himmler aggravated Hitler's fears by constantly feeding him information about Roehm's impending coup. (Ibid.)

As Chancellor, Hitler was worried that the regular army, the Wehrmacht, had not sworn an oath of allegiance to him. In fact, he was aware that many German army generals had a low regard for him as he had "only achieved the rank of Corporal" during WW1. (History Learning Site: 2015)

The regular army hierarchy saw the SA as a threat, especially as Roehm had openly spoken about taking over the Wehrmacht by absorbing it into the SA. Such talk alarmed the army's leaders who viewed the Storm Troopers as a brawling mob of undisciplined street fighters with "corrupt morals".

Reports of a huge cache of weapons in the hands of SA members caused them further concern. Not surprisingly, the entire German army officer corps opposed Roehm's suggestion of taking over the regular army, insisting that discipline and honor would vanish if the SA gained control of the Wehrmacht

Death list

Nazi historian C.N. Trueman (History Learning Site: 2015) revealed that by the summer of 1934, Hitler had decided that Roehm was indeed a "threat" and he made a pact with the Wehrmacht that if Roehm and other SA leaders were removed, the rank and file Storm Troopers would come under the control of the German army, but the army would be obliged to swear an oath of allegiance to him.

When German army generals agreed to swear an oath to Hitler, Roehm's fate was sealed.Top Nazis including Goering, Himmler, Heydrich and Viktor Lutze drew up lists of people inside and outside the SA's ranks marked for death.

Historian, Paul R. Maracin, (Night of the Long Knives: 2004) said once the death list was started, it expanded rapidly: "With utmost secrecy a death list was compiled. Heydrich was in control of the master list, which was expanded almost daily as they added more names to the 'enemies of the party'.'

Working out of Gestapo headquarters, Heydrich meticulously correlated the planning for the operation which was assigned the innocuous code name of 'hummingbird'." (spartacus-educational.com: 2015)

Hermann Goering also contributed to the list of people outside the SA he wanted killed. These included Gregor Strasser [who had openly criticized Hitler and the Nazi Party], Kurt von Schleicher, Hitler's predecessor as Chancellor [who had evidence of Hitler's homosexuality] and Gustav von Kahr who had crushed the Beer Hall Putsch in 1923. (Ibid.)

Joseph Howard Tyson (Surreal Reich: 2010) said that Roehm had one fatal weakness which was his hedonistic craving for revelry and the fact that he made no effort to tone down his homosexual activity.

"He continued to frequent Turkish bathhouses and gay hangouts such as the Nurnberger Bratwurstgloeckl Cafe, Kleist Casino and Silhouette Lounge. In addition to drinking heavily, he had a predilection for adolescent boys between fourteen to nineteen years old."

True to form, Roehm and a large group of his SA companions went on holiday to a resort in Bad Wiessee in late June 1934 which presented the ideal opportunity to arrest him and his SA associates.

On June 28, 1934 Hitler phoned Roehm and asked him to gather all the SA leaders at the Hanselbauer Hotel in Bad Wiessee on June 30 for a conference.

Roehm agreed and apparently had no suspicions about what was to unfold. What became known as the "Night of the Long Knives" began at dawn on June 29.

Whip in hand, Night of the Long Knives

On that day, Hitler, accompanied by Theodor Eicke [eventual Kommandant of the Dachau concentration camp] and selected members of the SS arrived in Bad Wiessee, where Hitler decided he would personally arrest Ernst Roehm.

Erich Kempka, one of Hitler's Berlin chauffeurs who himself had the nickname "Queen of the Reich", witnessed what happened (I Was Hitler's Chauffeur: 1951): "Hitler entered Roehm's bedroom alone with a whip in his hand. Behind him were two detectives with pistols at the ready. He spat out the words; 'Roehm, you are under arrest!' Now the bus arrives. Quickly, the SA leaders are collected from the laundry room and walk past Roehm under police guard. Roehm looks up from his coffee sadly and waves to them in a melancholy way. At last, Roehm too is led from the hotel. He walks past Hitler with his head bowed, completely apathetic."

Emil Maurice, who also accompanied Hitler to Bad Wiessee, was responsible for shooting Edmund Heines, Roehm's deputy and boyfriend on June 30, 1934.

He also murdered Father Bernhard Stempfle who had publicly criticized Hitler's relationship with his niece, Geli Raubal. (spartacus-educational.com: 2015)

A large number of SA officers were shot as soon as they were captured but Hitler decided to pardon Roehm because of his past services to the movement. After much pressure from Goering and Himmler however, Hitler agreed that Roehm too should die.

SS chief, Heinrich Himmler ordered Theodor Eicke to carry out the job.

Theodor Eicke and his adjutant, Michael Lippert traveled to Stadelheim Prison in Munich where Roehm was being held.

Apparently, Eicke placed a pistol on the table in Roehm's prison cell and told him that he had ten minutes in which to use the weapon to kill himself.

Roehm replied: "If Adolf wants to kill me, let him do the dirty work himself."

According to Paul R. Maracin, author of Night of Long Knives (2004): "Ten minutes later, SS officers Eicke and Lippert appeared, and as the embittered, scar-faced veteran of Verdun defiantly stood in the middle of the cell, stripped to the waist, the two SS officers riddled his body with revolver bullets "

The next day, Otto Dietrich, Nazi Party Press Chief, gave a blood-curdling account of the slaughter to the press and described "Hitler's sense of shock at the moral degeneracy of his oldest comrades". (Ibid.)

From June 30 to July 2, 1934 the entire SA leadership was wiped out, along with many other political adversaries of the Nazi Party.

Two naked boys

The blood purge of the SA in 1934 was legalized with a one-paragraph decree called the "Law Regarding Measures of State Self-Defense". No public reference was ever made to the alleged threat of a Storm Trooper rebellion, but only generalized references to "misconduct", "perversion" and "some sort of plot". [There has never been a shred of evidence to suggest that Ernst Roehm was planning a coup against Hitler.]

The extent of the purge was kept secret until it was announced by Hitler on July 13, 1934. It was during this speech that Hitler gave the slaughter its name,

the "Night of the Long Knives" [a line from a popular Nazi song].
Hitler claimed that 61 Storm Troopers had been executed while 13 had been shot resisting arrest and three had committed suicide. Others have argued that as many as 400 people were killed during the purge.

LONG ARMS OF THE LAW: A dead body being removed through a window by SA men the day after the Night of the Long Knives

In his speech, Hitler explained why he had not relied on the courts to deal with the conspirators:
"In this hour, I was responsible for the fate of the German people, and thereby I became the supreme judge of the German people. I gave the order to shoot the ringleaders in this treason." (Ibid.)
For the execution of his old comrade, Ernst Roehm, Hitler cited his "immoral sexual behavior" but explained the broader purge as mainly a "defense against treason" and the need to rid the Party of "undesirable elements".
Years later, Hitler told Albert Speer (Inside The Third Reich: 1970) how he was feeling as he and his henchmen entered the hotel at Bad Wiessee: "We were

unarmed, imagine, and didn't know whether or not those swine might have armed guards to use against us." Hitler also claimed the homosexual atmosphere in the hotel had disgusted him.

He told Speer: "In one room we found two naked boys!"

In an attempt to erase Roehm from German history, all known copies of the 1933 propaganda film Victory of Faith, in which he starred with his Storm Troopers, were destroyed on Hitler's orders.

The following year, a new film, Triumph of the Will showed an altered Nazi hierarchy, with the SS as the premier uniformed paramilitary group with Roehm replaced by Viktor Lutze as leader of a depleted SA.

William L. Shirer (The Rise and Fall: 1960) summed it up well: "The Roehm purge was largely implemented by homosexuals against other homosexuals".

After the Night of the Long Knives, the Nazi Party began to use the charge of homosexuality to discredit and undermine their political opponents. In a 1935 propaganda campaign and two show trials in 1936 and 1937, Nazi officials alleged there was "rampant homosexuality in the priesthood".

The Party wanted to undermine the power of the Roman Catholic Church in

Germany, an institution which many officials considered their most powerful potential enemy.

Then in 1938, Hermann Goering used trumped-up accusations of homosexual improprieties to unseat army supreme commander, Werner von Fritsch, who had publicly criticized Hitler's military policy. (Holocaust Memorial Museum: 2015)

Hitler's revenge

The Nazi's also continued to eliminate opponents who knew of Hitler's homosexuality as far back as WW1. Hans Mend, a fellow dispatch runner during the Great War became an obvious target. He had publicly threatened the Fuhrer on a Munich street and said he would let the world know "what Hitler used to be".

"Listen, Adolf, why are you ignoring me? Have you forgotten your benefactor? To whose credit is it that you are here at all? We'll talk about that later, you half-man, you jumped-up knife grinder. You're going to get it in the neck from me tomorrow, in writing. I'm warning you, Adolf, don't tempt me!" Mend said. (Hidden Hitler: 2001)

Mend then wrote a letter to Hitler, castigating him, and published it in the anti-Nazi newspaper, Der Gerade Weg [The Right Way].

In 1936, Hans Mend was arrested without warning by the Gestapo and interrogated relentlessly. He was charged with "sexual offenses against children" and sentenced to two years hard labor. While he was being interrogated, his home was searched and ransacked, and many important documents concerning Hitler were confiscated, including several Hitler art works. A female friend said: "He [Mend] said the Gestapo was out to get him and that Hitler wanted to get hold of his pictures at all costs."

After Mend's release from prison [1938], he must have felt that he had nothing further to lose as his reputation had been damaged beyond repair. In 1939, a secret document was apparently sent to German diplomat, Werner Otto von Hentig, from London which eventually led one section of the German resistance to move against Hitler.

What became known as "The Mend Protocol" was an important part in the movement's plans.

Hitler would be taken alive and examined by a medical board of inquiry, and the results would be published as widely as possible in Germany. Testimony from Mend, which related mainly to the years 1914 to 1919, was recorded during the interrogation process and placed on file. (Schmid-Noerr: 1939)

During the interview, Mend categorized Hitler as "misogynistic"; implied that his war medals, including the Iron Cross were fake and said Hitler only ever wanted to serve as far away from the front as possible. (Hidden Hitler: 2001).

Mend also said Hitler had forged strong acquaintances with three men during WW1, the last of which, Schmidt, was on "a very intimate level".

Before German intelligence could implement their outrageous plan to take Hitler alive to examine him, the participants were either imprisoned or obliged to leave Germany to avoid arrest.

In 1940, Hans Mend was accused of various sexual offenses against women and sentenced by a special court to two years imprisonment. He died on February 14,

1942, in Zwickau penitentiary with his hatred of Adolf Hitler still burning in his heart.

NEW ANTI-GAY LAWS

Richard Plant's book (The Pink Triangle: 1988) first outlined both the homophobia and homosexuality of Nazi Party leaders including Hitler.
Then Scott Lively and Kevin Abrams (The Pink Swastika: 1995) suggested that when the Nazis persecuted homosexuals, the homosexuals were almost exclusively the effeminate members of the gay community.
They said that much of the mistreatment was administered by masculine homosexuals who despised effeminacy in all its forms.
As part of the Nazis' attempt to purify German society and propagate an 'Aryan master race', they condemned homosexuals as 'socially aberrant.'
Soon after taking office on January 30, 1933, Hitler banned all homosexual and lesbian organizations. Brown-shirted Storm Troopers raided the institutions and gathering places of homosexuals.
"This subculture had flourished in the relative freedom of the 1920s, in the pubs and cafes of Berlin, Hamburg, Munich, Bremen, and other cities.
The Storm Trooper leadership was predominantly homosexual - the irony was that gay men were raiding and closing down homosexual meeting places."
(Holocaust Memorial Museum: 2015)

Pink lists and world domination
In 1934, a special Gestapo (Secret Police) division on homosexuals was set up. One of its first acts was to order the compilation and delivery of police "pink lists" from all over Germany. [German police had been compiling these lists of suspected homosexual men since 1900.]
On September 1, 1935, a harsher, amended version of Paragraph 175 of the Criminal Code, originally framed in 1871, went into effect, punishing a broad range of "lewd and lascivious" behavior between men.
In 1936, SS-leader, Heinrich Himmler created a Reich Central Office for the Combating of Homosexuality and Abortion called the Special Office IIS. The linking of homosexuality and abortion reflected the Nazi regime's population policies to promote a higher birthrate of its "Aryan" population. (Holocaust Memorial Museum: 2015)

One-way ticket to the grave
Himmler spoke to a group of high-ranking SS officers about the dangers homosexuality posed to the German birth rate on February 17, 1937.
"I would like to develop a couple of ideas for you on the question of homosexuality. There are those homosexuals who take the view: 'what I do is my business, it is a purely private matter'. However, all things which take place in the sexual sphere are not the private affair of the individual, but signify the life and death of the nation. The nation which has many children has the candidature for world power and world domination. A people of good race which has too few children has a

131

one-way ticket to the grave, for its insignificance in 50 or 100 years, for burial in 250 years. Therefore we must be absolutely clear that if we continue to have this burden in Germany, without being able to fight it, then that is the end of Germany, and the end of the Germanic world." (Racial State: 1993)

Paragraph 175
An estimated 1.2 million men were homosexuals in Germany in 1928. (Holocaust Memorial Museum: 2015) Under the revised Paragraph 175 and the creation of the Special Office IIS, the number of prosecutions against gay men increased sharply, peaking in the years 1937-1939.
Half of all convictions for homosexual activity under the Nazi regime occurred during these years. The police stepped up raids on homosexual meeting places, seized address books of arrested men to find additional suspects, and created networks of informers to compile lists of names and make arrests.
While lesbian bars were closed, few women are believed to have been arrested. In fact, Paragraph 175 did not mention female homosexuality. Lesbianism was seen by many Nazi officials as alien to the nature of the Aryan woman and nothing more, though in some cases, the police arrested lesbians as "a-socials" or "prostitutes."
Between 1933-45, an estimated 100,000 men were arrested for being homosexual, and of these, some 50,000 officially defined homosexuals were sentenced. Most of these men spent time in regular prisons, and an estimated 5,000 to 15,000 of the total sentenced were incarcerated in concentration camps. (Ibid.)
In addition, Hitler authorized an edict in 1941 prescribing the death penalty for SS and police members found guilty of gay activity.
How many of the 5,000 to 15,000 "175-ers" perished in concentration camps will probably never be known. Historical research to date has been very limited. One leading gay scholar, Ruediger Lautmann, author of the controversial Desire for a child (1994) believes that the death rate for "175-ers" in the camps may have been as high as 60 per cent.
All prisoners of the camps wore marks of various colors and shapes, which allowed guards and camp functionaries to identify them by category. The uniforms of those sentenced as gay bore various identifying symbols, including a large black dot and a large "175" drawn on the back of the jacket.
Later a pink triangular patch [rosa Winkel] was used.

Medical experiments
Conditions in the camps were generally harsh for inmates, many of whom died from hunger, disease, exhaustion, exposure to the cold and brutal treatment. Many survivors testified that men with pink triangles were treated particularly severely by guards and other inmates because of widespread bias against homosexuality. Some homosexuals were also victims of cruel medical experiments, including castration.
Nazi doctors often used gay men for quasi-scientific experiments in an attempt to locate "a biological basis for homosexuality", purportedly to cure any future Aryan

children who might be gay.

Jonathan Zimmerman, former history professor at New York University said: "To win their release from the camps, some gays were forced to undergo castration. Others were mutilated or murdered in so-called medical experiments by Nazi doctors, who insisted that homosexuality was 'a disease that could be cured'. At Buchenwald concentration camp, SS physician Dr. Carl Vaernet performed operations designed to convert men into heterosexuals. These operations involved the surgical insertion of a capsule which released the male hormone testosterone. Such procedures reflected the desire by Himmler and others to find a medical solution to homosexuality." (Holocaust Memorial Museum: 2015)

Lothar Machtan (Hidden Hitler: 2001) claimed Hitler and his party's opposition to homosexuality was most likely a defense mechanism against his own "internalized homophobia". He came to the conclusion that "Hitler allowed the persecution of gays in order to disguise his own true colors"

GAY NAZIS MARRIED OFF

"Homosexual boys are the best because they are the most manly. Some say they are shameless but they are wrong. It requires compulsion to overcome their natural disinclination to marriage and pro-creation. They are quite content to live with one another unwed." (Bisexuality in the Ancient World 2002)

Hitler put pressure on his gay and bisexual Nazi colleagues to get married. He even acted as a "matchmaker" for some of the gay men in his circle. It was all part of Joseph Goebbels's propaganda drive to clean up the image of the Nazi Party and ultimately to bolster his own opportunities for advancement.

Rudolf Hess

Hess was released from Landsberg prison just nine days after his lover Adolf Hitler. During the 1920s, homosexuality was accepted within the Nazi Party but "effeminate homosexuals" like Hess were frowned upon. (Pink Swastika: 1995) He was therefore disliked or even shunned by some within the Nazi hierarchy because he was seen as "pathologically sensitive, weak, and impressionable" with many feminine qualities. (Hidden Hitler: 2001)

Hess had been given various Nazi Party job titles, but he could never shake off the gay nicknames "Fraulein Anna" and "Black Emma" (and also "Fraulein Paula" according to some sources) he had earned during his time in Landsberg.

In effect, he had become an embarrassment to the Nazi machine and was eventually sidelined by the man he adored, his Fuhrer. In December 1927, at Hitler's suggestion, Rudolf Hess married a woman called Ilse Prohl, an acquaintance from his Munich University days. His wife would later complain that her life with him "was much like that of a convent schoolgirl". After ten years of marriage, the couple had their only child, a son they christened "Wolf "in honor of the Fuhrer.

In May 1941, desperate to restore Hitler's personal and sexual interest in him, Rudolf Hess attempted to set up a peace agreement between Germany and Britain without telling anyone about his plans.

He put on a Luftwaffe uniform and flew a German fighter plane toward Scotland on May 10, 1941. He intended to see the Duke of Hamilton, who he had met briefly during the Berlin Olympics in 1936 to discuss a peace plan between the two countries.

He successfully navigated the five hour, 900 mile flight across the North Sea and managed to get within 30 miles of the Duke's residence near Glasgow. When he bailed out of his plane at 6,000 feet and parachuted safely to the ground, he came across a bewildered Scottish farmer and said in English, "I have an important message for the Duke of Hamilton."

He told his British interrogators that Hitler had no wish to destroy a fellow "Nordic" nation such as Britain. (History Learning: 2015)

Rudolf Hess was declared "insane" by Adolf Hitler (and also by Winston Churchill), and he was effectively disowned by the Nazis who struggled to explain his actions. Hitler said that if Hess ever attempted to return to Germany, he should be shot as a traitor as soon as he crossed the border.

Hess displayed increasingly unstable and paranoid behavior during his four years in British custody, and at one point, believed his food was being poisoned. After WW2, he was returned to Germany to stand trial at Nuremberg.

CRACKING UP: Rudolf Hess during his Nuremberg trial in 1946, watched closely by his court-appointed psychiatrist

At his trial, he suffered from dizzy spells and claimed to have amnesia then he said he had been faking it. In his final speech, he said he had no regrets about his devotion to Adolf Hitler and if he got the chance, he would do it all again: "It was granted me for many years to live and work under the greatest son whom my nation has brought forth in the thousand years of its history. Even if I could I would not expunge this period from my existence. I regret nothing. If I were standing once more at the beginning, I should act once again as I did then, even if I knew that at the end I should be burnt at the stake."

In the early 1980s, his son Wolf Hess tried to have his father released from prison on the grounds of his old age and fragile mental state. He was not successful. In 1991, he publicly refuted the rumors of his father's homosexuality. He claimed that the KGB had tried to damage his father's reputation by releasing documents which said Rudolf Hess was known as "Black Bertha" in the gay underworld in Berlin before the outbreak of the war.

Hess was convicted of "crimes against peace" and transferred to Spandau Prison, Berlin in 1947. Over the next four decades, he had plenty of time to think about the "beautiful human experience" he had shared with Adolf Hitler.

Rudolf Hess died in August 1987 in Spandau prison's summer house. He had taken an extension cord from one of the lamps and strung it over a window latch so that he could hang himself. He was 93 years old.

Baldur von Schirach (b.1907-d.1974) joined a military cadet group at the age of ten and became a member of the Nazi Party circa 1924. He became leader of the National Socialist German Students' League in 1931. Two years later, Hitler appointed him as head of the Hitler Youth and in 1933 gave him a senior Storm Trooper rank. As with other youth organizations at that time, homosexuality was common, if not encouraged within the Hitler Youth, to increase a feeling of male bonding and to improve overall morale.

Some of von Schirach's young boys were sent to Ernst Roehm and his Storm Troopers so they could be used in the SA's sex orgies.

One of Hitler's strongest critics, Gregor Strasser, dismissively described Baldur von Schirach as "a young effeminate aristocrat upon whom Hitler had bestowed both Henriette Hoffmann as a gift and the Hitler Youth position".

Adolf Hitler personally arranged the marriage between von Schirach and 19-year-old Henriette Hoffmann which took place on March 31, 1932.

The von Schirach family, who were descended "from noble stock" and through Baldur's mother, directly related to two signatories of the US Declaration of Independence, were violently opposed to the marriage and did their best to prevent it, but Hitler insisted. (Nizkor Project: 1943)

It was therefore a marriage that suited everyone except von Schirach's parents. Henriette Hoffmann, who had been a victim of Hitler's unwanted sexual attention as a girl, had fallen into prostitution after her mother's death and the marriage saved her from a life on the streets; at the same time, a veil was thrown over Baldur von Schirach's homosexual history and Hitler was no doubt relieved that "Henny" was now a respectable married woman and much less likely to gossip about any sexual indiscretions he had inflicted upon her.

Ernst Roehm attended the wedding while Rudolf Hess and Adolf Hitler took on the role of "best men".

Hitler then appointed Baldur von Schirach as gauleiter of Vienna in 1936. Years later, at his Nuremberg trial, von Schirach was one of only two men to denounce Hitler. (The other was Nazi architect, Albert Speer).

In the final year of WW2, boys as young as 12 were recruited from the Hitler Youth to fight in depleted German army units. One army unit made up almost entirely from its ranks fought in Normandy in 1944. The unit was later accused of committing several war crimes.

Baldur von Schirach was sentenced to 20 years in prison at Spandau in Berlin where he served out his time with Rudolf Hess. His wife Henriette divorced him in 1949. When he was released in September 1966, von Schirach retired quietly to southern Germany and published his memoirs, ironically called, I believed in Hitler. He died aged 67 on August 8, 1974 in Krov, Rhineland-Palatinate.

THREESOME: Henriette Hoffmann, Rudolf Hess, Baldur von Schirach

Albert 'Bubi' Foerster

In 1934, Albert Foerster, (b.1902-d.1952) the top Nazi official for Danzig-West Prussia married Gertrud Deetz following an order to do so from Adolf Hitler. The hastily arranged wedding took place in the Berlin Chancellery in May 1934, with both Adolf Hitler and Rudolf Hess presiding as witnesses.

The Nizkor Project noted that Foerster was "a known homosexual" who was addressed as "Bubi" by other Nazi officials including Hitler. "Hitler calls Foerster 'Bubi', which is a nickname employed by homosexuals in addressing their partners. More condemning would be the remarks dropped by Foerster, that deal with Hitler's impotence as far as heterosexual relations are concerned." (Ibid.)

During Albert Foerster's administration of Danzig-West Prussia, the local non-German population suffered ethnic cleansing, mass murder, and "forced

Germanization". Foerster was also responsible for the mass murders in Piasnica where approximately 12,000 to 16,000 Poles, Jews, Czechs and Germans were killed in the winter of 1939-1940. He was sentenced to death for crimes against humanity and executed in Poland in 1952.

Gerhard Rossbach

In 1912, Hans Blueher wrote the book, The German Wandervogel Movement as an Erotic Phenomenon, which told how the organization was used to recruit young boys into homosexuality.

Gerhard Rossbach (b.1893-d.1967) worked his way up through the Wandervogel [German Boy Scouts] and was involved in several successful WW1 military campaigns. Immediately after the war, he was one of many former army officers placed in command of a Freikorps unit.

Konrad Heiden, (Hitler's Rise to Power: 1944) a leading authority on early Nazi history, wrote that the Freikorps "were breeding places of perversion" and that "Rossbach's troop was especially proud of being homosexual".

His adjutant was Edmund Heines, a convicted pederast and murderer and noted for his ability to procure boys for sexual orgies. At one time, Rossbach claimed to have recruited Ernst Roehm into a gay lifestyle.

Historian Dr. Robert G. L. Waite (Psychopathic God: Adolf Hitler: 1977) described Rossbach as a "sadist, murderer and homosexual".

Most scholars agree that Rossbach was the bridge between the Wandervogel and the Nazi Party (Modern History Project: 2015) and he is generally credited with inventing their brown colored uniforms (using surplus tropical khaki shirts).

Rossbach took part in the Beer Hall Putsch in December 1923, mobilizing students and cadets but when the coup failed he fled to Austria.

Like other gay and bisexual Nazis, Rossbach married under pressure from Hitler. His first marriage took place circa 1933 but it quickly ended in divorce. He eventually remarried and had at least one child. His second marriage also ended in divorce. Hitler recruited him into the Storm Troopers but he fell out of favor and was imprisoned as part of the Roehm Purge in 1934. When he was released, he no longer had any influence within the Nazi machine. When the Allies arrested him after WW2, his ignorance of the Nazi regime was enough to save him from a custodial prison sentence.

In the post war era, he operated an import export company near Frankfurt and organized Richard Wagner festivals in Bayreuth. He died aged 74 in 1967.

Emil Maurice

Enigmatic bisexual, Emil Maurice (1897-1972) had known Hitler from the earliest days of the Nazi Party. They had served time and shared intimacy in Landsberg prison; they had also taken part in the "Night of the Long Knives" together and most important of all, they knew each others secrets.

Maurice knew of Hitler's liaisons with other homosexuals, including his earliest bodyguards – he too had been obliged to satisfy Hitler's sexual urges – and he also knew about Hitler's attempts to have relationships with underage girls - even worse, he knew about Hitler's incestuous and perverted relationship with his niece, Geli Raubal. He too had an affair with her.

When Hitler sacked him as his Munich chauffeur in 1931, Maurice transferred from the Storm Troopers to the more elite and prestigious Black Squadron or SS. But as a single man, he remained a link to Hitler's homosexual past and the German leader encouraged him to marry.

In 1935, Emil Maurice, aged 38, married Hedwig Ploetz, a beautiful 22-year-old medical student. Before the wedding could take place, the groom was obliged to submit details of his family history to Heinrich Himmler (because he had Jewish ancestry). Adolf Hitler did not attend the nuptials.

In 1936, Maurice was elected as a Reichstag deputy for Leipzig; and became chairman of Munich's chamber of commerce the following year. He later served with distinction in the Luftwaffe from 1940-42.

After WW2, he was sentenced by the Allies to four years in a Labor camp. He appealed his conviction, saying he had been "merely a chauffeur" and knew nothing of the SS or what they had done. His appeal was successful and he was released in 1948.

HANDSOME COUPLE: Emil Maurice and his bride; he successfully blackmailed Hitler over his sex life in 1927

He returned to work as a watchmaker in Munich where he lived with his wife and their two children. Witnesses said their family living room was decorated with paintings and portraits of his Jewish ancestors.

When Emil Maurice died in 1972, his wife Hedwig sold his collection of letters and other memorabilia connecting him with Hitler to a private bidder.

CHAPTER 8: THE MALE LOVE OF HITLER'S LIFE, JULIUS SCHRECK

"Even today, Hitler derives pleasure from looking at men's bodies and associating with homosexuals." (Nizkor Project: 1943)

FROM THE LATE 1920s onward, Hitler tried to present himself to the German people as a contented heterosexual bachelor (having been advised to do so by propaganda chief, Joseph Goebbels) but this "false personality" was very far from the truth.

While the Nazi machine began to persecute homosexuals, to imprison them and then to murder its own gay SA leaders, Hitler was enjoying a secret gay relationship with Julius Schreck, his personal Munich chauffeur and former bodyguard who would be his last male companion.

Schreck is one of the forgotten men in Hitler's love life; he was written out of history on the orders of Joseph Goebbels. Why? Because Schreck and Hitler conducted an on-off love affair for more than ten years.

Julius Schreck (b.1898-d.1936) took on the role of Hitler's personal chauffeur, based in Munich, after Emil Maurice was sacked from the job in 1931.

But from 1921 onward, Schreck had been a prominent member of every one of Hitler's bodyguard units created during the Nazi era.

These units changed their names every few years and included the Ordnertruppe [Steward Troop], the Saalschutz [Hall Protection], the Stabswache [Staff Guard], the Stosstrup [Shock Troop], the Schutzkommando [Protection Command] and finally the Schutzstaffel [Protection Squadron], the latter is better known as the infamous "Black Order" or SS.

As Schreck was a member of every one of Hitler's bodyguard units from the early 1920s and it is known that bodyguards were obliged to satisfy Hitler's sexual urges as and when necessary, it is highly likely that he and his boss had intimate knowledge of each other prior to 1931.

They may also have shared sexual intimacy in 1924 when they were both imprisoned in the sexual free-for-all that was Landsberg prison. In fact, it is known that Schreck had started working as one of Hitler's unofficial personal chauffeurs as early as 1926. (Jewish Virtual Library: 2015).

But their regular sexual relationship began in earnest in 1931 and their devotion to each other continued until Schreck's sudden death from meningitis in 1936.

Julius Schreck was born in Munich, Bavaria on July 13, 1898 which made him almost ten years younger than Hitler.

Like so many other WW1 soldiers, he was disillusioned when the war ended and developed right-wing views about Germany's future. He, like so many other disaffected soldiers, joined the Freikorps [Free Corps], a right-wing paramilitary army with a homosexual ethos.

At the time, Ernst Roehm was one of its most prominent commanders, and in March, 1919, the Freikorps took part in the successful overthrow of the Bavarian Socialist Republic. (spartacus-educational.com: 2015)

SECRET TRYSTS: Schreck became his loyal servant, occasional sex partner and bodyguard in the 1920s, in 1931, the relationship became more exclusive and they enjoyed long weekends together in the Bavarian mountains

Schreck joined the National Socialist German Worker's Party (NSDAP), in 1920 and is documented as "member number 53".
Soon afterward, Hitler and Schreck developed "a deep and enduring friendship". (Jewish Virtual Library: 2015).

Rubber bludgeons
From the time Hitler became Nazi party leader in 1921, Schreck played an important role in Hitler's rise to political power. He became known in those early days as a brutish SA thug who could always be relied upon to take part in street violence even at short notice.
Julius Schreck helped to organize the Nazi Party's first bodyguard unit, the Ordnertruppe [Steward Troop] whose task was to keep order at their indoor

political meetings.

It later became known as the Saalschutz [Hall Protection] within the larger Athletic and Sports section of the party. Over the next couple of years, its role and name changed and it specialized in guarding Nazi Party speakers, especially Hitler. In 1921, Schreck and Ernst Roehm helped to set up the Storm Troopers (SA) whose job it was to intimidate and physically subdue Nazi Party opponents. He also helped form the Stabswache [Staff Guard], which was an early company of SA troops assigned as Hitler's bodyguards.

At about this time, according to Peter Fotis Kapnistos, he earned the nickname "pistol Schreck" because of his apparent "mania for handguns". (Hitler's Doubles: 2015) He would use the butt of his gun to render and opponent senseless.

John Toland (Definitive Biography: 1991) said that like Emil Maurice, he was part of the muscle or "street fighter" element in the Storm Troopers - "the brawn rather than brains" within the SA and among the men who used "rubber bludgeons and knives" to intimidate and subdue Nazi Party opponents.

On one occasion, in October 1922, Hitler decided to make a display of force in Coburg, a town in Upper Bavaria, over 160 miles north of Munich.

The occasion was a "German Day" celebration which had been organized by a group of folk societies. Hitler, who was invited to attend and to "bring an escort", chose to interpret this invitation literally, and he left Munich in a special train with 600 SA men and a forty-two piece brass band. (Ibid.)

Historian John Toland said: "The train stopped for half an hour at Nuremberg to pick up more adherents. The band struck up again and the men shouted as they waved swastika flags from the windows. Jews in another halted train jeered at the swastika flags until Julius Schreck, 'leaped into the midst of them, laying about him.'"

"With military precision, the SA paraded into town. Just behind, a row of men carrying large red and black flags came behind Hitler and his entourage, followed by 800 men armed with rubber bludgeons or knives; their only common distinction was a swastika band on the left arm."

"Hitler himself was the epitome of the common man with his belted trench coat, slouch hat and ridiculous calf-high boots." (Definitive Biography: 1991)

In 1923, Schreck participated in the Beer Hall Putsch and was incarcerated at Landsberg prison along with other top Nazis but, unlike Hitler, he was released after only a few weeks.

When the Nazi Party was re-founded in 1925, Emil Maurice asked Schreck to help him form yet another new bodyguard unit for their boss. The Nazi leader wanted a small group of tough ex-soldiers like Schreck, who would be loyal to him.

This new unit was briefly called the Schutzkommando [Command Squadron] but was later renamed as the infamous Schutzstaffel [Protection Squadron] or SS. At first, it consisted of a group of eight men with Schreck being assigned SS Member number 5.

As Dr. Louis L. Snyder has pointed out: "The name was universally abbreviated to SS, not in Roman or Gothic letters but written as a lightening flash in imitation of ancient runic characters. The SS became widely known as the 'Black Order.'" (spartacus-educational.com: 2015)

Hitler soon appointed Schreck as Reichfuhrer-SS (SS chief) the highest rank available, though Schreck never referred to himself by this title and did not do very well in the job. (Jewish Virtual Library: 2015). He said he was only interested in protecting Hitler which he could do as his personal bodyguard and chauffeur.

SEEING DOUBLE: Julius Schreck grew a toothbrush mustache so that he would look more like his boss and lover; he was often attacked because of his doppelganger role

In 1926, he stood down as SS-chief to make way for more capable leaders such as Joseph Berchtold, and Sepp Dietrich, who eventually made way for the notorious Heinrich Himmler.

Schreck remained on the SS payroll but in reality, he was already working as Hitler's unofficial private chauffeur in Munich (when Emil Maurice was unavailable). In 1930, after the SS had begun to expand under Himmler, Schreck was appointed as an SS-Standartenfuhrer which meant he was responsible for a unit of between 300-500 men though he did not show much enthusiasm for the job. His final SS rank was Oberfuhrer but he had little actual power.

Schreck as body double

By the early 1930s, Hitler began to employ a string of doppelgangers to confuse the prying media and to prevent assassination attempts and Julius Schreck became one of them.

He grew a "toothbrush mustache" to mimic that worn by his boss and apparently, always had a trench coat, slouch hat and a pair of knee high boots ready so he could carry out his decoy job at a moment's notice.

Schreck was unusual as a "Hitler decoy" given his senior SS status because other Hitler doubles were mostly low-ranking soldiers or SA men who nobody really knew.

Peter Fotis Kapnistos (Hitler's Doubles: 2015) said Schreck was probably "the highest-ranking doppelganger within the Third Reich and on occasion was assaulted because of their resemblance".

Then in 1931, Schreck became Hitler's official private chauffeur (in Munich) even though he had been doing this job on a casual basis as early as 1926. According to Albert Speer, the author of Inside the Third Reich (1970), during this period, "pistol Schreck" was very much part of Hitler's inner circle in Munich.

"In the evenings, he [Hitler] usually had some trusty companions about including Schreck, his chauffeur for many years; Sepp Dietrich, the commander of his SS bodyguard; Dr. Otto Dietrich, the press chief; Bruckner and Schaub, his two adjutants; and Heinrich Hoffmann, his official photographer."

"Since the table held no more than ten persons, this group almost completely filled it. I saw very little of Himmler, Roehm or Streicher at these meals, but Goebbels and Goering were often there." (spartacus-educational.com: 2015)

Death's head skull

Julius Schreck was not known for his leadership skills but he is remembered for reintroducing ancient Germanic symbols into the Nazi uniform. When he became leader of the Stabswache [Hitler's earliest bodyguard unit], he resurrected the use of the Totenkopf skull and crossbones as the unit's insignia. It later became the insignia for the SS.

The Totenkopf symbol is internationally recognized as a warning of death, the defiance of death, danger and piracy. It consists usually of the human skull with or without the mandible and often includes two crossed long-bones (femurs), behind some part of the skull.

The symbol had first been used during the reign of German King Frederick II perhaps better known as Frederick the Great.

Both Hitler and Schreck adored the former German monarch and the Fuhrer had a large portrait of the homosexual king hanging in his Munich office. (Surreal Reich: 2010)

Both men were also admirers of King Frederick's writing, particularly his poetry and his love letters to Voltaire. They believed that their relationship mirrored the most important gay relationships in the former king's life.

In one of Frederick the Great's erotic poems, he wrote: "A moment of climax for a fortunate lover is worth so many eons of star-spangled honor". According to Philip Mansel (SpectatorOnline: 2015) "after Frederick's accession to the German throne in 1740, he repeatedly humiliated his wife as 'this incorrigibly sour subspecies of the female sex' and effectively 'came out' as being gay. He spent most of his time far from prying eyes in Potsdam, south- west of Berlin, and enjoyed 'intimate relations' with young officers, as well as his first valet Fredersdorf."

During Frederick's reign, the Totenkopf had been used as a German military symbol when the Hussar cavalry in the Prussian army used it as its emblem. This regiment adopted a black uniform with a skull and crossbones which was worn during the War of Austrian Succession and the Seven Years' War.

The symbol had also been widely used by the Freikorps of which Schreck had been a member during the inter-war years.

Andrew Mollo, author of To the Death's Head: The Story of the SS (1982) said: "[At first] SS men were expected to provide their own uniforms which also differed from those of the SA. SS men wore the brown shirt but, unlike the SA, they had a black cap adorned with a silver death's head, a black tie and black breeches."

SS-leader, Heinrich Himmler said of the Totenkopf: "The skull is a reminder that you shall always be willing to put yourself at stake for the life of the whole community."

Once the Schutzstaffel (SS) adopted the symbol, they continued to use the death's head skull to the very end of their history. It is one of the few innovations for which Schreck is given credit.

Car lovers

As well as their love for Frederick the Great, Hitler and Schreck also shared a fascination with fast cars. Hitler had developed his love for Mercedes Benz while at Landsberg from where he considered buying a "Benz 11/40" or a "16/50 with a more powerful engine" with "wire wheels".

Time magazine (June 1, 1936) said: "When Hitler drove out in his huge Mercedes-Benz, the man at the wheel was usually Julius Schreck, muscular, slit-eyed, sub-commander of the Schutzstaffel (SS), who wore an imitation Hitler mustache."

There are many pictures of the two men wearing the leather helmets worn by racing car drivers of that era.

There are also many images of the Fuhrer, who did not know how to drive, endorsing or inspecting the first production of luxury Mercedes Benz, including the sports models, from the mid-1930s up to the outbreak of WW2.

Although Hitler enjoyed viewing fast cars and owning them, he did not want to be driven fast.

PETROL HEAD: Hitler did not know how to drive but loved Mercedes Benz, he often complained to his chauffeur Schreck that he drove like a lunatic

According to Nerin E. Gun (Hitler's Mistress: 1969), Hitler and his chauffeur often argued over the speed at which Schreck chose to drive. "Hitler had a distrust of Schreck who was fond of speeding. Hitler, who never sat behind the wheel of a car, liked to be driven at a comfortable, middle-class pace."

During their relationship, Schreck "endorsed a German Grand Prix race car and organized the expansion of the Autobahn motorway" so that German drivers could increase their speed on the roads. (Hitler's Doubles: 2015)

But despite Schreck's need for speed and his boss's fear of it, he and Hitler often enjoyed leisurely drives around the Bavarian mountains near the Fuhrer's summer residence in Obersalzberg and the longer trips between Munich and Berlin, where they often stopped for the night at one of Bayreuth's secluded hotels for romantic interludes. (Surreal Reich: 2010)

Speeding

Nerin E. Gun (Hitler's Mistress: 1969) said that on the day of his niece, Geli Raubal's suicide, Hitler was rushing to be ready for his Hamburg trip because he did not want to give Schreck the excuse to start speeding if he was running late. On the day of her death, a car registered in Hitler's name, driven by Schreck, received a speeding ticket.

As the registered owner of the Mercedes, Hitler received the speeding ticket and later a summons from a traffic officer by the name of Probst on September 19, 1931,. (Daily Mail: 2011)

The speeding offense happened in the tiny hamlet of Baar-Ebenhausen, south of the city of Ingolstadt and apparently Hitler tried to get out of paying the fine by saying his lookalike chauffeur, Julius Schreck was driving the Mercedes at the time.

GOING ALL THE WAY: Schreck helped organize the expansion of the Autobahn in Munich

The registration plate number 11 A: 19357 of Hitler's personal car was sent to traffic headquarters in Munich and Probst wrote: "The speed of the vehicle was determined by two officials with stop watches. The car drove over a measured distance of 200m in 13 seconds, which resulted in the average speed of 55.3 km per hour (34.3mph). (Ibid.)

This was twice the permitted limit at that time and should have resulted in an immediate ban. Three days later, Probst received the information that the car belonged to one A. Hitler, who lived at Prinzeregentstrasse. There was, however, another document found in the archive with the word "settled" stamped on it. Apparently Hitler told officials he had instructed his chauffeur Schreck to drive as fast as possible without him being in the car without explaining why.

The Daily Mail (UK) and other newspapers have speculated that Hitler asked Schreck to speed on that day in a blind panic to get back to his Munich apartment because his niece Geli Raubal had shot herself there with his gun. Or, did Hitler use Schreck as a decoy to confuse police so he could have an alibi for her murder? More later.

PEOPLE WAGON: This drawing is believed to be Hitler's vision for a German family car; he drew it in a Munich restaurant in 1932 while arguing with Schreck about its design

Trysts at Hotel Bube

Ever since his time with August Kubizek, Adolf Hitler was a big fan of Richard Wagner's music and before the outbreak of WW2, he never missed the annual Wagner Festival in Bayreuth. Newsreel footage and photographs show him surrounded by adoring followers, SA men and curious onlookers in the town during the festivities.

But there was another reason why Hitler liked the Bayreuth district as it was where he and Julius Schreck spent many happy nights together away from prying eyes. Their favorite hideaway was the Hotel Bube in Bad Berneck near Bayreuth which overlooked a magnificent river. It also had the romantic backdrop of mountains and fir trees.

The Hotel Bube is roughly the midway point between Berlin and Munich, a route Hitler was obliged to travel frequently. What better cover could the loved-up couple have to conduct their steamy affair than to stop for the night midway through their 383-mile journey between the two cities? The Hotel Bube was secluded, romantic and the perfect place for illicit sex.

Joseph Howard Tyson (Surreal Reich: 2010) said: "Hitler and this trusted servant stole away by themselves for intimate weekend vacations in Obersalzberg, Bad Godesburg, Weimar and Bayreuth. One of their haunts was the Bube Hotel, a resort popular with homosexuals during opera festivals."

Gay lawyer, Erich Ebermayer also hinted at Hitler's fondness for the Hotel Bube and its sexual ethos (Ebermayer Diary: 1959):

"My sources stressed the homoerotic orientation of the Fuhrer and his inner circle, and have stated that the Fuhrer himself no longer indulges his inclinations. Only occasionally, on car journeys, notably at the Hotel Bube in Berneck does he get an opportunity to relax during trips from Berlin to Munich."

SECRET HIDEAWAY: They often went to the Hotel Bube for romantic weekends

Hitler's gay fantasies

Hitler was upset when, due to poor health, Schreck resigned as his private chauffeur in 1934, though the two men remained in regular contact.

When Schreck developed meningitis and died suddenly on May 16, 1936 in a Munich hospital, Adolf Hitler was devastated. Schreck was only 38 years old. Witnesses said Hitler was so distraught, he could not stop weeping for several days.

Schreck had fulfilled Hitler's fantasies about the great love between a powerful man and his obedient servant. (Surreal Reich: 2010)

One of Hitler's most treasured possessions was a love letter written by the homosexual Bavarian-King Ludwig to his coachman and lover for 20 years, Richard Hornig, for which he had paid a fortune when it came up for auction. The Bavarian monarch had refused to marry in spite of the pressure exerted on him by his family and government ministers and he apparently held orgies with the troopers under his command. Eventually, a secret Bavarian parliamentary committee discovered that their king had a weakness for "muscular country lads" and was declared insane by a special court. [He was found dead in his bath with one of his attendants in 1886, three years before Hitler was born].

Confusion over Schreck's death
Ignoring, the advice of his propaganda minister, Joseph Goebbels, Hitler immediately ordered a state funeral for his former bodyguard and chauffeur. While arrangements were being made for the ceremony, the Nazi propaganda machine set to work to bury Schreck's private life, in particular, his long-term homosexual relationship with their Fuhrer.

TERRIBLE TWINS: Hitler's associates said their boss adopted what he hoped was a "Napoleonic look" when he thought he was being observed

Goebbels deliberately fed misleading information to the foreign press who naturally wanted to know why a state funeral was being held for a mere chauffeur. (In the end, most foreign newspapers did not report on the funeral until years later). Goebbels also told Germany's media outlets that reporting on the ceremony would be severely restricted.
Meanwhile, members of the SS seized and destroyed Schreck's personal documents and any souvenirs connecting him with Hitler.

Author Peter Fotis Kapnistos (Hitler's Doubles: 2015) said "to confound Schreck's notice of death, several foreign news outlets reported that he died in a traffic accident in 1936" and three years after his death, several US newspapers continued to speculate about what really happened.

The Chicago Times (October 1, 1939) reported that he had been killed as part of an assassination attempt.

The newspaper said: "Julius Schreck, aged 38, was formerly Adolf Hitler's lookalike or double, a Bavarian, who also acted as the Chauffeur of the Fuhrer's giant Mercedes".

The article noted "his devotion to the Fuhrer" and added that "during election campaigns, Schreck sometimes slept in his clothes for weeks at a time."

BAVARIAN KING: The gay monarch had sex with his bodyguards and coachman; he was one of Hitler's heroes; King Ludwig 11 was a great sponsor of the arts and helped to promote Richard Wagner's career

The article concluded: "Schreck and Hitler were traveling in a car to the town of Bernau on May 15, 1936. They reached a railway crossing and slowed up. As they did so, shots fired with unerring accuracy, burst from the roadside. The man in the passenger seat slumped. The wrong man had been assassinated."

Primitive and brutal

By contrast, the Pittsburgh Press, (June 11, 1942) published a story with a different slant. The article blamed Schreck's death on his imitation toothbrush mustache: "Sabotage Howls Hitler at Error in Mustache Size".

According to their report, Schreck had contracted an abscess while taking one of Hitler's Mercedes cars from Berlin to Munich and had "a great swollen jaw". The newspaper said "He [Schreck] was a primitive, brutal, animal-type of man utterly devoted to Hitler. He took a screw-driver from his tool-case, gouged and scraped the infected tooth, broke open an abscess losing four teeth, amidst horrible pain, tried to pull the worst tooth with a pair of pliers and started to Munich with a temperature of over 100. When Schreck arrived in Munich, he was taken to a hospital and subsequently died of the infection. The word was that Hitler wept bitterly at his chauffeur's death." (Hitler's Doubles: 2015).

Adolf Hitler was indeed inconsolable after the death of his loyal friend and lover and ordered all the Nazi top brass to attend the specially arranged state funeral. The ceremony took place at Grafelfing cemetery near Munich on May 27 with Hitler delivering the eulogy. Joseph Goebbels' had warned the German media that no part of Hitler's "personal eulogy" could be quoted in German newspapers. As a result, the Munich Observer (May 28, 1936) merely confirmed the event with plenty of photographs but provided few details about Schreck's life.

TOP BRASS: All the Nazi hierarchy turned out for Schreck's funeral during which restrictions were placed on media reporting

It said: "Julius Schreck, one of the earliest members of the Nazi Party and a founding member of the SS, served as Hitler's personal chauffeur. He died of meningitis on May 16, 1936, and received a Nazi state funeral and burial at the cemetery in Grafelfing, a suburb of Munich. His casket was borne to the grave by 'Old Fighters' and SA and SS members."

"Adolf Hitler delivered the eulogy at Schreck's graveside. Also attending were Rudolf Hess, Christian Weber, Victor Lutze, Joseph Goebbels, Hermann Goering, Wilhelm Bruckner, Heinrich Himmler, Otto Dietrich, Franz Xavier Schwarz,

Wilhelm Frick, Martin Bormann, Julius Streicher, Julius Schaub, Max Amann, Fritz Todt, Robert Ley, Walter Darr, Adolf Huhnlein, Josef "Sepp" Dietrich, and other Nazi leaders."

Valhalla
Under the heading "Chauffeur to Valhalla", Time magazine (June 1, 1936) also reported on the funeral and remarked on the number of Nazi "bigwigs" at the graveside.
"White-faced and shaking, Adolf Hitler last week stood beside an open grave in Grafelfing cemetery near Munich. Massed behind him, were most of Germany's Nazi bigwigs. The Realm leader had come to bury his chauffeur, Julius Schreck, 32 [he was in fact aged 38], dead of inflammation of the brain." The report continued: "Julius Schreck was the first commander of the SS, a special police force that originated as a strict bodyguard company for Hitler. After the SS began to expand under Heinrich Himmler, Schreck remained on the SS payrolls and worked as Hitler's private chauffeur and political decoy."

It was quite a send-off for a man of humble origins who, to the outside world at least, had merely been Hitler's personal bodyguard, chauffeur and occasional body double.
Joseph Howard Tyson (Surreal Reich: 2010) said: "Schreck's sudden death from meningitis in May 1936 affected Hitler deeply. He placed a picture of him in his study next to the one of his mother Klara."
It was indeed the end of an era as Julius Schreck would be Hitler's last long-term, gay partner.

PART THREE – HITLER'S FEMININITY & HEALTH: ADDICTIONS & OBSESSIONS

CHAPTER 9: HITLER'S FEMININE CHARACTERISTICS

The psychiatric experts who examined Hitler's character and psyche suggested that the entire "Fuhrer personality" was a grossly exaggerated and distorted conception of masculinity as Hitler believed it to be. In other words, he acted the way he thought men were expected to behave.

They said: "Undoubtedly he would like to be such a [masculine] person in reality and believes that he actually is that person but he deceives himself. This personality has been created unconsciously as a compensation and cover-up for deep-lying tendencies which he despises. This mechanism always serves the purpose of denying the true self by creating an image which is diametrically opposite [to reality] and then identifying with the image." (Nizkor Project: 1943)

"The great difference between Hitler and thousands of other hysterics is that he managed to convince millions of other people that the image was true. The more he was able to convince them, the more he became convinced of it himself on the theory that 80 million Germans can't be wrong." (Ibid.)

Dr. Jekyll and Mrs. Hyde
The psychiatrists also claimed there were "two people" at work inside Hitler who were constantly battling each other for dominance.

"This is not one person but two which inhabit the same body and alternate back and forth. The one is a very soft, sentimental and indecisive individual who has little drive and wants nothing quite so much as to be amused, liked and looked after. The other is just the opposite, hard, cruel and decisive who knows what he wants and is ready to go after it and get it regardless of costs."

"It is the first Hitler who weeps profusely at the death of his canary, and the second Hitler who can say with great conviction: 'There will be no peace in the land until a body hangs from every lamp-post'." (Ibid.)

"His extreme sentimentality, his emotionality, his occasional softness and his weeping, even after he became Chancellor, may be regarded as manifestations of a fundamental feminine pattern which had its origins in his relationship to his mother, his gait, his hands, his mannerisms and ways of thinking. His choice of art as a profession might also be interpreted as a manifestation of a basic feminine identification."

These experts noticed that Hitler gained considerable pleasure from spending time with the Hitler Youth, but they said his attitude toward them was "more that of a woman than a man".

They also noted that his voice often had "a rasping-quality which broke into a shrill falsetto when he became aroused" (Ibid.).

One of Hitler's assistants, Josef Wagner described his boss in the following way: "His gait was not that of a soldier. It was a very ladylike walk. Dainty little steps.

Every few steps he cocked his right shoulder nervously, his left leg snapping up as he did so."

And former Nazi, Ernst Hanfstaengl (The Missing Years: 1957) said that when he showed psychologist, Dr. Carl Jung a specimen of Hitler's handwriting in 1937, the latter immediately exclaimed that it was a typically feminine hand which had "the characteristics of someone with essentially feminine instincts".

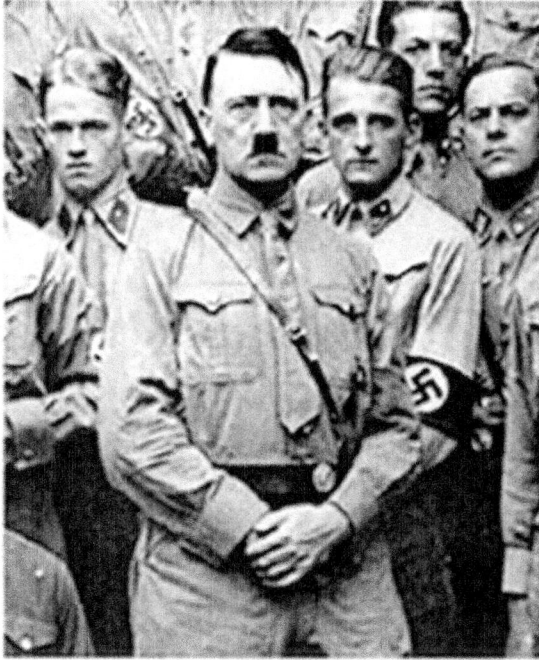

MUM'S THE WORD: Hitler took on a mothering role with the young boys in the Hitler Youth

William L. Shirer (Rise and Fall: 1960) said "Though Hitler reflexively acted with brutality, the Fuhrer exhibited many traits associated with homosexuality, including heightened aesthetic sense, intuition, mental acuity, dramatic flair and duplicity."

Indeed, breaking down in floods of tears, having regular tantrums and using emotional blackmail to manipulate others might be considered more feminine characteristics than masculine ones and these were all character traits which the "manly Fuhrer" regularly displayed.

Many of Hitler's associates admitted that he often wept openly in front of them.

Weeping like a baby

Historian Will D. Bayles (Caesars in Goose Step: 1940) said "when he finds himself in difficult situations, the great dictator who prides himself on his decisiveness, hardness and other leadership qualities, breaks down and weeps like a child appealing for sympathy".

Herman Rauschning (Voice of Destruction: 1939) agreed that Hitler often lost control emotionally when he was under pressure or he was frustrated:

"In 1934 as in 1932 he complained of the ingratitude of the German people in the sobbing tones of a down-at-the-heel music-hall performer! 'If the German people don't want me...!' A weakling who accused and sulked, pleaded and implored, and retired in wounded vanity instead of acting."

And journalist Konrad Heiden (Hitler: a Biography: 1936) described a scene at a Nazi Party leaders' meeting at which Hitler heard of a colleague's disloyalty to him: "He [Hitler] cried, and laid his head on the table and sobbed. Tears came to the eyes of many of those present, as they saw their Fuhrer weeping."

Former Nazi, Otto Strasser (Gangsters around Hitler: 1942) also confirmed the Fuhrer's penchant for losing control. On one occasion, he took both of Strasser's hands in his: "His voice was choked with sobs, and tears flowed down his cheeks."

This particular episode happened during a Nazi Party meeting in the early 1930s. There is also newsreel footage showing Hitler weeping on stage during his speeches to the German nation in what might be described as a non-masculine way.

Submissive, feminine role

Hitler's mother Klara had been submissive to Alois Sr. and the psychiatric experts who examined Hitler's life suggested she must have had a strong submissive and even masochistic streak to have endured the constant beatings and the abuse of her children with such "a stoic and uncomplaining attitude". (Nizkor Project: 1943)

So too her son, Adolf. They said there was a strong submissive [feminine] as well as masochistic element in his character.

He was submissive to his superior officers during WW1 and took on the "woman's role" of washing their undergarments and uniforms, fetching and carrying whatever they wanted and doing their menial chores (much to the disgust of other soldiers) and he continued to be servile to them immediately after the war.

He was willing to do anything they asked, even to the point of spying on his own comrades and then condemning them to death [just before the foundation of the Nazi Party].

"It is an excellent example of Hitler's willingness to submit to the leadership of strong males who guided and protected him." (Ibid.) Just as a woman might do if she had no family or partner to support her.

When his officers singled him out to do special propaganda work because they believed he had a talent for speaking, he was "overjoyed" and Hitler said, for the first time in his life, he felt "appreciated and loved".

Nor did he behave in a "manly" way in the presence of royalty. He was star struck, nervous and always submissive when he met anyone with a title; he bowed and scraped (much to the embarrassment of some of his Nazi colleagues) as he did with President Paul von Hindenburg and several royals.

Also, when in the company of young girls he felt attracted to, witnesses said he groveled at their feet and often said he "was not worthy" to be near them. Again, this type of behavior was submissive and unmanly and these girls were prone to laughing at the Fuhrer's bizarre behavior behind his back.

Hitler's rages (chewing the carpet)

Almost everyone who knew him commented on Hitler's rages. "These are well known to all of his associates and they have learned to fear them. The descriptions of his behavior during these rages vary considerably. The more extreme descriptions claim that at the climax he rolls on the floor and chews on the carpet." (Nizkor Project: 1943)

William L. Shirer (Rise and Fall: 1960) said that in 1938 he did this so often that his associates frequently referred to him as "Teppichfresser" [carpet eater].

"Even without this added touch of chewing the carpet, his behavior was still extremely violent and showed an utter lack of emotional control. In the worst rages he undoubtedly acts like a spoiled child who cannot have his own way and bangs his fists on the tables and walls. He scolds and shouts and stammers and on some occasions, foaming saliva gathers in the corners of his mouth." (Nizkor Project: 1943)

They said "His rages are brought on whenever anyone contradicts him, when there is unpleasant news for which he might feel responsible, when there is any skepticism concerning his judgment or when a situation arises in which his infallibility might be challenged or belittled". (Ibid.)

Herman Rauschning (Voice of Destruction: 1939) described one of Hitler's uncontrolled exhibitions: "He was an alarming sight, his hair disheveled, his eyes fixed, and his face distorted and purple. I feared that he would collapse or have a stroke."

And in a series of articles in 1939, Karl Von Weigand ("Hitler Foresees His End") said there was a tacit understanding among his personal staff: "For God's sake don't excite the Fuhrer, which means do not tell him bad news, do not mention things which are not as he conceives them to be."

F. A. Voigt also (Unto Caesar: 1938) said: "Close collaborators for many years said that Hitler was always like this, that the slightest difficulty or obstacle could make him scream with rage. Occasionally, he will look around sheepishly, as if to see if anyone is laughing, and then proceeds with other matters, without the slightest trace of resentment."

Dr. Walter C. Langer et al said : "Some of his closest associates have felt that he induces these rages consciously to frighten those about him."

According to some eyewitnesses, the rages would often end with the Fuhrer screeching in a high-pitched, hysterical [female] voice.

Emotional blackmail

There is no doubt that Hitler used emotional blackmail and fear to control those around him. He gained control of the Nazi Party in 1921 by threatening to leave and never come back.

According to Munich journalist, Konrad Heiden, he did this: "To break all resistance for good, he left the party for three days, and the trembling members obediently chose him as the first, unlimited chairman, for practical purposes responsible to no one, in place of Anton Drexler, the modest founder, who had to content himself with the post of honorary chairman [July 29, 1921]." (spartacus-educational.com: 2015)

Threats of suicide

Hitler's frequent threats of suicide were yet another form of emotional blackmail, a trait perhaps more prevalent in women than in men. By using his "feminine wiles" and playing on the emotions of others, Hitler was able to manipulate and control their behavior to his own satisfaction.

As a teenager, he had threatened to throw himself into the Danube over his fantasy relationship with Stefanie Isak, and the option of suicide as a reaction to unpalatable events or circumstances continued throughout his adult life.

During the Beer Hall Putsch, he told the officials he and his associates were holding as prisoners: "There are still five bullets in my pistol, four for the traitors, and one, if things go wrong, for myself," (Ibid.)

He threatened to commit suicide in front of Mrs. Ernst Hanfstaengl directly after the failure of the Putsch, while he was hiding from police in the Hanfstaengl home. Then in Landsberg Prison, he went on a (very brief) hunger strike and threatened to martyr himself in imitation of Terence McSwiney, Lord Mayor of Cork who starved himself to death for the cause of Irish nationalism. (spartacus-educational.com: 2015) Hitler's hunger strike lasted less than one day.

In 1931, he again threatened to commit suicide after the death of his niece, Geli Raubal. Apparently, his bodyguards were obliged to watch over him every minute in the weeks that followed in case he carried out the threat. Rudolf Hess is also reported to have removed a pistol from his beloved Fuhrer's hand to prevent him doing so.

In 1932, he again threatened suicide if Gregor Strasser carried out his threat to split the Nazi Party.

In 1933, he threatened to end his life if he was not appointed Chancellor immediately, and in 1936, he promised to kill himself if the Occupation of the Rhineland failed. There were many other examples of his hysterical "I will end it all" if such-and-such does not happen.

Dr. Langer and his team predicted Hitler's death by suicide (in 1943) and claimed it was inevitable given his particular character traits. They concluded that Adolf Hitler was both an hysteric and a borderline schizophrenic.

"From what we know of his psychology, it is the most likely outcome; his rages will increase in frequency; his public appearances will become less and less as he is unable to face a critical audience; his mental state will deteriorate."

"The course he will follow will almost certainly be the one which seems to him to be the surest road to immortality and at the same time drag the world down in flames. It is probably true that he has an inordinate fear of death, but being a hysteric, he could undoubtedly screw himself up into the super-man character and perform the deed."

CHAPTER 10: HITLER'S PHYSICAL PROFILE

HITLER ONCE ORDERED a team of phrenologists to take measurements of his skull. The phrenologists concluded that his skull was "just like Napoleon's" and they had seen "nothing like it since Frederick the Great".

But when Hitler was put on trial for attempting to overthrow the government, Professor Max von Gruber of the University of Munich, the most eminent eugenicist in Germany reported:

"It was the first time I had seen Hitler close at hand. Face and head of inferior type, cross-breed; low receding forehead, ugly nose, broad cheekbones, little eyes, dark hair. Expression, not of a man exercising authority in perfect self-command, but of raving excitement."

The Nizkor Project (1943) authors also gave him a very unflattering description. With the exception of his "hypnotic glance" they believed he had nothing to recommend him by way of his physique.

"His hips are wide and his shoulders relatively narrow. His muscles are flabby; his legs short, thin and spindly, the latter being hidden in the past by heavy boots and more recently by long trousers. He has a large torso and is hollow-chested to the point where it is said that he has his uniforms padded. From a physical point of view, he could not pass the requirements to join his own elite guard."

His close associates also said he had a tic in his face which caused the corner of his lips to curl upward.

Friedelinde Wagner (who knew him when she was a child) said his dress sense, in the early days, was very unattractive. "He frequently wore the Bavarian mountain costume of leather shorts with white shirt and suspenders. These were not always too clean and with his mouth full of brown, rotten teeth and his long dirty fingernails, he presented rather a grotesque picture; his dark brown hair was parted in the middle and pasted down flat against his head with oil."

When Joseph Goebbels became his propaganda minister and media guru in the late 1920s, Hitler's appearance underwent a radical transformation.

Hitler's lederhosen [short trousers with suspenders] were banished, his hairstyle changed to a side parting; he began to wear high boots to hide his spindly legs and long trench coats over his own clothes or uniform to give him a more manly physique.

Goebbels was unable, however, to convince his boss to get rid of his toothbrush mustache which became a source of ridicule for his enemies and detractors - his trademark - which remained in situ for the rest of his life.

Height, weight and missing testicle
Documents discovered in 2010 (Hitler's time in jail: 2010), as part of Landsberg Prison's intake book stated that in April 1924, when Hitler arrived to serve his sentence, his medical examination showed that he had "health of moderate strength"; his height was measured at 1.75 meters (5'9") with weight measured at 77 kilograms (169 lbs. or 12.15 st.). He was 35 years old at the time.

While at Landsberg, he was examined by Dr. Josef Brinsteiner who discovered that

Hitler had only one testicle. The prison recorded that Hitler suffered from an undescended right testicle, or "right-side cryptorchidism". If the condition is not diagnosed in the first year of a child's life, it is too late, as in Hitler's case, to rectify the problem.

Today, treatment for the condition usually involves a simple operation called an "orchidopexy" to move the testicle into the correct position; an operation not widely available or understood during Hitler's life time.

General health

Almost from birth, Hitler suffered from very poor health. He had been a sickly child but survived several illnesses from which his siblings had perished. His friend August Kubizek confirmed his poor physical condition (The Young Hitler I Knew: 1953): "Adolf was of middle height and slender. His physique was far from sturdy, rather too thin for its height, and he was not at all strong. His health, in fact, was rather poor, which he was the first to regret. He had to take special care of himself during the foggy and damp winters which prevailed in Linz. He was ill from time to time during that period and coughed a lot. In short, he had weak lungs." And then in 1905, he was stricken by Consumption but survived.

In Vienna, he lived close to starvation at times, surviving on handouts from soup kitchens which could not have helped his condition and during WW1, he was wounded by shrapnel in the upper thigh and poisoned by mustard gas shortly after that.

His physician, Dr. Theodor Morell also said Hitler had longstanding abdominal problems which included stomach cramps, gas, constipation and diarrhea. For these chronic gastrointestinal problems, Dr. Morell said Hitler took large amounts of a drug to fight flatulence [farting].

Historians have also recorded that the German leader had polyps removed from his vocal chords twice; had high blood pressure and suffered from hepatitis, which was triggered by a blockage around his gall bladder.

Some of the unusual medical remedies Hitler resorted to included enemas for his constipation and leeches for blood complaints.

Parkinson's disease

As early as 1935, Hitler developed a tremor in his left arm and leg. The palsy or shake became very severe over time and debilitating during WW2.

In an attempt to disguise the problem, Hitler would wring his hands while speaking or clasp them tightly together (either in front or behind his back} so the tremor would go undetected. In most Nazi era photographs, Hitler does indeed have his hands tightly clasped either in front or behind his body but newsreel footage shows the tremors in his hand as well as his shuffling walk. Several German doctors, including Ernst-Gunther Schenck gave a diagnosis of Parkinson's disease.

Then in September 1944, Hitler suffered a minor heart attack and was forced to spend several days in bed. This exacerbated his Parkinson's disease.

After his heart attack, several Berlin witnesses claimed Hitler now "dribbled from the sides of his mouth" when he tried to speak more than a few sentences. They

also said the Fuhrer could only walk a few paces before becoming tired. (spartacus-educational.com:2015)
All of this was kept hidden from the German people but in the end, Hitler had so many medical complaints that Dr. Morell administered every type of drug available at the time just to keep the German leader functioning.

By late 1944, Hitler had become unhappy with Dr. Morell's medical treatments so he dispatched him back to the army to do general medical work. Morell was replaced by Dr. Karl Brandt who became Hitler's final physician - constantly on hand to administer painkilling and amphetamine injections during the final months of his life.
Hitler also had many psychological problems - real and imagined - which are dealt with in the next chapter.

Hitler's unusual diet
Hitler had peculiar dietary habits, consuming "tremendous quantities of sweets,

candies, cakes, whipped cream, in addition to his vegetable diet". (Nizkor Project: 1943)

"He eats large quantities of eggs prepared by the best chefs in Germany and there are always a large variety of fresh vegetables prepared in unusual ways. In addition, Hitler consumes incredible quantities of pastries and often as much as two pounds of chocolates in the course of a single day." (Ibid.)

He also loved pasta dishes, his favorite being asparagus tips in a cream sauce.

Witnesses said that Hitler rarely smiled and when he did so, he never showed his unsightly teeth.

His personal dentist, Dr. Johannes Blaschke reported that the Fuhrer had rotten teeth, bad breath, abscesses, and gum disease and "dreaded going to the dentist to the point of it being a phobia".

Vegetarian

As far as being vegetarian was concerned, Herman Rauschning (Hitler Speaks: 1939) said that Hitler attributed much of the decay of civilization to meat-eating and that the decadence "had its origin in the abdomen, chronic constipation, poisoning of the juices, and the results of drinking to excess".

Hitler said that "he was confident that one day all nations would arrive at the point where they would not feed any more on dead animals".

Yet, his childhood friend, August Kubizek said Hitler ate meat when they knew each other between 1904 and 1908.

In fact, Hitler only became a vegetarian immediately after his niece, Geli Raubal's death in September 1931 and some of his Nazi colleagues said that he only became a vegetarian because "the smell of meat reminded him of Geli's corpse" when he viewed it in Munich's morgue. (But there is no actual evidence that Hitler ever viewed his niece's corpse.)

The Nizkor Project said: "In clinical practice, one almost invariably finds compulsive vegetarianism setting in after the death of a loved object."

They also attributed his vegetarianism to his perversions: coprophilia and urophilia.

"In terms of unconscious symbolism, meat is almost synonymous with feces and beer with urine. The fact that there is a strict taboo on both [for Hitler] would indicate that these desires are still present and that it is only by refraining from everything symbolizing them that he can avoid arousing anxieties [in himself]."

In the 1930s, several witnesses confirmed that Hitler continued to drink red wine, especially when in the company of women, in particular, actress Renate Mueller and his half-niece, Geli Raubal .

Hypnotic eyes

Hitler's "hypnotic eyes" have been the subject of much comment by so many writers. His eyes were blue [like his mother's] and not brown or hazel as so many people have assumed.

Some of his associates reported that at their first meeting, Hitler "fixated them with his eyes as if to bore through them".

His childhood friend August Kubizek said: (The Young Hitler I Knew: 1953) "The eyes were so outstanding that one didn't notice anything else. Never in my life have I seen any other person whose appearance was so completely dominated by the eyes. They were the light eyes of his mother, but her somewhat staring, penetrating gaze was even more marked in the son and had even more force and expressiveness. In fact, Adolf spoke with his eyes, and even when his lips were silent one knew what he wanted to say. When I introduced him to my mother, she said, 'What eyes your friend has!' And I remember quite distinctly that there was more fear than admiration in her words. If I am asked where one could perceive, this man's exceptional qualities, I can only answer, 'In the eyes'."

Nazi propaganda minister, Joseph Goebbels was so captivated by Hitler's eyes that he turned from a skeptic to a believer once he met him face-to-face.

Apparently, at first, Goebbels did not have a high opinion of his Nazi boss; did not like his methods as leader or the way he treated senior party members.

Then, he described their first one-to-one conversation at a Nazi Party gathering in his diary: "Shakes my hand. Like an old friend. And those big blue eyes. Like stars. He is glad to see me. I am in heaven. That man has everything to be king."

The OSS report claimed Hitler's eyes were "bordering on violet" with a hypnotic glint. But people who met him for the first time, sometimes commented that when they met his gaze, and held it, Hitler often turned his eyes up to the ceiling and kept them there for the rest of the conversation.

And former Nazi, Herman Rauschning (Hitler Speaks: 1939) wrote a cautionary note:

"Anyone who has seen this man face-to-face, has met his uncertain glance, without depth or warmth, from eyes that seem hard and remote, and has then seen that gaze grow rigid, will certainly have experienced the uncanny feeling: 'That man is not normal'."

CHAPTER 11: HITLER'S HEALTH - ADDICTIONS & OBSESSIONS

Obsession with syphilis

Adolf Hitler was obsessed by syphilis and devoted many pages in Mein Kampf (1925) to its perils. The Nizkor Project authors and other scholars have suggested that his mother Klara's side of the Hitler family may have carried a strain of the disease.

In his autobiography, Hitler said: "The fight against syphilis demands a fight against prostitution, against prejudices, old habits, the first prerequisite for even the moral right to combat these things is the facilitation of earlier marriage for the coming generation. In late marriage alone lies the compulsion to retain an institution which, twist and turn as you like, is and remains a disgrace to humanity."

In Mein Kampf, he blamed foreigners for the spread of the disease: "Nothing but a stroke of the pen, and a Mongolian slave is forthwith turned into a real German. Not only is no question asked regarding the race to which the new citizen belongs; even the matter of his physical health is not inquired into. His flesh may be corrupted with syphilis; but he will still be welcome in the State so long as he may not become a financial burden or a political danger."

Hitler continued his tirade: "Running parallel to the political, ethical, and moral contamination of the people, there had been for many years, a no less terrible poisoning of the health of the national body. Especially in the big cities, syphilis was beginning to spread more and more, the attitude of the leadership of the nation and the state can only be designated as total capitulation."

"Thus, by the use of all propagandist means, the question of combating syphilis should have been made to appear as the task of the nation. To this end, its injurious effects should have been thoroughly hammered into people as the most terrible misfortune, until the entire nation arrived at the conviction that everything; future or ruin, depended upon the solution of this question. For, seriously to attack this plague, tremendous sacrifices and equally great labors are necessary."

In his essay, "Mein Kampf, a translation controversy" (2009), Michael Ford claimed the Fuhrer's obsession with syphilis was fed by his fears that he had contracted the disease during WW1.

"There is much controversy over why he spent so many pages on the matter. Medical reports discovered after World War 2 indicated that he may have suffered from syphilis. At any rate, he believed he had syphilis and his doctor administered treatments that were common for syphilis sufferers at the time."

These treatments included mild doses of arsenic, mercury or even an injection of malaria. Even though the earliest form of Penicillin was created in the late 1920s, it was not widely used to treat syphilis until after WW2.

US investigators suggested Hitler's obsession with the disease revealed his fear of genital mutilation, a throwback to a deep-rooted fear of his father.

"Throughout Mein Kampf, he comes back to the topic of syphilis again and again, in almost all cases, we find that a fear of this sort is rooted in a fear of genital injury during childhood; he uses the horrors of syphilis as a justification for his unconscious fear of that genital sexuality is dangerous for him."

Blow-up sex dolls
Hitler was so obsessed by his fear of syphilis that he wanted to provide Nazi soldiers with blow-up sex dolls to combat the disease. The dolls were smaller than life-size and could easily fit into a soldier's backpack.
The Nazis initially approached Hungarian actress, Kathe von Nagy to serve as a model for the dolls but when she refused, they settled on a blue-eyed blonde prototype to comfort soldiers.

The story of the blow-up sex dolls was revealed in a 2011 article in the Huffington Post which said: "The French Resistance and Allied bombers were not the only threats Nazi soldiers faced in Paris during WW2. The syphilis spread after dalliances with French prostitutes presented a more clandestine danger. To combat Nazi soldiers' temptations and Parisian joie de vivre, Hitler gave the go-ahead to manufacture blow-up sex dolls as a more hygienic alternative to using prostitutes."
Author Graeme Donald (Mussolini's Barber: 2010) who first discovered Germany's sex doll project said: "Hitler had ordered them to be made as ever more

troops were laid low by disease rather than by bullets. Syphilis was a problem Hitler was aware of and he was rumored to have suffered from it himself."

The sex dolls were part of "The Borghild Project", a top secret 1940 mission inspired by SS chief, Heinrich Himmler who claimed "the greatest danger in Paris is the widespread and uncontrolled presence of whores,"

The project focused on creating smaller than life sized dolls that would fit into a soldier's backpack and could then be taken out and pumped full of air, as and when required.

After endless tests by Nazi troops on the island of Jersey, blow-up dolls were manufactured for a selection of Himmler's troops.

But the project was postponed when soldiers refused to carry the dolls which they said would cause them great embarrassment if they were ever captured by the Allies.

Himmler's sex doll factories were destroyed during the Allied bombing of Dresden in February 1945.

Bed Compulsion and insomnia

Hitler had developed a taste for expensive living in the mid-1920s when private funding for the Nazi Party started rolling in. He collected paintings and Mercedes cars, furnished his apartments in Munich and Berlin with the latest designer materials and fabrics and lavished gifts on himself and his friends.

The only modest thing about his living arrangements were his bedrooms in Berlin, Munich and Berchtesgaden. These bedrooms were always furnished in the same way with a metal bed (decorated with yellow ribbons at the head), a painted chest of drawers and a few straight chairs.

Friedelinde Wagner and Ernst Hanfstaengl (The Missing Years:1957) both described his Munich bedroom in the same way, namely that it was a room "a lowly maid might have rather than a Chancellor."

Herman Rauschning (Voice of Destruction: 1939) also claimed that Hitler had "a bed compulsion" which demanded that the bed be made in a particular way with the quilt folded according to a specific pattern and that "a man must make the bed, before he could go to sleep".

Along with his bed compulsion, Hitler seemed to have a peculiar aversion to going to bed at a normal hour and being alone late at night.

Dr. Walter C. Langer et al said: "Sleep is no longer a refuge from his fears; he is afraid to sleep. He wakes up in the night shaking and screaming."

He had the habit of taking "a sleeping powder every night before retiring" an antidote to the "terrifying nightmares from which he awakes in a cold sweat and acts as though he were being suffocated". (Nizkor Project: 1943)

Hitler would often ring for his adjutants in the middle of the night after his guests had gone home and demand that they sit up and talk to him. It was not that he had anything to say and often the adjutants would fall asleep listening to him but as long as one of them remained awake, he was not offended.

"Even after he has dismissed his adjutant and goes to bed, he usually takes an armful of illustrated periodicals with him." (Ibid.)

Being attacked from behind

Herman Rauschning (Voice of Destruction: 1939) claimed Hitler's personal staff knew that their boss often woke in the middle of the night convulsing, shrieking and shouting for help.

"He sits on the edge of his bed, as if unable to stir. He shakes with fear, making the whole bed vibrate. He shouts confused, unintelligible phrases. He gasps, as if imagining himself to be suffocating. On one occasion Hitler, stood swaying in his room, looking wildly about him. 'He! He! He's been here!' he gasped. His lips were blue. Sweat streamed down his face. Suddenly he began to reel off figures, and odd words and broken phrases, entirely devoid of sense."

"It sounded horrible. He used strangely composed and entirely un-German word-formations. Then he stood still, only his lips moving. Then he suddenly broke out 'There, there!' In the corner! Who's that?' He stamped and shrieked in the familiar way."

The Nizkor Project authors suggested that Hitler's homosexual tendency found expression in his nightmares including "imagery concerning being attacked from behind or being stabbed in the back".

They said: "His nightmares, which frequently deal with being attacked by a man and being suffocated, also suggest strong homosexual tendencies and a fear of them."

Hypochondria

But fear of sleep was not the end of it. Other fears which contradicted the image of the brave and manly Fuhrer cropped up again and again.

Dr. Langer and his research team said images continued to appear in his mind and shook his confidence.

"Underneath, Hitler is a bundle of fears. He may rationalize these fears or displace them but they continue to haunt him."

For example, he had a morbid fear of cancer [because it killed his mother] and also of taking tablets, so his doctors were obliged to administer his medication by syringe.

Several outstanding specialists in cancer treatments assured him his fears of cancer were without foundation. Even so, he continued to believe he had been stricken by the disease in spite of all the expert testimony to the contrary.

"If our hypothesis is correct, namely, that a fear of death is one of the powerful unconscious streams which drive Hitler on in his mad career, then we can expect that as the war progresses and as he becomes older, the fear will continue to increase," (Nizkor Project: 1943)

Hitler had many other fears to deal with they said: "fears of being assassinated, fears of losing his health, fears of gaining weight, fears of treason, fears of losing his mystical guidance, fears of anesthetics, fears of premature death, fears that his mission will not be fulfilled." (Ibid.)

Hitler demanded of his doctors and close associates that "every conceivable precaution must be taken to reduce these dangers, real and imagined.

In addition, as his career progressed, he developed a "pathological fear of poisoning by mouth" and tried to solve the problem with an obsessional preoccupation with mouth-washing. (Ibid.)

Master of the syringe

On top of all his other health problems, Hitler became addicted to "uppers and downers" and many other drugs.

According to Jonathan Lewy (Drug Policy of the Third Reich: 2008), drug addiction was viewed as a "curable disease" in Nazi Germany. The use of most drugs among non-persecuted groups was perfectly legal as long as individuals had a medical prescription.

Many German drug addicts in the 1920s and 1930s were veterans of WW1 including Hermann Goering, who, in 1925, was locked up in a Swedish mental hospital for detoxification from a serious morphine addiction.

During WW2, Nazi soldiers were provided with substantial amounts of mind-altering drugs which the leadership believed enhanced their soldiers' abilities to be ruthless killers, and their fighter pilots to be more daring. The use of Pervitin was widespread among the German population after it was introduced in 1938. [Pervitin is a methamphetamine drug which triggered a heightened state of alert, increased self-confidence and the willingness to take risks.]

Hitler's doctors gave him Pervitin so that he could be more alert, more self-confident and clear in his thought processes. Today, a different form of the drug Pervitin is known as Crystal Meth.

In 1935, Eva Braun's boss, Nazi photographer, Heinrich Hoffmann, was treated by army doctor, Theodor Morell for gonorrhea; Hoffmann told Hitler about his new physician and eventually Morell was asked to examine the Fuhrer.

Hitler's drug addiction began almost from that moment.

Dr. Morell specialized in skin disorders, venereal diseases and sexual dysfunction and according to his detailed medical notes, when he first examined the Fuhrer, he was suffering from lower abdominal cramps and a "complete exhaustion of the lower intestinal system" which caused him headaches, stomach cramps, excessive gas, nausea, shivering fits and diarrhea.

At first, Morell recommended vitamins, hormones, phosphorus, and dextrose but later prescribed live bacteria for Hitler's stomach.

When his stomach problems eased, Hitler made Morell his primary physician.

He said: "No one has ever told me precisely what is wrong with me. Morell's method of cure is so logical that I have the greatest confidence in him."

Soon afterward, the doctor prescribed powdered cocaine to soothe the Fuhrer's throat and clear his sinuses.

Over the next nine years, the physician tested dozens of relatively unknown drugs on the dictator. These included "biologicals" from the intestines of male animals and high doses of barbiturates, amphetamines and, at the height of WW2, Pervitin.

According to the book, Was Hitler ill? (2012) by Eberle & Neumann, Hitler was having up to 82 different types of drugs injected into his body.

By the war's end, even Luftwaffe chief Hermann Goering, himself a morphine addict, gave his boss the unflattering nickname "Reich syringe master".

Also, after WW2, Nazi architect, Albert Speer who denounced the Nazi regime during his trial at Nuremberg, claimed Hitler's "addiction to amphetamines was the cause of his increasingly inflexible decision making", for example, never allowing German military retreats.

In other words, from circa 1935 until his death ten years later, the man responsible for the deaths of more than 70 million people was a "junkie".

Female hormones and bull semen

As early as 1943, the Nizkor Project authors suggested that Hitler was most probably impotent as far as heterosexual relationships were concerned and he had a deep seated fear of genital mutilation which prevented him from having penetrative sex.

In 1944, Hitler's private physician, Theodor Morell, began giving his boss injections of testosterone, especially when Eva Braun was around. In fact, before meeting Braun, the Fuhrer often asked Morell to inject his bloodstream with an extract derived from "the seminal vesicles and prostate glands of young bulls". This was a primitive form of Viagra. (Was Hitler ill?: 2012)

Then in 2013, medical notes sold at auction in the USA, confirmed what had long been suspected about the most hated man in history. He was probably impotent with women.

An article in the Washington Examiner under the heading "Hitler was definitely gay according to doctors" with the subheading "Took female hormones" provided further evidence of Hitler's sexual inclinations [predominant homosexual]; his poor physical health and his lack of intimacy with Braun.

The article by Ryan Lovelace said the Fuhrer was pumped up with female hormones and given experimental drugs by his doctors.

The information was based on a US Army interview with Hitler's doctors who confirmed the "madman had homosexual tendencies, did not sleep in girlfriend Eva Braun's bedroom, and was doped up with multiple drugs".

The medical notes were written in erratic shorthand, by US army interrogator Herman Merl, a Vienna-born medical technician enlisted to interview Hitler's doctors, including Theodor Morell [who treated Hitler for almost a decade] and Karl Brandt [who treated him in the last year of his life].

Merl scribbled "Homosex" in his notebook where he sized up the mass murderer's sexuality.

He then wrote: "Eva Braun equals separate rooms" before adding "female hormone, injection 50,000 units."

The Washington Examiner article continued: "Merl's notes confirm the other post-war interviews with Hitler's caretakers that he was 'hysterical' and 'megalomaniac.'" They also suggested that Hitler had suffered from Parkinson's disease for a number of years before his death.

Manic depression

Both August Kubizek and Reinhold Hanisch described how Hitler raged and then sank into deep depressions. They also noticed his laziness, his penchant for late nights and his inability or unwillingness to get up early in the mornings.

When Germany surrendered at the end of WW1, Hitler was in hospital having been temporarily blinded by British mustard gas. Hospital witnesses said he cried uncontrollably for several days; turned his face to the hospital wall and refused to speak to anyone. This was one of the first outward signs of the depression that would plague him in later life.

The Nizkor Project (1943) confirmed that he fell into a deep depression at the end of WW1 and again after the death of his niece, Geli (in 1931) when they said "he went into a severe depression which lasted for months".

He already had an irregular sleeping pattern which became more pronounced when the tide of WW2 turned against Germany.

Most experts agree that by 1942, (perhaps earlier) Hitler had already become totally dependent on anti-depressants to get him through each day, and in the years that followed, he often slept long into the daytime hours.

According to Hitler's last physician, Dr. Karl Brandt, "the Fuhrer was always tired". He said: "Hitler rarely got out of bed before 11 am. At noon, he was informed of the latest military developments and after quickly considering the news, he issued his orders to the relevant military personnel. His lunch was then followed by a two-hour afternoon nap. When Hitler was asleep, no one was allowed to disturb him. Even when important events were taking place, such as the Allied landing in Normandy, Hitler was left to carry on sleeping. When he did get out of bed, his secretaries were ordered 'not to mention the war' in his presence." (spartacus-educational.com: 2015)

A lack of personal hygiene is also one of the signs of manic depression and several Berlin bunker witnesses said that Hitler's sweat "smelled like rotten meat" at the very end of his life.

Given all of his medical problems – both psychological and physical - it is extraordinary that this man, could command anyone's sexual interest, let alone lead a nation of 80 million people into the most devastating war in history.

PART FOUR: HITLER'S DARK SIDE & HIS VIEWS ON WOMEN

CHAPTER 12: HITLER'S DARK DESIRES

NAZI DEFECTER, Otto Strasser (Gangsters around Hitler: 1942) said Hitler was not a homosexual in the ordinary sense but was probably impotent with both sexes. "His perversion has quite a different nature which few have guessed. He is an extreme masochist who derives sexual pleasure from having a woman squat over him while she urinates or defecates on his face."

In his article, "Hitler's Doomed Angel" (1992), respected historian Ron Rosenbaum said Hitler's sex life "took a form so bizarre and aberrational that they [women] found it, quite literally, unspeakable."

Sadomasochist

Dr. Langer and his team suggested Hitler derived a perverse pleasure from antagonizing his father even though when he did so, he knew he would be punished with either a whip or a belt. They said Hitler played the passive role; "his behavior was submissive and masochistic in the extreme as he derives sexual pleasure from punishment inflicted on his own body."

Four decades later, Dr. Robert G. L. Waite (Psychopathic God: 1977) agreed with this early assessment:"Hitler showed a tendency to stereotype male and female traits which is an expression of sadomasochistic impulses. In private conversation and public speeches he revealed how constantly his mind swung between masochism (weakness, submission) and sadism (brutality, strength, mastery)."

He liked to "talk about physical punishments and he liked to act them out".

His first boyfriend, August Kubizek admitted that Hitler talked by the hour about deviant sexual behavior and the actress, Renate Mueller said he talked about methods of torture before he asked her to act out his sadomasochistic fantasies.

Hitler's whip

Hitler's sadomasochistic impulses were carried over directly into his conduct with women. His father Alois Sr., carried a whip, and used it to beat his son and others in the family, including the dog. Hitler also used his whip on his dogs but it seems he preferred or wanted other people to use the whip on him.

Dr. Waite (Psychopathic God: 1977) said: "The whip that he [Hitler] habitually carried for many years is of course, a traditional symbol of sadomasochism. Hitler's whips were at first associated with mother substitute figures; his three favorite ones were all given to him by motherly women. We also know that he used whips violently in scenes involving women."

The first known incident with his whip occurred in June 1923 in Berchtesgaden, where he was staying at the Pension Moritz.

The proprietor's wife, Frau Buehner, was a striking, six-foot-tall, blonde who towered over Hitler and "inflamed him sexually".

He tried repeatedly to attract her attention by striding up and down in front of her as he swung his whip and beat it against his thigh.

"The more she ignored him, the more agitated he became; he lashed about him with his whip", then during a long monologue which Frau Buehner ignored, he started comparing himself to Jesus Christ and his travails against the Jews.

[The story was related by Dietrich Eckart, a former close friend and Hitler admirer who later said that "when a man starts comparing himself to Jesus Christ, as Hitler did, you know he is insane".]

Dr. Waite said that during this incident, Hitler did not use his whip to lash out at others but instead "whipped himself, beating his boots or thighs in moments of excitement".

The historian also noted in 1926, that in order to impress Maria Reiter, a 16-year-old convent girl whose mother had recently died, he whipped his own dog so savagely that she was shocked by his brutality.

Another incident with Hitler's whip occurred in 1928 with Heinrich Hoffmann's daughter, Henriette. She remembered clearly that when she was a 15-year old in pigtails and a flannel nightgown, Hitler, who was visiting the family home, asked her for a good-night kiss.

When she refused to give him one, his response was to beat his own hand viciously with his whip.

Dr. Waite noted: "Even after he stopped carrying it, he told his valet that he considered the whip to be his personal symbol." (Ibid.)

Toilet training

"Psychoanalysts have shown that the mothers of boys who become sexual perverts often were overly stringent about toilet training. As already noted [by the Nizkor Project], Klara Hitler had a reputation in Leonding and Linz for having had 'the cleanest house in town' and keeping her children 'absolutely spotless'."
(Psychopathic God: Adolf Hitler: 1977)

The implication is that she must have been very strict with her son when it came to his toilet training.

The OSS report said there is no doubt such a woman: "employed rather stringent measures during the toilet training period".

They said this type of toilet training usually resulted in "a residual tension in the anal area; experienced by the child as a severe frustration, arousing feelings of hostility, which, coupled with his infantile aggression found an avenue for expression through anal activities and fantasies. These usually center on soiling, humiliation and destruction, and form the basis of a sadistic character".

They said the experience was more intense in Hitler's case than in the average child due to the strong attachment and spoiling of his mother in his early infancy.

"His anal region has become highly sexualized and both feces and buttocks become sexual objects. Due to early toilet training, certain inhibitions have been set up which prevent their direct expression." (Ibid.)

"That a residual tension from this period still exists in Hitler is evidenced by the frequency of imagery in his speaking and writing which deal with 'dung' and 'dirt' and 'smell', words frequently used in his book, Mein Kampf."

Urine and feces

Hitler apparently enjoyed the reaction he got from women when he talked about "sewer water" which seems to have been his euphemism for urine. His secretaries were suitably shocked, for example, when he told them that their lipstick was made from "Parisian Abwasser".

Hitler's perversion [fascination with feces and urine and deriving sexual pleasure from them] though not a common one "is not unknown in clinical work".

The four collaborators on the Nizkor Project and Dr. Raymond de Saussure author of The Unknown Hitler, Psychoanalysis and Sexuality (1943) all had experiences from other case studies of this perversion. All five agreed that the information concerning Hitler's coprophagia and urophilia was true "in view of their clinical experience and their knowledge of Hitler's character".

These experts claimed that Hitler's perversion was a compromise between psychotic tendencies to eat feces and drink urine on the one hand, and to live a normal socially adjusted life on the other.

"The struggle between these two diverse tendencies continues to rage unconsciously within Hitler though he does not gratify his strange perversion frequently. Patients of this type rarely do and in Hitler's case it is highly probable that he has permitted himself to go this far only with his niece, Geli."

It is highly likely, they also claimed, that Hitler viewed the practice of his own perverse sexual inclinations "as the lowest depths of degradation". (Ibid.)

"In most patients suffering from this perversion, the unconscious forces only get out of control to this degree when a fairly strong love relationship is established and sexuality makes decisive demands."

"In other cases where the love component is less strong, the individual contents himself with less degrading activities." (Ibid.)

According to Dr. Robert Waite, Hitler also had a fascination with his own anus. He said: (Psychopathic God: 1977) "Hitler's fixation on the anus and his special interest in feces, filth and urine coincide with this sexual perversion [coprophilia]. Sexual pleasure can be stimulated by the rectal mucous membrane and the retention or expulsion of the feces ... and it is quite possible he found sexual pleasure from the expulsion of feces and urine from his own body".

Living in his own filth

It was perhaps symbolic that Hitler smeared his school failure certificate with his feces and sent it back to the principal aged 16; that he washed his superior officers' undergarments during WW1 and that while in Vienna, he enjoyed living in his own filth.

He gave the impression in Mein Kampf (1925) that he endured a terrific struggle against overwhelming odds while he lived there but he could have left Vienna at any time but he chose not to do so.

The Nizkor Project authors said "this existence yielded him considerable gratification in spite of its hardships" and "from a psychological point of view, his perversion was in the process of maturation and was finding gratification in a more or less symbolic form."

Infantilism

Dr. Waite noted that other aspects of Hitler's personality fit the psycho-pathology of sexual perversion. "The infantilism we have found in him is one necessary ingredient. As Freud was first to notice, 'perverted sexuality is nothing else but infantile sexuality magnified and separated into its component parts'. Infantilism is clearly marked when, as with Hitler, the perversion involves a reversion to the anal stage." (Psychopathic God: 1977)

He said patients with perversions tend to be infantile; they have un-reconciled Oedipus complexes; and they all display castration anxiety, and Hitler certainly had all of the chief symptoms.

He also said childhood experiences with both parents gave Adolf Hitler a lifelong fear and abhorrence of genital sexual intercourse.

"He saw it as dangerous, evil, depraved, something that must be avoided. He avoided genital intercourse by redirecting his sexual energies in deviate ways." Dr. Waite concluded, as other experts have done, that Hitler, on occasion, had "young ladies urinate or defecate on his head".

Unquestionably he suffered severe guilt reactions from his perverse tendencies, interminable struggles with his conscience which incapacitated him to a considerable extent. "It was an expression of the fetid underside of his grandiose, moralistic public image; it expressed the degraded, guilt-ridden self which pleaded for punishment and humiliation."

Degrading himself

The psychiatric experts have also said as soon as Hitler was aroused, he felt "compelled to degrade himself in the eyes of the loved object and eat their dirt figuratively, if not literally".

"These tendencies disgust him just as much as they disgust others when they get out of control; he despises himself and condemns himself for his weakness." (Nizkor Project: 1943)

They said these "copraphagic tendencies" were not as prominent during casual sexual encounters. "The only way in which Hitler can control these copraphagic tendencies or their milder manifestations is to isolate himself from any intimate relationships in which warm feelings of affection or love might assert themselves."

They said Hitler's outstanding defense mechanism [against his own perversion] was one commonly called "projection", a technique where an individual's ego defends itself against unpleasant impulses or characteristics by denying their existence in himself while attributing them to others.

"From a psychological point of view as the perversion developed and became more disgusting to Hitler's ego, its demands were disowned and projected upon the Jew. By this process, the Jew became a symbol of everything Hitler hated in himself."

He became more and more convinced that the Jew was a great parasite on humanity which sucked its life-blood and if a nation was ever to become great, it must rid itself of this pestilence. Translated back into psycho-sexual terms this would read: "My perversion is a parasite which sucks my life-blood and if I am to become great I must rid myself of this pestilence." (Ibid.)

Back to his mother's womb

In her description of her sexual experiences with Hitler, his niece Geli Raubal stressed the fact that "it was of the utmost importance to him that she squat over him in such a way that he could see everything".

He wanted to get back into his mother's womb. Apparently, Hitler's many sexual problems derived from this desire to return to his mother Klara. "When the home environment is harsh and brutal, as it was in Hitler's case, the small child often envies the position of passivity and security the unborn child enjoys within the mother". (Nizkor Project: 1943)

Klara was pregnant with Hitler's brother Edmund when he was five years old. "Sometimes a child fantasizes about finding a way in to the longed for claustrum and ousting his rival in order that he may take his place. These fantasies are usually of very brief duration because, as the child believes, he would have nothing to eat or drink except feces and urine. The thought of such a diet arouses feelings of disgust and consequently he abandons his fantasies in order to avoid these unpleasant feelings." (Ibid.)

In many psychotics, however, the psychiatrists said these fantasies often continue over a long duration – sometimes many years - and strive to express themselves overtly.

The Eagle's Nest

The psychiatrists claimed another piece of evidence proving that Hitler had this fantasy could be found in the Kehlstein or Eagle's Nest which he had built near Berchtesgaden in the shape of a "claustrum" or womb for his fiftieth birthday [it was supposed to be a gift from his assistant Martin Bormann but Hitler took over the architectural design].

EAGLE'S NEST: It was Hitler's version of a claustrum or womb where he went to commune with his subconscious and to get away from the real world

"There is a long hard road, then a heavily guarded entrance, a trip through a long tunnel to an extremely inaccessible place. Then one can be alone, safe and undisturbed, and revel in the joys that Mother Nature bestows." (Ibid.)

"If one were asked to plan something which represented a return to the womb, one could not possibly surpass the Kehlstein."

They said Hitler "often retired to this strange place" to await instructions from his higher instinct or subconscious concerning the course he should take during WW2.

Andre Francois-Poncet, one of the authors of the French Yellow Book (1938-9) a series of diplomatic surveillance papers on the Fuhrer was one of the few "outsiders" invited there. He gave an extremely vivid description of the strange location and the building: "The approach is by a winding road about nine miles long, boldly cut out of the rock, the road comes to an end in front of a long underground passage leading into the mountain, enclosed by a heavy double door of bronze. At the far end of the underground passage lies a wide lift, paneled with sheets of copper. Through a vertical shaft of 330 feet cut right through the rock, it rises up to the level of the Chancellor's dwelling place. Here is reached the astonishing climax. The visitor finds himself in a strong and massive building containing a gallery with Roman pillars; an immense circular hall with windows all around; it gives the impression of being suspended in space, an almost overhanging wall of bare rock rises up abruptly. The whole, bathed in the twilight of the autumn evening, is grandiose, wild, almost hallucinating. The visitor wonders whether he is awake or dreaming."

Francois-Poncet concluded that "only a madman would conceive of such a place, let alone try to build it".

CHAPTER 13: THE FEMININE MASSES

AS EARLY AS JANUARY 1934, Rodney Collin of The Spectator summarized the abnormality of German thinking and Hitler's sexuality: "Distorted sex showed itself in Jew-baiting, persecution and ultra-puritanism. The psycho-historical situation in Germany threw up representative leaders, Hitler in whose life there has been no other woman but his mother - Hitler, a sexual abnormal with a childhood fixation unable to conceive the normal ideal of full and heterosexual love and marriage. The tragedy lies in the power wielded by such abnormals over average people."

When Hitler was young and in reasonably good health, he enjoyed a homosexual lifestyle. By the time he "decided to go straight" in his late thirties, his health was already in serious decline and he had already become a drug addict. It is therefore no surprise that his efforts to live a heterosexual lifestyle only served to increase his paranoia and the bouts of anxiety and nervous tension he often displayed. (Surreal Reich: 2010)

In fact, Hitler's attempts at being a heterosexual were always disastrous, particularly for the women involved. The majority of the women he had intimate contact with committed suicide.

GOODBYE TO BEING GAY: Hitler tried to become completely heterosexual in his late thirties

HITLER'S VIEWS ON WOMEN

But Adolf Hitler knew how to manipulate women in the political sphere and he knew how to manipulate an audience.

Many of his early followers claimed that his eyes and his voice had hypnotic qualities and with the help and guidance of some of his Nazi associates, he had studied the psychology of crowd manipulation and effective speech-making.

In Mein Kampf (1925) he said: "The people, in an overwhelming majority, are so feminine in their nature and attitude that their activities and thoughts are motivated less by sober consideration than by feeling and sentiment."

On a practical level, he understood the value of women because they made up half the German electorate.

In 1923, Hitler told former confidant, Ernst Hanfstaengl (The Missing Years: 1957): "Do you know the audience at a circus is just like a woman? Someone who does not understand the intrinsically feminine character of the masses will never be an effective speaker. Ask yourself: 'What does a woman expect from a man?' Clearness, decision, power and action. What we want is to get the masses to act. Like a woman, the masses fluctuate between extremes. The crowd is not only like a woman, but women constitute the most important element in an audience. The women usually lead, then follow the children and at last, when I have already won over the whole family, follow the fathers."

Dr. Walter C. Langer et al summarized his talent as follows:

"He knew the importance of courting the lower classes, the inestimable value of winning the support of youth, and recognized the role of women in advancing a new movement; that the reactions of the masses as a whole had many feminine characteristics."

They also noticed that Hitler's talent as a speech-maker seemed to rob people of their common sense. "His magnetic quality wins the allegiance of people and seems to rob them of their critical functions even in the face of evidence that he is not always what he pretends to be."

In Mein Kampf Hitler wrote: "The psyche of the broad masses does not respond to anything weak or half-way. Like a woman, whose spiritual sensitiveness is determined less by abstract reason than by an indefinable emotional longing for that reason, [a woman] prefers to submit to the strong rather than the weakling, the mass, too, prefers the ruler to a pleader."

Hitler's aphrodisiac effect

Pauline Kohler, author of The Girls Who Knew His Love (1940) said Hitler owed his position to women as they "flocked to his meetings long before he was much more than a soapbox speaker".

"It was the woman's vote that swept him to increasing victories at the polls. The wives of the great Ruhr financiers met him and were fascinated. Their husbands' money soon afterward began to flow into the Nazi till."

The many German casualties suffered during WW1 meant that there were large numbers of German widows and spinsters in the country and many of them found Hitler's "bachelor image" very appealing.

As the Nizkor Project pointed out: "From the earliest days of his political career, he had steadfastly refused to divulge anything about his personal life, past or present but this only made him more 'mysterious' and appealing to his followers" particularly women.

Even though historian David Pryce-Jones (Unity Mitford: 1976) described Hitler as "deficient in sexuality" he recognized the "aphrodisiac effect" he had on women of all ages, and even suggested that the Fuhrer provided them with a license to perform "public masturbation".

He said: "Women by the thousand abased themselves at Hitler's feet, they tried to kiss his boots, and some of them succeeded, even to the point of swallowing the gravel on which he had trod. They moaned, they were hysterical; they fainted, for an introspective bachelor deficient in sexuality."

The author also said that "In one respect, Hitler was a final item in an intimate treasure-hunt, the object which could never be brought home, and in another respect he was a historical 'Big Daddy', patting the heads of blonde children. Restraint was impossible, in the frustration of apparently approaching the unapproachable; this was, so to speak, a masturbation of the spirit."

Lashing himself into a frenzy

Herman Rauschning (Voice of Destruction: 1939) said that before Hitler could act "he must lash himself out of lethargy and doubts into a frenzy; having lashed himself into this state of mind he can play the Fuhrer to perfection".

"When the transformation takes place in his personality, all his views, sentiments and values are also transformed. The result is that as 'Fuhrer' he can make statements with great conviction which flatly contradict what 'Hitler' said a few minutes earlier."

In his essay in the Literary Digest (1933), Stanley High compared the transformation in Hitler while he gave a speech to the climax of an orgasm: "When, at the climax, he sways from one side to the, his listeners sway with him; when he leans forward they also lean forward and when he concludes they either are awed and silent or on their feet in a frenzy."

US magazine Newsweek simply reported that Hitler as a speaker knew how to give the people what they wanted: "Women faint, when, with face purpled and contorted with effort, he blows forth his magic oratory..."

Mother figures

Hitler confided to his Nazi colleagues that he "detested women who dabbled in politics". But he saw the value in flattering and then using wealthy, older women during the Nazi Party's formative years, especially when it needed financial support to promote its ideas and to achieve political power.

The older women he wooed in this way often became besotted by him and his right-wing ideas but the only role he afforded them was as "mother figures" who were allowed to dote on him and "financiers" who supported his career.

The Nizkor Project noted that as early as 1920, Carola Hofman, a 61 year old widow from Munich, took him under her wing and for years played the part of his "foster mother".

Other supporters included wealthy benefactors, like Hermine Hoffmann from Munich's Solln neighborhood, who was nicknamed "Hitler's Mommy" and Helene Bechstein, the wife of a Berlin piano manufacturer who apparently called Hitler "my little Wolf" even though he was 35 years old at the time.

Dr. Langer said : "Helene Bechstein spent large quantities of money on Hitler in the early days of the party, introduced him to her social circle and lavished maternal affection on him."

She often said that she "wished that Hitler was her son" and while he was imprisoned in Landsberg, she claimed that she was his "adopted mother" so she could visit him.

According to Otto Strasser (Hitler & I: 1940), Hitler would often "sit at her feet and lay his head against her bosom while she stroked his hair tenderly and murmured, 'Mein Woelfchen' [my little wolf]".

BIG SIS: Angela Raubal became a mother figure for him until they fell out over money

Throughout his political career, Hitler often used the pseudonym "Herr Wolf" especially when he wanted to avoid public recognition and to dupe the German media. He named his headquarters in east Prussia "Wolf's Lair" and "Wolf's Headquarters" and even named his favorite German shepherd puppy "Wolf".

According to one witness, Helene Bechstein, was the only woman in Germany who could "carry on a monologue in Hitler's presence and would actually tell him what she thought".

Apparently, during these scoldings, Hitler would "stand there like an abashed schoolboy who had committed a misdemeanor".

Then, along came Victoria von Dirksen [the Berlin widow of the magnate who built the city's Underground], who is alleged to have spent a fortune on him and his career.

There were other older women who did exactly the same.

They appeared in his life in the 1920s, when Hitler and the Nazi Party needed funds and there is no doubt these women helped the Nazis to become a political powerhouse. Hitler used them to get money and allowed them to pamper him, but he fell out with them or forgot about them once he had achieved his goals.

Then his older half-sister, Angela, who kept house for him at his Munich apartment and later in Berchtesgaden, took on the mothering role into the mid-1930s, until they had a disagreement over money. (Strangely, she continued to work for him after her daughter Geli's suspicious "suicide".)

When he fell out with his sister circa 1935, it was then Magda Goebbels, wife of propaganda minister Joseph Goebbels, who took over the surrogate mothering role; she looked after his comforts, supervised his household and baked the delicacies [cream cakes] of which he was particularly fond. (Nizkor Project: 1943) Magda Goebbels was apparently so besotted by "mein Fuhrer" that Nazi Party officials joked that "they could hear her ovaries rattle every time she was near Hitler". She also tried (and failed) to act as a matchmaker, so he might marry one of her friends, which she believed would increase the bond between them.

RATTLING OVARIES: Magda Goebbels was so besotted by Hitler that she poisoned her six children when she knew the war was lost

Fear of humiliation

People close to Hitler often commented on the fact that he seemed uncomfortable with women his own age. Baldur von Schirach, leader of the Hitler Youth, described one incident [in 1923] which took place when Hitler was 34 years old. "Else Brummer was one of the most beautiful girls in Germany, with a gold fringed dress and the first silk stockings. She deliberately went up to Hitler, who looked at her unsuspectingly. She embraced him and kissed him tenderly on the mouth. The others watched. They found it funny that Hitler was being kissed so openly: He was already known at this time, but there was no talk about his being involved in any love affair. It would have been the most natural thing for him to kiss the girl back, but he didn't do that. As she moved away from him, he gazed at her solemnly, turned round and fetched his mackintosh. He took his black hat and without wishing anyone a happy new year, went out into the night." (spartacus-educational.com: 2015)

The author of Caesars in Goose Step (1940) Will D. Bayles described a similar incident when the Fuhrer [aged 47] simply did not know what to do when a woman hugged and kissed him in public.

On this occasion, he became so flustered, he left what was supposed to be "the greatest show on earth", the Berlin Olympics in 1936.

Bayles said: "His enjoyment of the Berlin Olympic Games was completely spoilt when a fanatical Dutch woman, who had achieved a personal presentation, suddenly clasped him in two hefty arms and tried to kiss him in plain view of 100,000 spectators. Hitler could not regain his composure or stand the irreverent guffaws of foreign visitors, and left the Stadium." (Ibid.)

Ronald Hayman (Hitler and Geli: 1997) claimed there was a regular pattern to Hitler's relationships caused by the fear of being rejected and the resulting humiliation.

"Though he found it easy during his twenties and early thirties to make friends with older women in their forties and fifties, he was nervous of being rebuffed or humiliated by women of his own age. But at thirty-seven, he was old enough to treat a teenage girl as if she were a child."

Here, Hayman is referring to the fact that at the age of 37, having had a string of gay relationships and casual sex with his chauffeurs and bodyguards for many years, Hitler met his first girlfriend, Maria Reiter, who was aged only 16.

In other words, Adolf Hitler, the great German Fuhrer, only felt comfortable with either much older or much younger women and never with women his own age.

Royalty and titles

The German leader's colleagues also noticed their boss appeared to become "star-struck" and unsure of himself to the point of being flustered when in the company of royals or anyone with "a title".

At such times, they observed that Hitler became so respectful, he behaved more like a sycophant than a great political leader.

Hitler was on friendly terms with several titled ladies. For several years, he counted Princess Stephanie von Hohenlohe (who was Jewish) among his royal confidants. During their meetings, she said Hitler was always deferential and exceedingly courteous in her company.

"Whenever I arrived or left he always kissed my hand, often taking one of mine into both of his and shaking it for a time to emphasize the sincerity of the pleasure it gave him to see one, at the same time looking deep into my eyes." (spartacus-educational.com: 2015)

At the time of their friendship, she was the mistress of Britain's Lord Rothermere and Hitler may well have been using her to get secret intelligence on the British.

INTIMATE: Princess Stephanie von Hohenlohe may have been a double agent; US intelligence described her as "intelligent and dangerous"

HAPPY TO GROVEL: Wallis Simpson and the Duke of Windsor - who abdicated as British Monarch in December 1936 - met Hitler at his country residence, Berchtesgaden, in 1937; it was a major propaganda coup for the Nazis

The princess advised the German leader on how he could best use his friendship with British aristocrat, Unity Mitford, for his own propaganda purposes.

She summarized her perception of Hitler's character as follows: "He was a master at the understanding of, and playing upon, the psychology of people, which I considered his greatest gift."

In her unpublished memoirs, princess Stephanie von Hohenloe admitted that she had been "physically intimate" with Hitler without ever having had sexual intercourse with him.

It is assumed by this comment that she allowed Hitler to paint an intimate nude portrait of her.

She also said that during all of their meetings, she had always assumed that Adolf Hitler was a homosexual.

Movie stars

Hitler liked the company of beautiful and frivolous women, especially movie stars; women who had no interest in politics. He had movie theaters installed in each of his residences in Berlin, Munich and Berchtesgaden so he could watch the latest German and American films. He also watched endless newsreel footage from Britain, the USA and of course the latest Nazi propaganda films.

In 1943, the Nizkor Project authors noted that "Hitler likes to be surrounded with pretty women and usually requests the moving picture companies to send over a number of actresses whenever there is a party in the Chancellery. He seems to get an extraordinary delight in fascinating these girls with stories about what he is going to do in the future or the same old stories about his past life."

"He also likes to impress them with his power by ordering the studios to provide them with better roles, or promising that he will see to it that they are starred in some forthcoming picture. Most of his associations with women of this type, and their number is legion, does not go beyond this point as far as we have been able to discover. On the whole he seems, to feel more comfortable in the company of stage people than with any other group and he often came down to the [film] studio restaurants for lunch."

Two film directors, Frank Wisbar and Adolf Zeissler, who worked in Germany during the 1930s revealed how Hitler spent a great deal of time visiting film sets and meeting with a variety of actresses. They both agreed that "Hitler had two consuming interests in film, as objects of Nazi propaganda and beautiful women". (Hitler's Mountain: 2010)

Frank Wisbar told the US Office of Strategic Services in 1943 that Hitler "frequently telephoned him about details of films in production and about even minor characters in the cast".

Wisbar got the impression at times "that Hitler devoted about an hour a day to politics and the rest of his time to movie details."

He said several times, Hitler intervened in film production, stopping and shelving films upon appeals from actresses. This happened so frequently, Wisbar said "that it was extremely difficult to manage the girls who were so often guests at the Chancellery; they threatened to complain to Hitler if they did not get the part they wanted or the scripts were not changed to suit their fancy." (Ibid.)

Adolf Zeissler had a similar experience.

He observed that "when Hitler did not come to the studio in person he frequently telephoned and held lengthy conversations about new films and the cast." He "often wondered when Hitler had the time to devote to affairs of state because he either spent so much time at the studios, on the telephone or looking at films that there seemed little time left for anything else."

Hitler frequently asked him to send actresses to the Chancellery but Zeissler said most of the young women thought Hitler was "extremely odd" due to the fact that he spent a great deal of time expounding on his ambitions and achievements.

"His chief object in all this was to impress the girls with his greatness and power," Zeissler said.

The Nizkor Project authors noted that actresses Renate Mueller (who committed suicide because of Hitler) and Leni Riefenstahl were frequent visitors to the Chancellery in Berlin.

"During their stay they were alone with Hitler behind closed doors so that not even his immediate staff knew what transpired between them."

Riefenstahl continued to be a guest at the Chancellery up to the outbreak of the war, though she always denied any sexual involvement with him.

She said their relationship was "work based" and their conversations centered on their shared fascination with film.

Indeed, Riefenstahl directed several Nazi propaganda films in the 1930s and at the beginning of WW2. And despite her "artistic"association with the Nazi regime and its leader, she went on to have a successful career (after the war) as a film director, writer and photographer.

By contrast, the actress Renate Mueller told director, Adolf Zeissler that on her visits to the Chancellery Hitler "threw himself on the floor, begging her to kick and beat him" and he "groveled in the most agonizing manner".

They continued to meet in Berlin at regular intervals for the next few years, even though what transpired between them disgusted the actress. When Mueller "consorted with a Jewish man", Hitler ordered the Gestapo to follow her, then had her name blacklisted in the cinema and theater worlds so she could no longer find work. More later.

S & M: Mueller tried to seduce Hitler but he
asked her to kick and beat him instead

WOMEN, PORNOGRAPHY & ART

Herman Rauschning (Voice of Destruction: 1939) also confirmed that Hitler loved nothing more than to while away his time watching films, often to the detriment of his government work.

"He dislikes desk work and seldom glances at the piles of reports which are placed on his desk daily. No matter how important these may be or how much his adjutants may urge him to attend to the particular matter, he refuses to take them seriously unless it happens to be a project which interests him. He seldom sits in a cabinet meeting because they bore him."

"On several occasions when sufficient pressure was brought to bear, he did attend but got up abruptly during the session and left without apology. Later it was discovered that he had gone to his private theater and had the operator show some film that he particularly liked." (Ibid.)

A number of Hitler's associates also commented on his delight at witnessing strip-tease and nude dancing numbers on stage. They said on such occasions he could never see enough to satisfy him and used opera glasses in order to observe more closely. (Nizkor Project: 1943)

"Strip-tease artists are frequently invited to the Brown House, in Munich, to perform in private and there is evidence that he often invites girls to Berchtesgaden for the purpose of exhibiting their bodies."

"On his walls are numerous pictures of obscene nudes which conceal nothing and he takes particular delight in looking through a collection of pornographic pictures which [Heinrich] Hoffmann has made for him."

Ernest Pope, author of Munich Playground (1941) said that Hitler frequently visited the Merry Widow theater show in which an American actress played the leading role.

"I have seen Hitler nudge his gauleiter, Wagner, and smirk when Dorothy does her famous back bending number in the spotlight. In this number, Dorothy's costume consists of a pair of transparent butterfly wings, or sometimes nothing at all."

"Hitler watches the performance through opera glasses and sometimes has command performances for his own private benefit." (Ibid.)

Back bending Jenny Jugo

There was another well-known actress who performed in private on stage for the Fuhrer. The woman's name was Jenny Jugo (1904-2001), an Austrian actress, who first came to light as one of Hitler's "intimate friends" in Pauline Kohler's book, The Girls Who Knew His Love (1940).

For almost two years, Kohler worked as a maid in Hitler's country home in Berchtesgaden, where she said even the Storm Troopers were allowed to engage in orgies [until the Roehm purge in 1934].

The former maid carefully recorded these relationships and had her book published once she managed to escape to Britain in 1939.

Kohler said: "Hitler has all the normal man's liking for a pretty face and a trim figure, though he dislikes women to use make-up or to be attractive in an artificial way, and even though it is true that the Fuhrer is not strongly sexed, I once heard him say to Goering, 'I know what women are for just as well as you do, Hermann'."

Hitler may have remained single "but to say that Germany is his only love is nonsense; he is discreet and his love affairs are not always the normal affairs of a healthy man."

Pornographic shows

In her book, Kohler said the Fuhrer enjoyed watching pornographic films in his private cinema at Berchtesgaden and that he particularly enjoyed the intimate company of Jenny Jugo, who had special gifts only her closest friends knew about. She described Jugo as "a small brunette and very pretty; from a poor family but a good Aryan."

Hitler first met Jugo under strange circumstances.

According to Kohler, one night the illegal "German Freedom Station" interrupted its radio program with a special announcement addressed to Joseph Goebbels wife which went as follows: "Frau Magda Goebbels. Do you want to know where your husband spends so much of his time? Well, it's easy to find out. Ask young Jenny Jugo. She should know."

Kohler said: "The station was right." Goebbels, who was married to frumpy Magda, was having an affair with the actress.

TEMPTRESS: Austrian actress, Jenny Jugo gave private striptease performances for Hitler

When Hitler heard about the broadcast, he called Goebbels to account for his "immoral behavior".

The propaganda minister responded by introducing the actress to the Fuhrer, and according to Kohler, "from that moment onward, she ceased to be Goebbels' mistress, becoming Hitler's instead".

Kohler claimed Goebbels decided if his Fuhrer ever wanted to marry, "it would be a woman whom he himself had chosen. In this way, the little doctor sought to strengthen his position."

During what Kohler called Jenny Jugo's "reign at Berchtesgaden" which lasted a few months, Hitler had a room fitted up as a studio with a small stage on which the actress could perform private pornographic shows. (Ibid.)

Apparently, the actress was "a contortionist" who enjoyed performing in front of the Fuhrer and his inner circle. Once she had stripped off her clothes, she bent forward and backwards "so that nothing was left to the imagination".

PRETTY AS A PICTURE: Joseph Goebbels had an eye for a pretty woman but was obliged to pass Jenny Jugo on to his boss

Her performances were filmed because Hitler declared "it was art" which also meant he could view her most intimate parts when she was unavailable in person. The former maid said Jugo was well rewarded for her efforts. "The presents I know he gave her were a diamond bracelet, a mink coat, a villa, two motorcars which were easily the most he has ever spent on a mistress." She estimated the total value of these gifts at $90,000.

The author said she doubted whether Jugo ever loved Hitler but she took advantage of his generosity: "she certainly tantalized him more than any other woman has dared to".

Rubber sausage

Kohler said the pretty actress was great fun to spend time with because she insisted on playing practical jokes.

On one occasion, she put a rubber sausage on Goering's plate before he sat down to eat. "He wrestled with it for a few minutes, then hurled it and the plate to the floor with a string of resounding oaths."

Another time she introduced a parrot into the Fuhrer's aviary. She had taught it to say: "I'm the Fuhrer! I'm the Fuhrer!" which caused a lively five minutes when it first spoke in Hitler's hearing.

The author said Jugo also sent outrageous wires to Hitler signed by Goebbels, [Robert] Ley and Goering.

"Anyone else would have died beneath the headman's ax." (Ibid.)

And of course, Hitler really appreciated Jugo's private stage performances.

One Christmas, Kohler said a select number of the staff were taken into the Fuhrer's private cinema.

SHOWING HER JUGS: Jugo was both innocent maiden and tantalizing Dominatrix in her films and real life

"We saw a long, dreary film about the achievements of the National Socialist regime, then a short film starring Jenny Jugo. This was a striptease act, at the end of which she faced the camera completely naked and, for ten minutes, did various exercises. Hitler saw this film, or one similar, nearly every night at the Berchtesgaden." (The Girls Who Knew His Love: 1940)

The author said nothing tragic happened at the end of Jugo's relationship with Hitler. "It just ended. She took up her normal life in Berlin, and the Fuhrer's famous friendship with Leni Riefenstahl [film director and actress] developed, but this relationship never became anything more than platonic."

Given Hitler's previous (lack of) sexual history with women, it is unlikely that the relationship with Jenny Jugo was ever consummated though she probably satisfied his yearning to see the inside of a woman's body which, according to Dr. Langer and his team, was part of his desire to "return to his mother's womb".

Jenny Jugo died aged 95 in 2001.

Nude paintings and drawings

Naturally, Hitler kept his love for strip-tease and pornography hidden from the German public but his intimate circle of Nazi colleagues knew and sometimes joked about it behind his back.

Herman Rauschning (Hitler Speaks: 1939) commented: "He can scarcely wait for the next edition of Der Stuermer [Julius Streicher's anti-Semitic magazine full of caricatures of Jews and explicit cartoons suggesting strange sexual practices] to appear on the news stands and when it reaches him he goes through it avidly. He seems to get great pleasure out of the dirty stories and the cartoons that feature in this magazine."

Hitler told Rauschning that Der Stuermer "was a form of pornography permitted by the Third Reich".

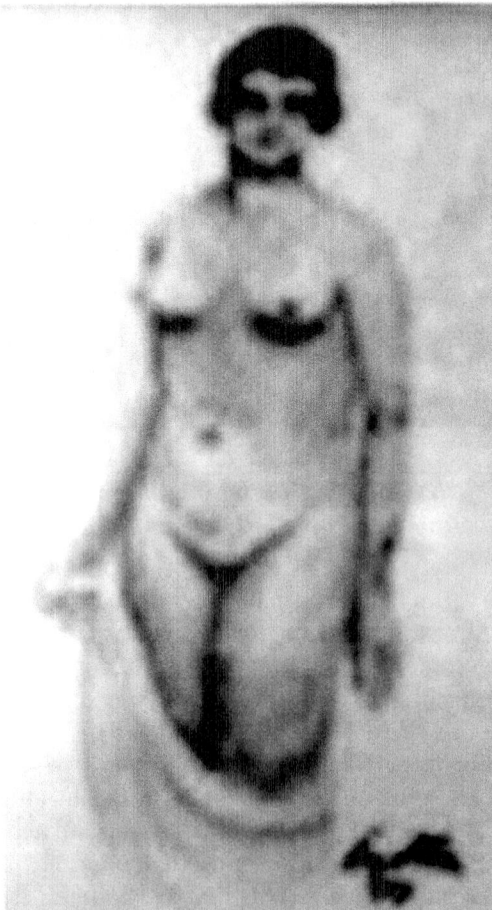

GELI NAKED: Hitler drew intimate sketches of his niece

He had drawn his own pornographic pictures of his niece, Geli Raubal which surfaced after her death and he continued to paint nude portraits of women including Princess Stephanie von Hohenlohe and the tragic singer and children's book author, Inge Ley. In addition, he had a large collection of nude paintings of women by other artists.

Rauschning (Ibid.) said his passion for collecting nudes meant "when his heart was set on one, the sky's the limit" as far as price was concerned.

Myth of the Aryan woman

By the time he became Fuhrer, Hitler's views on the "perfect woman" had not changed since his teenage years; the days of his fantasy relationship with the Jewish girl, Stefanie Isak in Linz. In fact, the woman he had never even spoken to continued to be his model for the ideal 'Aryan' along with his mother Klara.

The Nizkor Project (1943) said Hitler's approach to women was the same as his approach to men. He only wanted the ideal version from his own imagination and nothing else.

"He often stated that young Aryan women, especially virginal ones, were the model of perfection but at the first sign of imperfection, he would treat these perfect women in a disgraceful manner."

When his propaganda minister, Joseph Goebbels said: "The mission of German women is to be beautiful and to bring children into the world" Hitler was in full agreement.

He had never believed in women's education, calling it "pointless" and under the Nazi regime, women doctors, teachers and civil servants were forced to give up their careers.

Hitler wanted a high birth rate, so the German population could provide more labor and increased production. The Nazis even considered making it law that families should have at least four children.

Girls were encouraged to keep fit but only to make themselves healthy for childbirth; they were discouraged from becoming too thin, because it was thought that slender women had trouble giving birth.

The "Law for the Encouragement of Marriage" gave newlywed couples a loan of 1,000 marks, and allowed them to keep 250 marks for each child they had.

Mothers who had more than eight children were given a "gold medal" and young, single women could volunteer to have a baby for a member of the SS.

Aryan women were also expected to emulate traditional German peasant fashions, plain peasant costumes, hair in plaits or buns and flat shoes.

They were discouraged from wearing make-up or trousers, using dye in their hair and smoking in public, in other words, the ideal Aryan woman was expected to be the complete opposite of the actresses and starlets Hitler slavered over in private.

Fear of producing a "cretin"

Hitler's private attitude to women of child-bearing age was complex. Though he wanted German women to produce as many children as they could, he feared the consequences of producing his own heir.

He always said in interviews that he never married because he was "married to

Germany" and he never had children because "German citizens were the only children he required" but in truth, given his family's history [of incest and insanity], he probably feared producing a deformed or mentally deficient replica of himself.

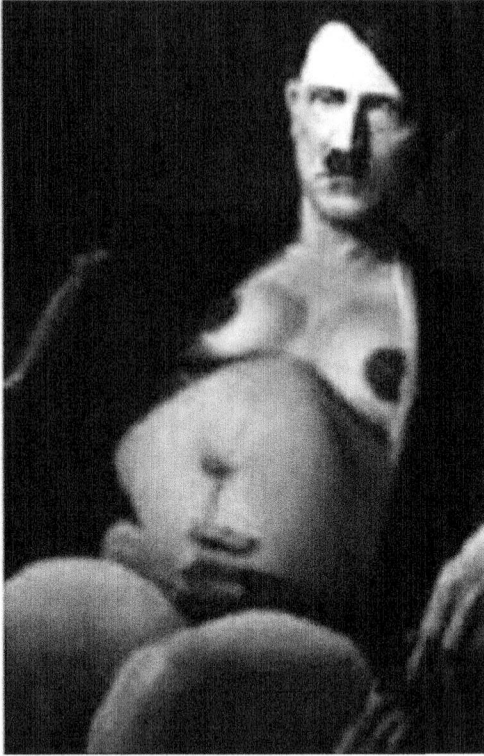

CRETIN: Hitler feared having a child of his own; this painting of him is by Indonesian artist, Ronald Manullang

He once told the German media that he was a bachelor who was "immune from such impulses" but understood that other men could not always exercise the same "self-control" and he said he felt sorry for other men and their "weakness for sex which made them appear foolish".
This contradicted his own policy which demanded German men and women marry young so they could produce children.
In his book, (Hitler and Geli: 1997), Ronald Hayman argued that the dark side of Hitler's sexual insecurity and fear of having children had several sources.
He often claimed that "it would be irresponsible to start a family when he was so busy".
But Hitler also said: "I'm aware that the children of a genius usually have a hard time in the world. They're expected to achieve the same stature as their famous father, and they're never forgiven if their achievement is only mediocre. Besides,

they're usually cretins."

Hayman concluded: "Though he was sincere in claiming to be a genius, his family background was such a well-kept secret that he could afford to talk like this, but, having so many relations who were deformed or mentally unbalanced, he was naturally worried about the genes he was carrying." (Ibid.)

The author also noted that the danger of producing a "cretin" would have increased if he and his niece Geli Raubal had ever produced a child, though "he may have found it reassuring that she came from the same tainted family" as he did.

Younger women - was Hitler a pedophile?

Before he was murdered in 1934, SA leader Ernst Roehm joked that his boss liked young women with large, round bottoms.

He said (Getting Hitler into Heaven: 1987): "Hitler is thinking about the peasant girls. When they stand in the fields and bend down at their work so that you can see their behinds, that's what he likes, especially when they've got big round ones. That's Hitler's sex life. What a man!"

Apparently, Hitler, who was present, did not move a muscle but stared at Roehm with narrowed lips.

Several historians and former Nazi colleagues also noticed that Hitler was attracted to teenage girls, and Catholic, convent-educated girls seemed to be the most appealing to him.

From the evidence available, his relationships with these girls involved little or no sex but did include his perversions and his penchant for sadomasochism.

Nazi historian, Joseph Howard Tyson (Surreal Reich: 2010) said: "Tales about Hitler's sex life come from enemies and disillusioned associates and although not always consistent, these accounts profile Hitler as a bisexual whose heterosexual preferences inclined toward adolescent girls, and youthful looking women."

"Sick and tired of being blackmailed [about his homosexuality], he curtailed his homosexual activity and began projecting the image of a heterosexual bachelor. A string of actresses and girls such as Henny Hoffmann, Mimi Reiter and Geli Raubal entered his life at this time."

As politics took up so much of his time, he abstained from sex for weeks or even months at a time and when he did indulge, his sexual activity was "deviant" except for the final "sexless phase" with Eva Braun, the author said.

Nazi historian, Ian Kershaw (Hitler 1889-1936: 1998) also suggested that Hitler's attempts at heterosexuality were "not normal" and that the Fuhrer especially liked "young ones".

Kershaw said: "Hitler's relationships with women, were in some respects abnormal. He liked the company of women, especially pretty ones, best of all young ones. He flattered them, sometimes flirted with them, called them in his patronizing Viennese petty-bourgeois manner: 'my little princess' or 'my little countess'. Occasionally, he made a clumsy attempt at some physical contact as in the case of Helena Hanfstaengl and Henriette Hoffmann."

The author suggested the Fuhrer preferred very young women so he could bully and manipulate them: "Like his father [Alois], he preferred women much younger than himself, girls he could dominate, who would be obedient playthings but not get in the way. The two women with whom he would become most intimately associated, Geli Raubal [19 years younger] and Eva Braun [23 years younger], fitted the same model, until that is, Geli became rebellious and wanted a level of freedom which Hitler was unwilling to permit." (Ibid.)

TEENAGE TARGETS: Hitler made advances toward pubescent girls when he was old enough to be their father, including clockwise from top left: Maria Reiter, Geli Raubal, Henriette Hoffmann and Eva Braun

On one occasion, Hitler confided to one of his Munich friends, Otto Wagener: "I can sit next to young women who leave me completely cold. I feel nothing, or they actually irritate me. But a girl like the little [Henriette] Hoffmann or Geli [Raubal], with them I become cheerful and bright, and if I have listened for an hour to their perhaps silly chatter, or I have only to sit next to them, then I am free of all weariness and listlessness and I can go back to work refreshed."
He also said: "A girl of eighteen to twenty is as malleable as wax. It should be possible for a man, whoever the chosen woman may be, to stamp his own imprint on her. That's all the woman asks for." (spartacus-educational.com: 2015)
Ernst Hanfstaengl, Otto Strasser, and Herman Rauschning (all authors of Hitler

books) reported on his submissive and masochistic tendencies in the company of certain young girls he liked.

They all agreed that even in the presence of other people, when Hitler was "smitten with a girl", he tended to "grovel at her feet in a most disgusting manner". "He insists on telling the girl that he is unworthy to kiss her hand or to sit near her and that he hopes she will be kind to him. From all this we see Hitler's constant struggle against complete degradation whenever any affectionate components enter into the picture."

His submissive behavior evidenced towards his superior officers during WW1 and towards anyone with "a title" in the early part of his career had found yet another outlet. (CrimeMagazine.com: 2013)

Hitler's second sexual indiscretion

In school, aged 12, Hitler so upset a little girl during his first reported sexual indiscretion that he was obliged to leave the school the following year. Hitler's next documented sexual indiscretion occurred with a teenager in a photographer's darkroom.

Henriette Hoffmann (1913-1992) was the daughter of the official Nazi Party photographer, Heinrich Hoffmann. He had been one of the German army's photographers during WW1, [his book of photographs was published in 1919] and he had taken a picture of the cheering crowds in Munich at the outbreak of the war.

Later, when Hitler became prominent in Munich politics, Hoffmann discovered Hitler in one of his pictures and called it to his attention.

Hitler was delighted and a close relationship sprung up between them. [Some have suggested Hoffmann deliberately faked the picture to gain favor with the Nazi boss].

Hoffmann's wife, the actress Therese Baumann was also very fond of Hitler and for a short time, one of the women who played a mothering role towards him, until her unexpected death in 1928.

The Hoffmann's daughter, Henriette first met Hitler in 1922 when she was nine years old and Hitler was a regular visitor to the family home. As he often did with young girls he knew, Hitler asked young Henriette to call him "Uncle" and he called her his "Princess".

But by the time Henriette reached puberty, his interest in her seems to have changed from the "avuncular" to something a bit more sinister.

According to several sources, Hitler made a sexual advance towards the teenager in her father's darkroom.

Former Nazi, Otto Strasser (Gangsters around Hitler: 1942) said Hitler began to molest Henriette Hoffmann when she was just 13 years old.

He said: "Hitler was frequently present at parties given in the Hoffmann home and became very friendly with Henriette who was known as 'Henny' to those who knew her well. The secret relationship between Hitler and Henny continued for some time until the teenager, who was a very garrulous person by nature, got drunk one night and began to tell others the strange things Hitler 'made her do for him.'"

"[Heinrich] Hoffmann had noticed Hitler's intense eagerness to help the thirteen-year-old girl develop plates in his darkroom. At first he considered it an indication of Hitler's great interest in photography. Then one day the little girl ran crying out of the darkroom and told her father what 'Uncle Adolf' wanted of her. Father Hoffmann went up to the libertine of the darkroom and made him the following proposal: either Hitler must appoint him sole photographer of the Nazi Party for life, or he would be compelled to report the affair to the authorities."

"Up to this time [1926], Hitler had steadfastly refused to have his photograph taken on the grounds that "it was better publicity to remain a mystery man" and also because if his picture appeared "it would be too easy to identify him when he crossed Communist territories". (Nizkor Project: 1943)

Fearing that Hoffmann would make good on his threat to go to the authorities, Hitler named him as the Nazi Party's official photographer and gave him the exclusive rights to photographs of him.

These privileges netted Hoffmann millions of dollars over the next 20 years as it is believed he took more than one million photographs of his boss.

The American psychiatrists noted sarcastically: "All differences between Hitler and Heinrich Hoffmann seem to have disappeared and today [1943] he is one of Hitler's closest associates and exerts a great personal influence on the Fuhrer."

Among Hitler's Nazi associates, it was supposed their boss had committed some kind of "sexual indiscretion with a minor" and Hitler bought Hoffmann's silence by granting him these exclusive rights. Of course, buying off blackmailers was not a new phenomenon, though such threats normally related to Hitler's homosexual affairs.

When Mrs. Hoffmann died in 1928, the Hoffmann family home apparently fell to pieces and became a kind of meeting place for homosexuals [of both sexes] and others from the demi-monde. There was a good deal of drinking and "a great freedom in sexual activities of all kinds". (Ibid.)

According to her Munich classmates, Henriette Hoffmann became "little more than a prostitute who could be had for a few German marks."

In 1931, when she enrolled as a student at Munich's university, Henriette became one of Hitler's part time secretaries for several months. Then in 1932, Hitler arranged her marriage to Nazi Youth leader, Baldur von Schirach, an alleged pederast and homosexual.

Over the years, Henriette became a friend and confidant to several of Hitler's suicidal girlfriends, including Geli Raubal, Unity Mitford and Eva Braun. She certainly had plenty of sexual gossip concerning the Fuhrer to share with each of them. More later.

PART FIVE - HITLER'S SUICIDAL GIRLFRIENDS

"Some have surmised that he suffered a genital injury during the last war, others that he is homosexual. As far as the German people know he has no sex life and this too is clothed, not as an abnormality, but as a great virtue. Apparently, the Fuhrer is above human weaknesses of this sort and has a profound contempt for the weakness in men for sex and the fools that it makes of them." (Nizkor Project: 1943)

Not exactly a sex god
LIKE SO MANY of the Hitler paintings floating around after his death, the Fuhrer personality was a fake. It masked the internal struggle raging between his masculine and feminine self. Women may have thrown themselves at his feet during his speeches but in reality, Hitler was an extreme turn-off as a sexual being. (Siobhan Pat Mulcahy: 2015)
As historian Joseph Howard Tyson said, it was only when he was sick and tired of paying off blackmailers who knew of his homosexuality that he decided in the late 1920s to "go straight". (Surreal Reich: 2010)
In fact, the first time he is known to have had a girlfriend, he was already 37 while the unlucky girl in question, Maria Reiter, was aged only 16.
Also, while he attempted to conduct his heterosexual relationships, Hitler continued to enjoy secret dalliances with men in the background.
When reviewing his character and his physical attributes, we already know that he had frequent tantrums or rages, wept openly and often in front of his close associates; he had bad breath, rotten teeth, passed gas at both ends, had Parkinson's disease [from 1935], and was a "syringe master" or drug addict.
He was a man obsessed with his health and afraid of death. He suffered from castration anxiety and while he shunned penetrative sex, his doctors were obliged to give him hormone injections so he might function in a "normal way".
He also had a poor sleeping pattern, suffered from nightmares and could only sleep in a bed made by a man. During WW1 he was subjected to sexual bullying by other soldiers because of his "underdeveloped genitals" and no doubt he was embarrassed by his small penis and withered testicle. With all these sexual, psychological and physical problems, he was a very unattractive prospect as a sexual partner for either men or women.

Going straight
It is known for certain that Adolf Hitler attempted to have at least seven "heterosexual" relationships.
Five of the seven women Hitler had sexual contact with committed suicide and two attempted suicide but failed. Four of the women were teenagers when he first made sexual advances toward them. [Henriette Hoffmann was aged only 13 but they did not have an ongoing relationship.}

Phallic symbols as a substitute for sex

Hitler's gifts to his women friends were a psychoanalyst's dream, phallic symbols representing his impotence in heterosexual relationships and obvious substitutes for what he could not provide. These gifts included cars, horses, houses and even a private aircraft for one actress.

He is unlikely to have had sex with Maria Reiter even though she claimed four years after her suicide attempt that they had shared one night of passion.

And it is almost certain that he did not have sex with Unity Mitford even though she seemed to be "mad for it". Their sex life, such as it was, amounted to her retelling the stories of her orgies with his SA men and his delighting in the details.

Hitler did have sexual relations with his niece Geli Raubal but these encounters involved his perversions rather than intercourse or what she called "the most disgusting practices". (spartacus-educational.com: 2015)

As for the actress Renate Mueller, she was obliged to act out some of his sadomasochistic fantasies, but again, there seems to have been no penetrative sex in their strange relationship.

With Inge Ley, he became her confessor and she allowed him to paint at least one intimate portrait of her. She may have been infatuated with Hitler but again it seems their relationship was never consummated.

And of course, there was the long-suffering and ever-loyal, Eva Braun, the woman he regularly ignored for months at a time, even before the outbreak of WW2; the woman he kept hidden in the background of his life.

Many insiders have said that they doubted very much whether Hitler and Braun ever had sex.

Martin Amis, author of Zone of Interest (2014) has claimed that Braun and Hitler may have had sex "without Hitler ever taking his clothes off" as he was mortified at the thought of being naked in front of her or anyone else.

And of course, Hitler's doctors, who labeled him as "homosex" were obliged to inject him with a primitive form of Viagra so that he might "occasionally fulfill his obligations" to her.

It is no surprise then that former Hitler confidant, Albert Speer said that Braun "would prove to be a great disappointment to historians". (Inside The Third Reich: 1970)

Sequence of suicidal women

As Hitler often played one woman off against another, the times at which he was "romantically involved" with them sometimes overlapped, therefore the seven suicidal women connected to him are discussed here in the order in which they attempted or succeeded in committing suicide.

CHAPTER 14: SUZI LIPTAUER

HITLER'S ABUSIVE CHILDHOOD, his mother fixation, his inner sense of failure and depression, his poor health, his warped philosophy and sexual impotence, his drug addiction and Parkinson's disease [from 1935], his predominant homosexual tendencies and his 'perversions' all affected his attempts to have romantic liaisons with the opposite sex. (Siobhan Pat Mulcahy: 2015)

Dr. Robert G. L. Waite (Psychopathic God: 1977) said: "The idea that Hitler had a sexual perversion particularly abhorrent to women is further supported by a statistic: of the seven women who, we can be reasonably sure, had intimate relations with Hitler, six committed suicide or seriously attempted to do so."

The mysterious Suzi Liptauer

Suzi Liptauer, a Viennese woman living in Munich in 1921 was Hitler's first known "attempted suicide". Some historians have said she tried to hang herself "after an all-night rendezvous with Hitler". Apparently this episode was quickly covered up by Hitler's cronies and for years, she remained under "Hitler's protection" even after her marriage.

The details about the Viennese woman's life are sketchy.

The name Liptauer is derived from the German name "Liptau" from the region of Liptove, a former county of the Austro-Hungarian Empire. Had Hitler known her from his days in Linz or in the Austrian capital?

In 1973, German magazine, Der Spiegel said Liptauer was from Vienna and "attempted suicide".

"Grief over Hitler was the reason for the suicide attempt of Viennese, Suzi Liptauer [the article listed other women who committed suicide or attempted suicide after spending time with him]." But the German magazine offered no other information about her.

Over the years, other writers and Hitler scholars have contradicted each other about whether Liptauer was a successful suicide or not.

Suicide culture

The fact that Suzi Liptauer attempted suicide over a man she spent only one night with [Hitler in this case] was not that uncommon in Munich in 1921. Single men were such a scarce commodity.

In fact, following Germany's defeat in WW1, the number of suicides among women increased alarmingly as widows found themselves without breadwinners and single women felt they would be obliged to remain as "spinsters" for the rest of their days.

According to historian, Christian Goeschel (Suicide in Nazi Germany: 2009) homelessness and "dislocation" were also factors in the higher suicide rate.

"In the short-lived Weimar Republic; social dislocation seems to have prompted ordinary people to kill themselves."

Hitler had also suffered in the immediate aftermath of the war and described himself as "a dog looking for a master". And even though he eventually achieved political success, his friends and acquaintances said that his "depressive episodes" became more extreme and his threats of suicide increased.

This "suicide culture" in Germany continued during the inter-war years and was adopted, even encouraged, under the Nazi regime - if a person had dishonored the country, the Nazi Party or their god-like leader Hitler, the only honorable thing to do was to end it all.

SLIPPERY BUT SLICK: Hitler in plain clothes shortly before becoming leader of the Nazi Party in 1921; he used emotional blackmail to get the job

Munich 1921

In the year the mysterious Suzi Liptauer attempted suicide, Hitler was living in a modest apartment in the Tiechstrasse district in Munich and had already proven his value as unofficial Nazi Party education officer. Though he was not rich, he had more money than he was used to and his political career could not have been going any better.

All his work-related fantasies had come true, "he was living and working among men ... his hour had struck, he was discovered and appreciated, singled out for his talent. He threw himself into this work with great enthusiasm always speaking to larger groups. His confidence grew with his success in swaying people." (Nizkor Project: 1943)

According to Robert Howard Tyson (The Surreal Reich: 2010) he continued to have casual sex with men, and his status as Nazi education officer afforded him extra opportunities for homosexual liaisons.

By 1921, he had already sent Communists to their deaths in Munich by testifying against them in court.

By threatening to leave the Party over an argument with its ruling committee, he had managed to insert himself as the Party leader with dictatorial powers. He was thriving among these Nazi men who followed and protected him and provided their sexual services to him. In fact, on a sexual level, Hitler was leading a dissolute life and regularly changed his male sex partners.

Though his long term boyfriend [from WW1], Ernst Schmidt had already left Munich, Hitler had formed new friendships with fellow Nazis, Emil Maurice and Julius Schreck while Ulrich Graf and Christian Weber, were also on tap to satisfy Hitler's needs as and when required. (Ibid.).

So, as the year 1921 was a year in the homosexual phase of Hitler's life and a year in which he was thriving in his new-found career among men, what was he doing associating with a young woman from Vienna? A young woman who attempted suicide, presumably after having had physical contact with him? It seems Hitler's life at the time was not just confined to his "glorious male community".

Young ballerinas and nude models

Eva Braun's biographer (Hitler's Mistress: 1969) Nerin E. Gun said that during 1921, when he was not immersed in politics, Hitler received pretty girls in his modest Munich apartment, located on the Tiechstrasse. The source for this information was Hitler's bisexual chauffeur, Emil Maurice who seemed happy to reminisce about the early years with Hitler in Munich and wanted to imply that his boss was most definitely "heterosexual".

He would of course want to create this impression given that he was one of Hitler's casual lovers at that time.

Maurice told Gun during their interview: "He [Hitler] always offered the girls flowers even when he was penniless. And we used to go and admire the ballet dancers."

He said Hitler enjoyed watching the ballet but did not like the male dancers as he believed they displayed a "manifest weakness". [In the Nazi Party, effeminate homosexuals were shunned in favor of masculine types].

According to Maurice, his boss had a predilection for "young ballerinas" and later in his political career, he wanted to introduce a type of social security scheme for them with guaranteed minimum salary and unemployment benefits. Maurice remembered that sometimes they used to go to Munich's Academy of Art to admire the female models posing in the nude and he said Hitler appeared "very much at ease among the nudity".

Young maids and secretaries

But Nerin E. Gun complained that there were so many rumors about Hitler's sex life around this time, including gossip from the sisters of his chauffeurs or servants, that he could not believe or document all of them.

"There were certain rumors for which it has been impossible to find any documented confirmation. But an unconfirmed rumor is not necessarily false."
"After all," he said, "for a long time, a mere whisper of a rumor, ignored by almost everybody was the only indication of Eva Braun's existence".

Unfortunately, the author devoted only a few paragraphs to Suzi Liptauer and her suicide attempt, immediately after the Braun reference above:

"Many men sleep with their secretaries or maids. A Viennese lady, Suzi Liptauer, who lived in Munich, apparently tried to hang herself in a hotel room in 1921 because Hitler had broken with her. I found this information in the highly respected British Museum Library in London. The photographer Hoffmann confirmed the episode and added that the lady subsequently married and enjoyed Hitler's protection." (Hitler's Mistress: 1969)

This would imply that Liptauer may have worked as one of Hitler's Munich servants or perhaps as his secretary. He had become Nazi Party leader in 1921 so he may have had some extra financial support to carry out his new role. But his Munich apartment on Tiechstrasse was described as "modest" so it is unlikely he had a maid at his disposal.

There is also the possibility that Liptauer worked as a maid at his favorite Munich hotel (at that time), the Vier Jahreszeiten but there is no record of her ever working there.

Gun suggested that Hitler dumped Suzi Liptauer once he had his wicked way with her but if that is the case, why was there a need to pay for the young Viennese woman's silence? Did Hitler reveal his perversions on that unhappy night in the hotel bedroom?

At least Eva Braun's biographer [Gun] has brought some clarity to the Suzi Liptauer mystery: she was single, not married as some authors have incorrectly stated.

Hitler had always viewed marital infidelity as "highly immoral" and admonished his married Nazi colleagues about their infidelities; therefore it is very unlikely he would have attempted to have sexual relations, even for one night, with a married woman.

Another fact we can be certain of is that she tried to hang herself in a hotel bedroom but she did not succeed (other writers have said she was a successful suicide). After her suicide attempt, she recovered sufficiently to marry an unnamed man of whom little is known. Hitler's cronies continued to pay Suzi Liptauer "silence money" even after her marriage to make sure she never spoke about what happened in the hotel bedroom.

The payment of hush money to cover up Hitler's sordid relationships with both men and women would become a regular occurrence for Nazi Party fixers over the next two and a half decades.

Other women?
Immediately after Gun's reference to Suzi Liptauer, the author moved forward to the "other women" Hitler was rumored to have had relationships with.
These included "the widow of Professor Troost, the Lady Bouhler and the Polish-born actress, Pola Negri". (Hitler's Mistress: 1969).

Helene Bouhler (b.1912-d.1945) was married to SS-Commander, Philipp Bouhler who was responsible for "Action T4", the euthanasia program which sent 70,000 disabled adults and children to their deaths during the war.

A loyal Hitler devotee, she threw herself from a window to her death in 1945. Her husband took a cyanide capsule.

Gerdy Troost (b.1904-d.2003), the daughter of an art critic, worked as a Nazi architect for the Third Reich and received 100,000 Reichmarks from Hitler in 1943. She died of natural causes aged 99.

Both women were too young, even for Hitler who had a predilection for teenagers, to have been involved in the Suzi Liptauer scandal in 1921.

Jealousy over Negri?

But the other woman Nerin E. Gun mentioned, Pola Negri (b.1897-d.1987), may have been the cause of Hitler's loss of interest in Liptauer. It would not be the first time he jilted one woman to pursue another.

Hitler first met the Polish-born actress and singer in 1921 when she was one of the most popular film stars in Germany. Her film, One Arabian Night (1920), in which she played a dancer sold into slavery in the Arab world had been a smash hit in both the USA and Germany.

POLISH BEAUTY: Pola Negri knew Hitler and met him for the first time in 1921; did Suzi Liptauer try to kill herself because of her?

Pola Negri was based mainly in Berlin for her film work but she was a frequent visitor to Munich. Hitler, who was already fascinated by actresses and an avid cinema-goer, was apparently entranced by the 24-year-old actress when she visited Munich on a film publicity tour.

In typically gushing fashion, Hitler apparently told her he had been completely transformed by her sultry performance in One Arabian Night.

After their initial meeting, Hitler and Negri remained in contact for almost two decades, even though, in September 1922, she signed a film contract with Paramount Studios and left Germany for Hollywood.

When her career in America began to decline, she returned to Germany circa 1933 to star in a French film called Fanatisme (1934) which was followed by the German film, Masurka (1935). In it, a woman is put on trial for murdering a predatory musician. Hitler claimed it was his "favorite film in years".

By this stage, Hitler had become German Chancellor and he and the actress renewed their acquaintance.

Like so many other actresses, she visited him at the Berlin Chancellery for late night suppers but she always claimed there was nothing sexual between them.

When Negri was photographed with him in public, the usual rumors began to circulate about a romantic relationship. One French magazine, Pour Vous actually printed a story which stated that the actress was "having a sexual relationship with the Fuhrer and had become pregnant with his child".

In 1937, Pola Negri sued the magazine for libel and won. Her friendship with the Fuhrer seems to have ended abruptly at that point.

Cover up

Did Suzi Liptauer attempt suicide because of Hitler's interest in the dazzling actress? Was it a case of simple jealousy? Several years after her suicide attempt, rumors of Hitler's sexual association with her resurfaced.

Heinrich Hoffmann, who confirmed the Liptauer episode, did not become Hitler's official photographer until the mid-1920s, so the rumors must have started some time after his appointment; otherwise he is unlikely to have been privy to them.

Even in those early years, Munich-based, anti-Nazi journalists were digging for dirt on Hitler in the hope of damaging his political career, so the story of a tragic young woman who tried to hang herself after a night of sex with him might prove very useful. But Hitler, who demanded "absolute loyalty" had plenty of sycophants to help him cover up the affair.

Whatever happened between Suzi Liptauer and Adolf Hitler in 1921, it was serious enough for her to attempt suicide and serious enough for Hitler to pay her off to keep her quiet. It was also serious enough for her to remain under "Hitler's protection" for years

Did Hitler dare to display his perversions [urophilia or coprophilia] during what appears to have been a one-night encounter? The Nizkor Project authors and other experts have said there had to be a "love component" in the relationship for him to reveal his darkest desires. In any event, in 1921, Hitler's perversions were apparently still only at their "naisant stage". (Ibid.)

Did he ask Suzi Liptauer to whip and beat him as he lay on the ground (as he did ten years later with the actress Renate Mueller)? This is also unlikely as Liptauer appears to have been from his own social class, therefore he would not have groveled in front of her.

Did he choose to make her suffer because she was from Vienna, the place where his perversions first materialized; a city he hated since his days queuing at soups kitchens, the place where his anti-Semitism first took hold? Or was it simply a case of jealousy over Pola Negri as previously suggested?

The answer to these questions may never be known.

Hitler's internal struggle

One thing is clear: in 1921, Hitler's life was full of contradictions and hypocrisy. Storm trooper chief, "Queen" Ernst Roehm said Hitler often contradicted himself "but he was never wrong". These contradictions seem to have carried over into his complex sexual psyche.

Hitler was enjoying casual gay encounters throughout 1921, yet he managed to get himself entangled in a "heterosexual episode" which had near fatal consequences for the woman and could have ended his political career.

Obviously at this time, he was not exclusively homosexual; if Emil Maurice is to be believed, he visited art studios to look at naked female models and he went to the ballet to ogle at "young ballerinas", hardly the actions of an uncomplicated sexual being.

Psychiatrists and psychoanalysts, Dr. Walter C. Langer and his colleagues have offered an explanation for the contradictions in Hitler's sexual character, saying that Hitler was "harassed by fears, anxieties, doubts; feelings of loneliness and of guilt". (Nizkor Project: 1943)

They said his mind was like a "battle-royale" with many conflicting fears and impulses pulling him this way and that. The result of these internalized conflicts was a narrowing of the sexual world in which he lived.

"Haunted by these fears, he distrusts everyone, even those closest to him. He cannot establish any close friendships for fear of being betrayed or being discovered for who he really is." (Ibid.)

In other words, casual sex became Hitler's preference in place of any form of real intimacy with either sex.

CHAPTER 15: MARIA REITER

THE FIRST SUICIDAL TEENAGER romantically linked with Adolf Hitler was Maria "Mimi" Reiter. (1911-1992). This fairly short-lived relationship was Hitler's first attempt at leaving his homosexual past behind him and "going straight".
Reiter gave her story to the Germany's Der Spiegel magazine in 1959.
According to her account of their relationship, the 37-year old Hitler made a "coarse sexual advance" towards her (when she was only 16 years old) shortly after they first met but she declined to say exactly what had happened.
During their time together, Hitler romped like a child in the woods with her, fed her cream cakes from a spoon, took her hand and placed it on his crotch during a drive in his Mercedes, horse-whipped his dog in front of her and asked her to call him "Wolf", the name he used when traveling incognito.
Maria Reiter tried to hang herself when Hitler lost interest in her but she said that five years later, they shared one night of passion together in his Munich apartment – an extraordinary experience she said she would never forget.
She is the only one of Hitler's suicidal girlfriends known to have lived until old age. She died in 1992, aged 81.

Adolf Hitler first met 16-year-old Maria Reiter in autumn 1926, in Berchtesgaden, Obersalzberg, one of his favorite holiday retreats. He was there to give a Nazi Party speech at the local hotel.
Apparently once he set eyes on her, Hitler wanted to impress her and invited her to a local concert but Maria's older sister Anni intervened, saying he was "too old" to spend time with such a young girl.
Undaunted, he refused to take no for an answer and continued to pursue her.
At the time, the convent-educated teenager was grieving for her mother who had died just two weeks earlier from cancer.
Her father, a local Nazi official, had taken his daughter out of Catholic boarding school one year early so she could help him run the family clothes shop.

First impressions
More than 40 years after they first met, Maria Reiter gave her first impressions of Adolf Hitler to Der Spiegel magazine. During the interview, she remembered that his toothbrush mustache made her giggle so much that she could hardly control herself. (Purple Velvet: 1959)
Der Spiegel said: "Maria confessed to have met the then 37-year-old Hitler in Berchtesgaden when she was aged only 16. She said: 'But heaven help me, I sympathized with his two black flies pasted on his face above his upper lip!' she said"
In his book (Hitler and Geli: 1997), Ronald Hayman said Maria's sister was now running the family dress shop and the two girls shared an apartment together.
"Maria was walking the family dog, Marco, in the Kurpark when Hitler was walking his Alsatian, Prinz. Like so many dog-owners who are introduced to each other by their pets, Hitler and Maria started chatting. He invited her to a concert, but she

could not accept without asking her sister, and when they went into the shop, Anni said Maria was too young to go out with an older man."

Hitler then invited Maria and her sister Anni to attend the Nazi rally in the local hotel: "Maria felt uncomfortable when he kept looking at her during his speech, but she said she had enjoyed listening to him. Immediately more relaxed, he started addressing her with affectionate Austrian diminutives, 'Mimi, Mitzi, Mitzerl'."

COME TO DADDY: Hitler romped like a child during his time with "Mimi" Reiter; he also whipped his dog in front of her

Hayman continued: "The favorable reaction to his speech encouraged him to start flirting, but he did this gauchely, saying that her eyes were like his mother's. He told her he too had been orphaned when he was sixteen [in fact he was almost 19 years old]. He said it must be significant that the date of her birthday [December 23] was the date on which his mother had been buried."

According to Der Spiegel: "They shared a meal of fried fish and Maria expressed a positive reaction to her sister Anni afterward: 'He looks so strong with his boots, pants and with his riding crop. He really has an impressive appearance. But those funny flies? I had to giggle again and again'."

Horse whipped

Reiter told Der Spiegel: "We went out into the night. Hitler was about to put his arm around my shoulders and pull me toward him when the two dogs suddenly attacked each other. Hitler suddenly intervened, like a maniac he hit his dog with his riding whip and shook him violently by the collar. He was very excited. I did not expect that he could hit his dog so brutally and ruthlessly, the dog which he had said he could not live without. Yet he beat up his most loyal companion." (Purple Velvet: 1959)

She asked him "How can you be so brutal and beat your dog like that?"

He replied "It was necessary."

After midnight, Reiter said they returned to the apartment she shared with her sister "where brutality turned to tenderness".

"Hitler came up very close to me and looked at me for a very long time I could feel his breath. Tenderly, he touched my shoulders, his mouth changed, his voice sounded sad. 'Don't you want to kiss me?' he asked."

Reiter told Der Spiegel magazine she wanted to kiss him but forced herself to say no, that "they shouldn't see each other again". She feared what her father might say as she was so young and he was so much older than her.

Hitler took the rejection badly. According to Reiter, he "turned cold, kindness disappeared from his face, abruptly he turned away said 'Heil Hitler!' and left."

In his book, Explaining Hitler: The Search for the Origins of his Evil (1998), Ron Rosenbaum said Hitler did not give up the chase. "He sent a confidant around to Mimi's store the next morning. The surrogate told Mimi, 'I have never seen him like that. Herr Hitler poured his heart out to me. Believe me: The man is on fire.'"

Mimi agreed to another meeting.

Rosenbaum said: "Mimi accedes to an excursion to the picturesque Starnbergersee, which is to be the scene of their first kiss, although Hitler begins the intimacy on the drive itself." (Ibid.)

With his chauffeur, Emil Maurice, up front at the wheel, Hitler sat very close to Mimi in the back.

Reiter explained: "He took my hand and put it into his lap, then he took my other hand as well and pressed it [down on his crotch]."

He put his right arm around me and tenderly placed his hand on my temple, pulled my head toward his shoulder and wanted to close my eyes with his fingers. He said I should dream."

Rosenbaum (Explaining Hitler: 1998) said: "This combination of coarseness [the hand in the lap] and tenderness worked its magic on Mimi who later said: 'I think that during those first minutes on our ride to Starnbergersee my reserve was broken.'"

Plaything he could dominate

In his book, Hitler 1889-1936 (1998) historian, Ian Kershaw attempted to explain Reiter's fascination with a man so much older than her and suggested she may have been "emotionally disturbed so soon after her mother's death".

"She had already heard that the famous Adolf Hitler had taken rooms in the hotel when he introduced himself one day as she was sitting on a bench in the nearby Kurpark, playing with her Alsatian dog, Marco."

"Soon, he was flirting with her. His manner of dress, complete with knee-length boots and whip, impressed her. Hitler demonstrated his domination by thrashing his own dog, an Alsatian called Prinz, when it misbehaved by fighting Mimi's dog. She was in awe of him, and plainly became completely infatuated."

"Hitler was evidently taken with the attractive, blonde young girl, charming in her naive, youthful way, flirtatious, hanging on his every word. He flattered her, and played with her affections. For Hitler she was 'Mimi, Mimilein, Mizzi, Mizzerl', whichever diminutive occurred to him. He also called her 'my dear child'." (Ibid.)

Kershaw believed that Hitler preferred women much younger than himself because he could then dominate them, "girls who would be obedient playthings but not get in his way".

Cate Haste, author of Nazi Women (2001), has agreed with Kershaw's assessment: "He pursued her, flirted with her, took her out on trips in his Mercedes and invited her to a meeting he was to address. She was impressed by his celebrity, and by his dress, by this time, breeches, light velour hat, riding whip and a coat held closed by a leather belt. In Reiter's later account, she recalls him taking her to dinner, feeding her cakes like a child, and touching her leg with his knee under the table. He told her that she reminded him of his own mother, especially her eyes."

Ronald Hayman (Hitler and Geli: 1997), said Maria Reiter fitted Hitler's type of woman as he hated people laughing at him: "What she had in common with Geli [Raubal, his niece] was that she was too young and inoffensive for him to feel threatened. If she laughed, it would mean that she was either embarrassed or having a good time."

Reiter told Der Spiegel (Purple Velvet: 1959) that Hitler wanted to visit her mother's graveside with her.

When they arrived, she said: "I looked again at the wreaths; then I started to cry because I realized that Herr Hitler was moved by something, something he wanted to tell me. I cried more and more. Then he turned to me, took my hands, folded them, held them to his chest and pushed my head towards him. Hitler sounded serious, like a friend in dire need: 'I'm not ready', he said."

"There was a pause, because Maria didn't understand what he was thinking." With his whip in one hand, he comforted the sobbing girl by putting the other arm around her shoulder.

Then Hitler said: "But my dear, listen, from today, I want us to address each other as 'you' [the more informal 'du' in German]" and "I would like you to call me 'Wolf'."

Reiter remembered "there was no kiss; no formal handshake, nothing."

Ronald Hayman (Hitler & Geli: 1998) said: "With Maria, once they were sufficiently relaxed in each other's company, there was nothing to stop them from making love." But he offered her nothing more than a paternal hug.

Woodland fairy

On their next date, Hitler's chauffeur, Emil Maurice, once again drove them to the nearby woods.

When they came to a clearing, the Nazi leader asked the ingenue to stand in front of a tall fir tree.

Reiter described his attempts at seduction as "awkward".

She told Der Spiegel (Purple Velvet: 1959): "Hitler put me standing under a tall tree. He turned me to the left, to the right. 'What should I actually see here under this great fir?' I asked amazed. 'Nothing. You should only stop to see how I made you. A gorgeous picture,' he said. 'Do you know what you are now? You're my woodland fairy ', he beamed."

"'What makes you suddenly think that I was a forest fairy? We're not in the theater', Maria said. 'You will understand much better later, Mimi, my child!' said Hitler. He told me not to laugh at him which made me giggle even more."

"Then, he came up to me, grabbed me and kissed me. He kissed me for the first time wild, wild, stormy. He pulled me in and said: 'Sweet girl, now I just cannot help myself.' He wrapped his hands firmly around my neck. He kissed me. He did not know what he should do. He said: 'I like you too much. What I feel for you, everything is easy. Mimi! Kiss me!' he asked. I wanted to stop living. I was so happy. The way Hitler looked almost frightened me. "

"He paused and then kissed me on the forehead, on the mouth, on the neck. I felt him clench his fists. I saw how he struggled with himself. 'Child', he said 'I could crush you, now, in this moment.' I did not try to resist."

Romping like a child
Lothar Machtan (Hidden Hitler: 2001) one of the first authors to out Hitler as a homosexual said of course Hitler did not know what to do.
"In default of any physical desire to guide him? It was only his quirky imitation of a painter that had lent him the courage to venture as far as he did."
Machtan said that Hitler once paid court to Lotte Bechstein, (the daughter of one of his financial patrons, Helene Bechstein) who later told her husband the reason why she and Hitler never had sex was because: "He couldn't kiss."
Lotte Bechstein said: "His fixation on his own sex was too strong and his self-imposed heterosexuality too dependent on an effort of the will. All his attempts to start a love affair with a woman had come to nothing."
Hitler and Reiter had several more dates during which he tried to be passionate towards her, and according to Christopher Nicholson (Richard and Adolf: 2007), on several occasions he enjoyed watching his "wood nymph" swimming nude while he sat on the river bank.
During another walk in the woods, Reiter said he made her "romp with him like a child". Then, according to Reiter, he said he wanted her "to be his wife, to found a family, to have blond children, but at the moment, he had no time to think of such things. Repeatedly, Hitler spoke of his duty, his mission".
But he made her a promise: "When I get my new apartment [in Munich], you have to stay with me forever. We will choose everything together, the paintings, the chairs; I already can see it all: beautiful, big lounge chairs of violet plush."

His apartment
Reiter told Der Spiegel of another rendezvous with the man she called "Wolf" - this time in Munich:
"During Munich's winter Figure Skating Championships, Reiter who was a member of the Berchtesgaden skating club, arrived in the city. After the show, she

met Hitler and accompanied him to his apartment."

Once again, he suggested that they would eventually set up home together.

"Wolf pressed his forehead down to her neck and told her: 'You can no longer be away from me, Mimi. Did you hear? When I will get my new apartment now, you have to stay with me always! We will select all together. The pictures, the chairs, I see everything in front of me. A beautiful large living room set with purple velvet with no expense spared'." (Purple Velvet: 1959)

Though she left his Munich apartment at 2am, she said they did not have sexual intercourse. Hitler attempted some heavy petting but once again his attempts at intimacy were awkward. She said she went back to her hotel and returned home to Berchtesgaden the following day.

But after making his declaration of love to her, Hitler completely forgot about her. This plunged the teenager into a deep depression.

At Christmas, she sent him hand-made cushions with Nazi Party emblems she had embroidered herself and he sent her a leather-bound copy of Mein Kampf.

But the "romantic" side of their association seems to have ended.

In any case, Reiter's father did not approve of their relationship and tried to intervene to end it. Apart from the obvious age difference, Hitler remained "on probation for treason" and would remain so until 1928.

Hitler wrote to Maria in February 1927 using her father as an excuse to end things.

"My dear, good child, I was truly happy to receive this sign of your tender friendship to me. I am given a constant reminder of your cheeky head and your eyes. As regards what is causing you personal pain, you can believe me that I sympathize with you. But you should not let your little head droop in sadness and must only see and believe; even if fathers sometimes don't understand their children any longer because they have got older not only in years but in feelings, they mean only well for them. As happy as your love makes me, I ask you most ardently to listen to your father. And now, my dear treasure, receive warmest greetings from your 'Wolf', who is always thinking of you."

In despair, the (now) 17-year-old attempted to hang herself.

She told Der Spiegel: "My whole world started tumbling down. I did not know what had happened, nothing. All sorts of pictures appeared in my mind; faces of other women and Hitler smiling at them.""I did not want to go on living."

Gunther Peis (Spies and Saboteurs: 1973) described her suicide attempt.

"In this depressed mood, she went to find a clothesline. One end of it she slung around her neck, the other around a door handle. Slowly, she glided to the floor. Slowly, she lost consciousness. Luckily, her brother-in-law arrived and saved her life at the last minute."

Sex with a minor

When he heard about her suicide attempt, Hitler sent a message that he was unable to see her because he was being blackmailed.

Reiter told Der Spiegel: "Hitler told my brother-in-law, that anonymous letters had been mailed to the party office saying that Hitler was having a relationship with a girl who was underage. The letter said 'Hitler seduces young, inexperienced girls. He just found a sixteen-year-old girl in Berchtesgaden who obviously will be his next victim.'"

Hitler told her he could not allow his relationship with her to "jeopardize the success of his political party".

In his book, (Hidden Hitler: 2001), Lothar Machtan confirmed that blackmail letters were being sent. "As early as 1927, Party headquarters had received some anonymous letters accusing Hitler of seducing a minor. It later transpired that their author was a certain Ida Arnold, a girlfriend of Emil Maurice [Hitler's Munich chauffeur], who had invited 'Mimi' to coffee and skilfully pumped her for information. Feeling cornered, Hitler forced Maria Reiter to make a sworn deposition to the effect that she had 'no relationship of any kind with him.'"

Machtan said: "Although this amounted to flagrant perjury, it must have seemed Hitler's only possible recourse. He was clearly under extreme pressure, because nothing could have presented a greater threat to him, as party leader, than revelations about his private life, and who knew more about that subject than Emil Maurice?"

INNOCENT: Maria Reiter aged 22

Adolf Hitler had a very good reason for losing interest in Maria Reiter and not just because of the blackmail letters; he had become obsessed with his beautiful teenage niece, Geli Raubal. This incestuous relationship which involved many of his sexual perversions would result in yet more blackmail letters being sent to Nazi Party HQ. Her death in 1931 led to accusations that Hitler had murdered his vivacious and talkative niece to keep her silent for good.

In 1930, three years after her suicide attempt, Maria Reiter married a local hotel keeper. The marriage broke down almost immediately and she left her husband in early 1931.

In her interview with Der Spiegel, she claimed that in the same year, Hitler sent Rudolf Hess to fetch her and she spent the night at Hitler's Munich apartment. "I let him do whatever he wanted to me. I was never as happy as that night," she said. (Purple Velvet: 1959)

She also claimed Hitler wanted her to remain in Munich as his lover; that he would buy her an apartment in the city, so she could be near him.

In hindsight, she said this would not have worked for either of them as "his sexual tastes were too extreme for her"; she wanted marriage and he only wanted a mistress.

[Note: Most historians have questioned the truth of Reiter's story concerning their night of passion in Munich. Up to her death in September 1931, Hitler only had eyes for his niece and is unlikely to have been unfaithful to her.]

SURVIVOR: Maria Reiter was one of the few to survive knowing Hitler

Later life

In 1936, Maria Reiter married George Kubisch, an SS officer who was killed in 1940 during the Battle of Dunkirk. Hitler sent her one hundred red roses when he heard of her husband's death. There was no further contact between them.

After the war, she lived for a while with Hitler's sister Paula and found work as a maid in a hotel in Berchtesgaden.

In 1977, she was living alone in Munich.

She died single and childless aged 81 in 1992.

CHAPTER 16: ANGELA 'GELI' RAUBAL

"From a consideration of all the evidence it would seem that Hitler's perversion is as Geli has described it. The great danger in gratifying it, however, is that the individual might get feces or urine into his mouth. It is this danger that must be guarded against [by Hitler]." Nizkor Project (1943)

"Nobody laughs with their eyes like my Geli does," Adolf Hitler.

ANGELA "GELI" RAUBAL (b.1908-d.1931), Hitler's half-niece, was the daughter of his older half-sister, also called Angela. Most historians agree that his niece, and not Eva Braun, was the heterosexual love of Adolf Hitler's life.

Geli was 15 years old when Hitler first began to take an interest in her. She visited him while he was in Landsberg prison and holidayed with him at his summer home in the Obersalzberg. They would eventually share an apartment together in Munich.

During their relationship, Geli Raubal told several people that her uncle made her do "disgusting things" when they were alone in her bedroom.

She said she was obliged to urinate (and possibly defecate) on his face while he masturbated and he made her pose naked so he could draw "depraved intimate sketches" of her private parts.

There is also a suggestion that he used his whip to beat her and himself during their sex sessions. She became a virtual prisoner in his Munich apartment between 1929 and 1931 during which time, he tried to control every aspect of her life. While Hitler was away from the apartment they shared, Geli Raubal managed to have secret sex sessions with other men, including Hitler's chauffeur, Emil Maurice and an un-named Jewish teacher from Vienna.

In September 1931, she committed suicide by shooting herself in the chest with Hitler's gun. But her death was extremely suspicious for a suicide:

"The bullet had entered above the heart and lodged in her lower back at hip level, meaning the gun had to be pointing downwards and the hand holding it higher than her heart, a strange way to commit suicide." (The Mirror: 2006)

Other commentators believe that she was murdered, either by Hitler or one of his Nazi henchmen to guarantee her silence. If she had lived to tell the world of his sexual perversions, his political career would have been ruined.

Femme fatale

Historian, Dr. Robert G. L. Waite (Psychopathic God: 1977) has said: "Part of the continuing fascination with Geli, this enigmatic femme fatale, is that she had such a pronounced impact on Hitler. and "an examination of their doomed affair might be a window into the 'mysterious darkness' of Hitler's psyche. With the single exception of his mother's death, no other event in his personal life had hit him so hard."

Dr. Waite believed, with his niece, he was able to express the darkest side of his sexuality, perhaps for the first and only time in his life.

In 1991, [sixty years after her death] Der Spiegel said: "There is no other story in the realm of Hitler studies where legend and fact are so fantastically interwoven. No other woman linked to Hitler has exerted the kind of fascination for succeeding generations."

DOOMED ANGEL: Geli would die in tragic circumstances; she was probably murdered on Hitler's orders because she knew too much about his darkest sexual appetites

The following year, Ron Rosenbaum (Vanity Fair: 1992) said: "She was beautiful but there was something unusual about her beauty, something peculiar - even frightening."
Rudolph Binion (Hitler Among the Germans: 1976) believed she was Hitler's

"single approximation to amour passion" but doubted the sexual relationship was ever consummated because of his fears about sexual penetration.

Murray Davies (The Mirror: 2006) put it a bit more crudely:

"Historical evidence suggests Geli and some other Frauleins treated Hitler to golden showers, and maybe a brown or two."

Early years

In 1908, Hitler's half-sister, Angela Raubal gave birth to a girl also called Angela, who soon became known as "Geli." At the time of her birth, Hitler was living in Vienna, a disaffected would-be artist, bitter about the series of rejections from the Academy of Fine Arts, scratching out a living selling postcards he painted of local landmarks. He had lost contact with his older half-sister Angela and the rest of the family as they were unrelenting in their view that he should become a civil servant.

Adolf Hitler had detested Leo Raubal, Geli's father, a civil servant who had put pressure on him to follow a similar career path. The two men had quarreled many times about Hitler's future which meant that up to the time of Leo Raubal's death in 1910, Hitler was not welcome in the Raubal family home.

It was not until after WW1, after Corporal Hitler returned to his adopted city Munich and became, at almost 34 years of age, the leader of the National Socialist Party, that he got back in touch with Angela and her family in Vienna.

More than ten years had passed since he had seen any of his family.

By then, Geli was a pubescent fourteen-year old; whose father had been dead for 12 years and whose mother Angela worked as a housekeeper at a convent school. Their life in a flat by the Westbanhof railway station [ironically, one of Hitler's former begging sites] in Vienna was austere and bleak.

Ron Rosenbaum said: (Vanity Fair: 1992) "Suddenly, teenage Geli had an exciting gentleman caller, a celebrity, her 'Uncle Alfie' as he had her call him."

Angela and her daughter Geli visited Hitler at Landsberg prison in 1924, and when in early 1925, he returned to Munich to plot his political comeback, he summoned Angela and Geli to serve as his live-in housekeepers, first at his mountain retreat in Berchtesgaden and later at his apartment in Munich.

By 1925, Geli had blossomed into something of a beauty and soon her uncle began to take notice of her in a way that went far beyond the avuncular. Geli was 17 years old and Hitler was 36.

Patrick Hitler, the Fuhrer's half-nephew, who met Geli during this period said: "Geli looked more like a child than a girl. She usually went without a hat and wore very plain clothes, pleated skirts and white blouses. No jewelry except a gold swastika given to her by Uncle Adolf." (spartacus-educational.com: 2015)

Anti-Nazi journalist, Konrad Heiden, described Hitler "squiring her around bucolic mountain villages, riding through the countryside; from time to time showing his niece how 'Uncle Alf' could bewitch the masses."

His Princess

But it soon became clear that it was Uncle Alf who was becoming bewitched by his young relative. Incestuous relationships were common in Hitler's background and as Cate Haste, author of Nazi Women (2001) said: "Any relationship between Hitler and Geli was incestuous... She called him 'Uncle Alf', and he called her his 'Princess'."

In Munich, Geli became a close friend of Henriette Hoffmann, the young daughter of Heinrich Hoffmann, Hitler's official photographer.

In summer, the two teenagers often went to the local lake together and after swimming naked they let the sun dry their bodies.

FORBIDDEN FRUIT: Geli, aged 16, attracted her uncle's attention but not in a good way

Henriette said: "One day a cluster of butterflies settled on the naked Geli. We made ourselves garlands of strawberry leaves and put them on. For us the world was a garden, a forest glade, with fairies dancing in the moonlight and fauns with goat feet making music. We thought life was a party that was just beginning. We didn't know the forest glade was a battlefield you couldn't leave till you were defeated. We didn't know the world was rough and mean and stupid." (spartacus-educational.com: 2015)

Ian Kershaw, author of Hitler 1889-1936 (1998) summed it up perfectly. "From the start, Hitler was attracted to his niece. She exuded a strong sexuality. She was full of life and full of fun, and Hitler was not exactly that type, but this contrast somehow had its appeal, and a very strong bond, certainly from Hitler to her, developed."

After she moved to Munich, 'Uncle Alf' set her up in her own apartment in the building next to his, leaving the housekeeping to her mother. Meanwhile, he

"paraded Geli around on his arm, escorted her to cafes and cinemas.
"He soon began to act like a Hearst-ian sugar daddy, paying for her lessons with the best voice teachers in Munich and Vienna, encouraging her to believe she could become a heroine of the Wagnerian operas he loved to distraction." (Ibid.)

UNCLE ALF: Hitler with his two nieces, pictured here circa 1923;
Geli's older sister Elfriede (right)

Ernst Hanfstaengl (The Missing Years: 1957) said Geli had the effect of making him behave like a teenager. "He hovered at her elbow in a very plausible imitation of adolescent infatuation."

Hanfstaengl said he once saw him "mooning at her" and when he noticed, Hitler quickly "switched his face to the Napoleonic look".

He also said Geli went around very well dressed at Hitler's expense, or, more probably, the [Nazi] Party's and never behaved in such a way in Eva Braun's company, rather he seemed mildly bored whenever he was with her. (Ibid.)

Ron Rosenbaum (Vanity Fair: 1992) said that in 1929 "something happened which changed the nature of their relationship".

Geli was now 21 years old. His political fortunes had improved and so had his financial situation. Hitler bought a nine-room luxury apartment in a building on Munich's fashionable Prinzregentenplatz not far from Munich's opera house. He sent Geli's mother off to semi-permanent duty at the Berchtesgaden retreat and moved Geli in with him.

"Outside that apartment, Geli seemed to revel in the attention her role as Hitler's consort brought her. And the power it gave her over him."

"Just twenty-one years old, the product of modest circumstances, she'd suddenly become a celebrity, flattered, catered to, the center of attention in the court of the man described as 'the King of Munich' who was on his way to becoming the emperor of the New Germany. She was the envy of untold numbers of women.

Some spoke resentfully of the spell she'd cast on Hitler."

As Hitler became more and more obsessed with her, he attempted to have himself or someone he trusted with her at all times, accompanying her on shopping trips, to the cinema, to dinner and the opera.

TOO CLOSE FOR COMFORT: Hitler took complete control of her life

After her college classes or singing lessons, she was collected by one of Hitler's cronies and therefore had little or no chance to form friendships or romantic relationships. And if she did make new friends, Hitler knew about them.

More and more obsessive

Pauline Kohler (The Girls Who Knew His Love: 1940) said: "Adolf, began to neglect his political work. He failed to turn up at meetings, preferring to spend his evenings walking in the Munich parks arm in arm with slim, dark-haired Geli. His days were spent in writing passionate letters."

Geli's friend Henriette Hoffmann, told historian John Toland (Definitive Biography: 1991), she was "irresistibly charming and if Geli wanted to go swimming it was more important than the most important conference."

This was confirmed by other Nazi colleagues who demanded Hitler be brought onto the carpet at the Brown House [Nazi HQ in Munich] to answer questions about his relationship with his niece and where he found the money to spend on her. The implication was that he was splashing Nazi Party funds on her. (spartacus-educational.com: 2015)

Gregor Strasser, felt that Hitler's relationship with his niece was causing poor publicity and was creating "a good deal of unfavorable talk". [Gregor Strasser was murdered during the Night of the Long Knives.]

And a low-ranking party official from Wuerttemberg called Eugen Munder complained that Hitler was "being excessively diverted by the company of his niece from his political duties." Hitler fired Munder in 1928.

Hitler Youth Leader, Baldur von Schirach said Geli's presence relaxed and released him.

BATHING BEAUTY: Geli Raubal was full of life and full of fun; the complete opposite of her "Uncle Alf"

"In front of favored guests, he let her perform her specialty act with the mountain jackdaw; when she called, the bird flew in through the open window, and he enjoyed seeing her romp about with his Alsatians Blondi and Muck. Geli was allowed to laugh at her Uncle Alf and adjust his tie when it had slipped. She was never put under pressure to be especially clever or witty. She could be simply what she was, lively and uncomplicated." (spartacus-educational.com: 2015)

In his book, Hitler & Geli (1997), Ronald Hayman said Hitler felt safe with Geli and was able to reveal himself fully.

"No one else was ever allowed to tease him as much as she did, because no one else made him feel so secure. He hated nothing more than being laughed at, but when Geli laughed, she was laughing with him, not at him."

According to Baldur von Schirach, Hitler followed her into millinery shops and watched patiently while she tried on all the hats and then decided on a beret.

"He sniffed at the sophisticated French perfumes she inquired about in a shop, and if she didn't find what she wanted in a shop, he trotted after her like a patient lamb. She exercised the sweet tyranny of youth, and he liked it."

Dirty rumors

In Munich [1928-9], rumors began to circulate among anti-Nazi journalists that he was having an affair with her and Nazi HQ had to work extremely hard, but ultimately failed, to prevent the story reaching the newspapers.

The rumors were helped along by the fact that they were now living alone together in Hitler's nine-room apartment.

As Geli's mother had been dispatched to Berchtesgaden to work, the loved up couple had more freedom in the apartment to do whatever they wanted together even though a new housekeeper, the always compliant and discreet, Anni Winter was brought in to manage his Munich home.

Weapons' training

As time went by, Hitler became more and more possessive of his niece. He insisted Geli and her friend, Henriette Hoffmann, received weapon's training. They were both encouraged to carry loaded pistols in their handbags for protection. They also practiced shooting on a rifle range just outside Munich. The young women learned how to use a safety catch and to clean a Walther 6.35 [the type of gun Geli used in her alleged suicide], taking the gun to pieces and putting it back together again. Henriette said they enjoyed this as it made them "feel like the characters in a Western movie".

Nazi photographer, Heinrich Hoffmann (Hitler Was My Friend: 1955) said Hitler wanted to control Geli from the very beginning.

Hitler apparently told him: "You know, Hoffmann, I'm so concerned about Geli's future that I feel I have to watch over her. I love Geli and could marry her. But you know what my viewpoint is; I want to remain single. So I retain the right to exert an influence on her circle of friends until such a time as she finds the right man. What Geli sees as compulsion is simply prudence. I want to stop her from falling into the hands of someone unsuitable."

Hoffmann (Ibid.) claimed that Geli gradually found Hitler's controlling behavior unpleasant: "The pressure under which she lives is burdensome to her and what makes matters worse is that she's prevented from saying how unhappy she feels. The ball [they attended together] gave her no pleasure. It merely reminded her of how little freedom she has. Certainly, it flattered her that her serious and unapproachable uncle, who was so good at hiding his feelings from everybody else, was fond of her. She wouldn't have been a woman if she hadn't been flattered by Hitler's gallantry and generosity. But it seemed simply intolerable to this child of nature that he should want to mother her every step and that she shouldn't be allowed to speak to anyone without his knowledge."

Virtual confinement

Geli lived with Hitler for over two years until her death in Hitler's apartment in September 1931.

Ron Rosenbaum (Vanity Fair: 1992) said she was obliged to pay a heavy price for knowing him, even before her death. "Part of the price was virtual confinement in a huge apartment with no company but Hitler and her pet canary, 'Hansi'."

"Geli too was a bird in a gilded cage, trapped within the stony fortress with an uncle twice her age, an uncle increasingly consumed with what Hitler biographer Alan Bullock calls jealous 'possessiveness' of her."

"Whatever the explicit form Hitler's affections took, it became increasingly evident that for Geli the rewards of her public celebrity could not compensate for the oppressiveness of her private confinement with Hitler. And that in the final months of her life, indeed within days of her death, she was making desperate efforts to escape."

Pauline Kohler (The Girls Who Knew His Love: 1940) said: "Although Geli was flattered by his love and had a real affection for him, already she felt what millions of others have since come to know; that Hitler cannot have his wishes slighted."

UNHAPPY COUPLE: Geli appears to be miserable in Hitler's company

Sex with the chauffeur

Their relationship was stormy and they accused each other of infidelity. Apparently, Geli was annoyed with her uncle because he had given a 17-year-old [Eva Braun] a lift in his motor car.

But according to Konrad Heiden (Hitler: a Biography: 1936), Geli was hardly an innocent rose floundering on the Nazi dung heap. He described her as "fascinating to many men, well aware of her electric effect and delighting in it. When relations to his niece Geli ceased to be parental. She looked forward to a brilliant career as a singer, and expected 'Uncle Alf' to make things easy for her."

Behind her uncle's back, Geli was promiscuous with other men. Before she moved into Hitler's apartment, she began a secret relationship with the handsome Emil Maurice, Hitler's Munich chauffeur and former bodyguard. Maurice had an artistic temperament, (he played the guitar and mandolin) and he and Geli, were immediately attracted to each other. They had first met during Geli's visits to Landsberg prison in 1924 to see her uncle.

Their clandestine affair was helped along by the fact that Maurice became Geli's personal chauffeur when Hitler was away from Munich on business. Under such circumstances, the cunning Maurice was able to woo and bed the enchanting Geli, by hiding in plain sight.

Maurice later told Nerin E. Gun, author of Eva Braun: Hitler's Mistress (1969): "Her big eyes were a poem and she had magnificent hair. People in the street would turn round to take another look at her, though people don't do that in Munich."

He also admitted that he was "madly in love with her and they decided to become engaged". Apparently Geli "gladly accepted" his proposal.

Her friend Henriette Hoffmann confirmed that Geli was in love with the dashing chauffeur.

"He was a sensitive man, not just someone who took pride in fighting, and there was a genuine tenderness behind his affability."

Soon, Geli told Henriette that she no longer wanted to be loved by Hitler and preferred her relationship with Maurice:

"Being loved is boring, but to love a man, you know, to love him, that's what life is about. And when you can love and be loved at the same time, it's paradise."

Geli wrote to Maurice, on December 24, 1928.

JIGGERY POKERY: Emil Maurice had much more success at winning Geli Raubal's heart than his Nazi boss did

"The postman has already brought me three letters from you, but never have I been so happy as I was over the last few days. Uncle Adolf is insisting that we should wait two years. Think of it, Emil, two whole years of only being able to kiss each other now and then and always having Uncle Adolf in charge. I can only give you my love and be unconditionally faithful to you. I love you so infinitely much. Uncle Adolf insists that I should go on with my studies."

Maurice was aware that Hitler was also trying to conduct a sexual relationship with Geli and knew of the perverted side of it as Geli had confided in him. Maurice said: "He liked to show her off everywhere; he was proud of being seen in the company of such an attractive girl. He was convinced that in this way he impressed his comrades in the party, whose wives or girlfriends nearly all looked like washerwomen."

At first, Hitler believed that the relationship between them was a mild flirtation but as Alan Bullock pointed out (A Study in Tyranny: 1962) he "was beside himself with fury when he discovered that Geli had allowed Emil Maurice, his chauffeur, to make love to her, when he forbade her having anything to do with other men." But Geli Raubal was not the monogamous type and the affair with Maurice had already ended by the time Hitler found out that they had been having regular sex.

Empty-headed slut
Anni Winter, Hitler's Munich housekeeper, said: "Geli loved Hitler. Naturally, she wanted to be become Frau Hitler. He was highly eligible but she flirted with everybody; she was not a serious girl."
Former Nazi, Ernst Hanfstaengl (The Missing Years:1957) went further and described Geli Raubal as "an empty-headed little slut, with the coarse sort of bloom of a servant girl."
Author Ian Kershaw (Hitler 1889-1936: 1998) said, even so, the situation for Maurice when his betrayal was uncovered was very serious and "there was such a scene that the chauffeur feared Hitler was going to shoot him."
According to Ronald Hayman (Hitler & Geli: 1997) there are several versions of what happened to Maurice after he was caught in the act.
The first is that Hitler "gradually started to freeze him out, fell behind in paying his wages, and in the end Maurice himself made the break." Another is that Hitler told Maurice he was never to set foot in the Munich apartment again, and the chauffeur replied: 'Sack me, and I'll take the whole story to the Frankfurter Zeitung! [Frankfurt News]'."
It is not clear which betrayal was greater for Hitler since he had sexual feelings for both his niece and his chauffeur.
He was of course unaware that Maurice and his friend Ida Arnold had successfully blackmailed him in 1927 [when he was with Maria Reiter] for attempting to have sex with a minor. In the blackmail letters, though Geli's name was never mentioned, they also referred to what she had confided about Hitler's "disgusting sexual habits". The Nazi leader never discovered that his crafty chauffeur had been involved in the extortion.

Getting rid of his rival
Hitler sacked Maurice in early 1931 when he discovered their illicit affair.
According to Ron Rosenbaum (Vanity Fair: 1992) he called Maurice a "skirt chaser" who ought to be shot "like a mad dog".
But the friendship between them proved resilient. They were bound by a mutual trust or perhaps mistrust.
To prove he was not afraid of Hitler, Maurice sued the Nazi Party for arrears of his salary amounting to 3,000 marks. When the case was heard at the Arbeitsgericht

in Munich, the court dealing with employment disputes ordered Hitler to pay his former chauffeur 500 marks which he used to set himself up as a watchmaker.

HITLER'S PERVERSIONS WITH GELI

Rumors of Hitler's strange sexual practices with his niece began to haunt him in much the same way that rumors of his "Jewish ancestry" and "homosexuality" had shadowed his rise to power.

Konrad Heiden, who wrote for the Frankfurt News at the time, was the first to claim that Hitler was a "sexual pervert" who obtained sexual pleasure from "undinism" and the first to suggest that Hitler was having a sexual relationship with his niece.

Former Nazi, Ernst Hanfstaengl (The Missing Years: 1957) attempted to explain Hitler's relationship with his niece and has claimed that Geli was a cure for Hitler's longstanding impotence.

"What particular combination of arguments her uncle used to bend her to his will, presumably with the tacit acquiescence of his half-sister Angela, we will never know."

"Whether he assumed that a young woman who was already no saint might be brought fairly easily to submit to his peculiar tastes, who went some way towards curing his impotence and half making a man out of him. What is certain is that the services she was prepared to render had the effect of making him behave like a man in love."

Ron Rosenbaum (Explaining Hitler: 1998) agreed with Hanfstaengl: "There are those who believe that with Geli Raubal, Hitler experienced the closest he came to real love, the closest he came to the emotional life of a normal person. But there are also those who believe that in his relationship with Geli Raubal, Hitler expressed the true, profound deformity of his moral nature in perverse sexual practices [paraphilia] that either drove Geli to suicide or led to her murder to prevent her from talking about them."

Hitler's dirty letter

Before Dr. Langer and his colleagues drew up their report outlining Hitler's coprophilia and urophilia completed in 1943, a Catholic ex-priest provided evidence which supported their findings.

Dr. Robert G. L. Waite (Psychopathic God: 1977) said this priest, Father Bernhard Stempfle, had befriended Hitler and helped edit Mein Kampf for publication. "He [Stempfle] asserted that in 1929 Hitler had written Geli a shockingly compromising letter which explicitly mentioned his masochistic and coprophilic inclinations."

Konrad Heiden (Hitler: a Biography: 1936) confirmed that when Geli was 21 years old, Hitler wrote a letter which betrayed his liking for coprophilia, urophilia or "undinism".

"[The] uncle and lover gave himself completely away; it expressed feelings which could be expected from a man with masochistic-coprophilic inclinations, bordering on what Havelock Ellis calls 'undinism'. The letter probably would have been repulsive to Geli if she had received it. But she never did. Hitler left the letter lying around, and it fell into the hands of his landlady's son, a certain Doctor Rudolph."

Nazi defector, Ernst Hanfstaengl (Unheard Witness: 1957) also heard about the letter in which Hitler apparently tried to end the perverted relationship with his niece. He said Carl Anton Reichel, an art expert who left the Nazi Party in 1936, told him Hitler had shown him a letter he had recently written to Geli.

"It was couched in romantic, even anatomical terms and could only be read in the context of a farewell letter of some sort. Its most extraordinary aspect was a pornographic drawing which Reichel could only describe as a symbol of Hitler's impotence." (spartacus-educational.com: 2015)

Hanfstaengl said that Reichel was not the sort of man to make up such a story. Konrad Heiden said the letter was bound "to debase Hitler and make him ridiculous in the eyes of anyone who might see it. Hitler seems to have feared that it was Dr. Rudolph's intention to make it public".

In other words, yet more blackmail and another serious threat to his political ambitions.

According to Heiden, several Hitler confidants including Nazi Party treasurer, Franz Schwarz, the shadowy ex-priest, Stempfle, and the gnome-like, Nazi-memorabilia collector J. F. M. Rehse, bought the letter from Rudolph, ostensibly for a projected collection of Hitler and Nazi Party memorabilia.

[The Rehse collection can today be found in the archives of the Nazi Party, now largely available on microfilm in the Hoover Institution and in the National Archives, USA.]

Indeed, Franz Schwarz's continued service and loyalty to Hitler [paying off blackmailers} helped make him one of the more influential, though publicly obscure figures within the Nazi Party. Hitler showed his "confidence in Schwarz" when he made him the sole executor of his personal will of May 2, 1938.

And there was another piece of circumstantial evidence that supported the ex-priest, Stempfle's knowledge of Hitler's perversions with his niece: "In June 1934, during the so-called Blood Purge [Night of the Long Knives], when Hitler settled his accounts with people who were in a position to embarrass him, Stempfle was found dead in the forest of Herlaching near Munich, with three shots through his heart. Emil Maurice had murdered him on Hitler's orders.

Hitler's porno drawings

Former Nazi, Ernst Hanfstaengl. (Unheard Witness: 1957) also said the next sign he was given that there was something wrong with the relationship between Hitler and Geli came in early 1930 from a depressed Franz Schwarz.

The two men met on a Munich street one day and according to Hanfstaengl, Schwarz was "very down-in-the-mouth". Schwarz took him to his flat and "poured out what was on his mind".

"He had just had to buy off someone who had been trying to blackmail Hitler, but the worst part of the story was the reason for it. This man had somehow come into the possession of a folio of pornographic drawings Hitler had made. They were depraved, intimate sketches of Geli Raubal, with every anatomical detail." (Ibid.)

Hanfstaengl said he was surprised when he found Schwarz still had possession of the ransomed Geli porn. "Heaven help us, man! Why don't you tear the filth up?" he asked the party treasurer.

"No," he quoted Schwarz as saying, "Hitler wants them back. He wants me to keep them in the Brown House safe [Nazi HQ in Munich]."

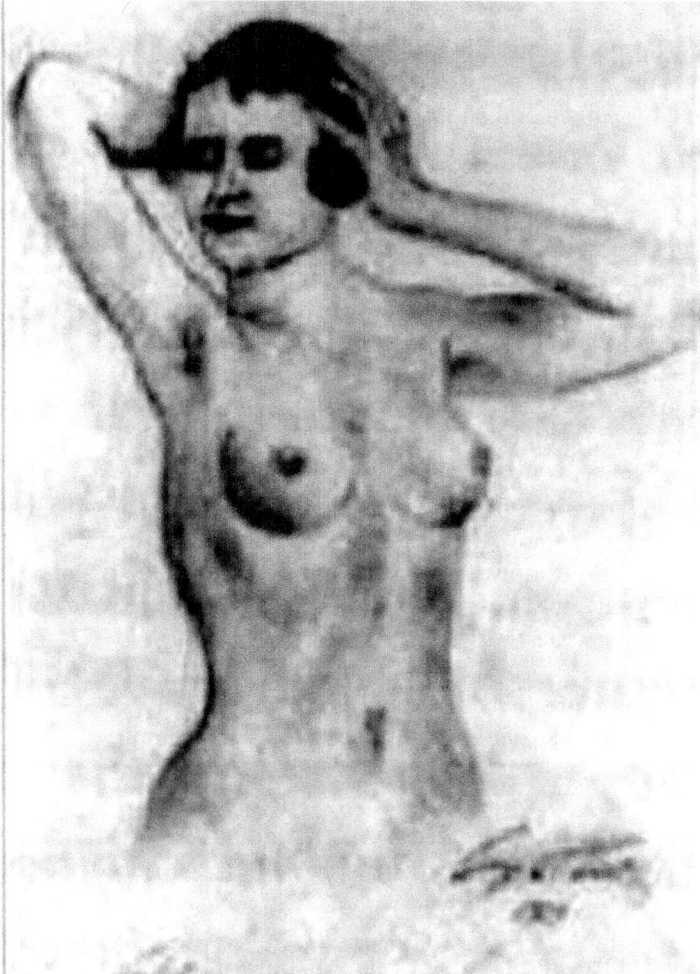

DEPRAVED: One of Hitler's drawings of his niece, Geli Raubal

He wanted to keep them as a memento of his time with his niece and believed the pornographic drawings had "great artistic merit".

Sexual confession
But even before the news of Hitler's dirty letter to his niece and before the pornographic drawings came to light, Geli Raubal had started talking about her

sex life with her uncle. Her sexual confession to Otto Strasser (another Nazi defector) revealed Hitler's "extreme form of masochism in which the individual derives sexual gratification from the act of having a woman urinate or defecate on him." (Psychopathic God: 1997)

Otto Strasser and his brother Gregor had been early Hitler allies, the leaders of a "left-wing" faction within the Nazi Party which emphasized the "socialism" in National Socialism.

Otto, and later Gregor, eventually broke with Hitler; with Otto setting up an exiled opposition movement called the Black Front, based in Prague. Otto Strasser eventually fled to Canada and supplied American intelligence agents with a number of damning stories about Hitler including Geli's Raubal's confession to him at the Chinese Tower in Munich's central park.

In May 1943, Otto Strasser was interviewed by the O.S.S. [forerunner of the CIA] in Montreal, Canada.

During his interview, he said: "I liked that girl [Geli] very much, and I could feel how much she suffered because of Hitler's jealousy. She was a fun-loving young thing who enjoyed the Mardi Gras excitement in Munich but was never able to persuade Hitler to accompany her to any of the many wild balls."

"Finally, during the 1931 Mardi Gras, Hitler allowed me to take Geli to a ball. Geli seemed to enjoy having for once escaped Hitler's supervision. On the way back, we took a walk through the English Garden. Near the Chinese Tower, Geli sat down on a bench and began to cry bitterly. Finally, she told me that Hitler loved her but that she couldn't stand it anymore. His jealousy was not the worst of it. He demanded things of her that were simply repulsive. When I asked her to explain it, she told me things that I knew only from my readings of Krafft-Ebing's Psychopathia Sexualis in my college days."

Sadism, masochism and squatting over Hitler's face

The book Psychopathia Sexualis (1886) was the first academic study of homosexuality and bisexuality, intended as a forensic text book for psychiatrists, physicians and judges in criminal cases.

Austro-German psychiatrist, Richard von Krafft-Ebing's book popularized the terms "sadism" from the brutal sexual practices of the Marquis de Sade and "masochism" from the name of Leopold von Sacher-Masoch.

During his interview with the O.S. S., Strasser recalled a tearful Geli telling him "after much urging" the nature of her relationship with her uncle.

"He demanded things from her that were simply disgusting and she said she had never dreamed that such things could happen."

"Geli said when night came, Hitler made her undress [while] he would lie down on the floor. Then she would have to squat down over his face where he could examine her at close range, and this made him very excited. When the excitement reached its peak, he demanded that she urinate on him and that gave him his sexual pleasure. Geli said that the whole performance was extremely disgusting to her and that although it was sexually stimulating it gave her no gratification."

This sexual practice is known as undinism or urophilia. [Undinism is the name Havelock Ellis gave to this practice after the water nymph Undine]. The authors of the only full length psychoanalytic biography of Hitler, Hitler's Psychopathology, compiled by medical writer Verna Volz Small and Dr. Norbert Bromberg, connected Hitler's undinism to what they described as an overly close confinement with his parents during which he witnessed "the primal scene."

Dr. Waite (Psychopathic God: 1977) said experts in this area [urophilia and coprophilia] have shown that sadomasochistic traits are a prerequisite for such perversions. "Hitler's tendencies are consistent with a coprophilic perversion, for in it masochism and sadism are united. By having young ladies defecate or urinate on his head, Hitler degraded both himself and others. In this act, he could unite with his victims, who became the personification of depraved self, as the persecutor who attacks a part of himself in his victims."

Dr. Waite said Hitler employed the same psychological defenses against perversion that he used against feelings of latent homosexuality and fears of Jewishness: "denial, projection, and punishment".

"In one particularly revealing turn of phrase, he accused Jewish journalism and literature of 'splashing filth in the face of humanity'."

Waite concluded that unnatural offenders generally turn into homicidal maniacs and should be subjected to the strongest possible punishment. He said such people "must be rendered harmless however young they may be".

Turning away from 'Uncle Alf'

Ernst Hanfstaengl (The Missing Years: 1957) believed Geli turned away from Hitler because of his perverted sexual needs. One night, he dined with Geli and Hitler at the Schwarzwalder Cafe in Munich:

"As we walked through the streets after the meal, Hitler emphasized some threat against his opponents by cracking the heavy dog whip he still affected. I happened to catch a glimpse of Geli's face as he did it, and there was on it such a look of fear and contempt that I almost caught my breath. Whips as well, I thought, and really felt sorry for the girl."

"She had displayed no sign of affection for him in the restaurant and seemed bored, looking over her shoulder at the other tables, and I could not help feeling that her share in the relationship was under compulsion," he said.

Her friend Henriette Hoffmann confirmed that Geli grew more and more indifferent to him while he grew more and more passionate about her. In secret, Geli began having sex with as many other men as she could.

This idea is supported by Wilhelm Stocker, the SA officer who was often on guard duty outside Hitler's Munich apartment.

Stocker told author Glenn Infield (Eva and Adolf: 1974): "Many times when Hitler was away for several days at a political rally or tending to party matters in Berlin or elsewhere, Geli would associate with other men. Hitler would have been furious if he had known that she was out with such men as a violin player from Augsburg or a ski instructor from Innsbruck."

Stocker also told Infield that he heard first-hand why she submitted to her uncle's sickening demands.

"She admitted to me that at times Hitler made her do things in the privacy of her room that sickened her but when I asked her why she didn't refuse to do them, she just shrugged and said that she didn't want to lose him to some woman that would do what he wanted. She was a girl that needed attention and needed it often. And she definitely wanted to remain Hitler's favorite girlfriend. She was willing to do anything to retain that status. At the beginning of 1931, I think she was worried that there might be another woman in Hitler's life because she mentioned to me several times that her uncle didn't seem to be as interested in her as he once was." (Ibid.)

DYING TO ESCAPE: Geli made several attempts to get away from her uncle but his cronies reported back to him on her every move

Beginning of the end

By 1931, Nazi Party chiefs were growing increasingly alarmed by Hitler's relationship with his niece. They believed the Nazi Party was on the verge of a major electoral breakthrough even though Hitler had not yet obtained German citizenship [he would not get it until February 25, 1932]; they feared that any sexual revelations involving Hitler's niece might scupper their leader's plans to become a true "German". Without citizenship, he would be unable to stand in national elections.

Geli was becoming much more difficult to control and there is plenty of evidence that by the end of her life, she was spilling the beans about her uncle's perversions to outsiders, including Otto Strasser, Henriette Hoffmann [who had her own strange experiences with Hitler], her former lover, Emil Maurice, SA officer, Wilhelm Stocker and possibly others.

To make matters worse for her, Geli met a man on a trip to Vienna and it seems she fell madly in love with him. It is almost certain that this man was Jewish.

Christa Schroeder, Hitler's private secretary, confirmed that Geli had fallen in love with a man she met in Vienna [who has never been named] saying only that he was Jewish and he wanted to marry her.

His love letter to Geli in 1930 demonstrates his frustration with "Uncle Alf" and is one of the few pieces of evidence that he ever existed.

"Now your uncle, who knows how much influence he has over your mother, is trying to exploit her weakness with boundless cynicism. He's putting obstacles in the way of our mutual happiness although he knows that we're made for each other. The year of separation your mother is imposing on us will only bind us together more closely. Because I'm always very strict with myself about thinking and behaving in a direct way, I find it hard to accept when other people don't do that. But your uncle's behavior towards you can only be interpreted as egoistic. He quite simply wants you to belong to him one day and never to anyone else. Your uncle still sees you as the 'inexperienced child' and refuses to acknowledge that in the meantime you've grown up and want to take responsibility for your own happiness. Your uncle is a force of nature. In his party they all bow down to him like slaves. I don't understand how his keen intelligence can mislead him into thinking his obstinacy and his theories about marriage can destroy our love and our willpower. He's hoping to succeed this year in changing your mind, but how little he knows your soul."

Hitler's humiliation

Ron Rosenbaum (Vanity Fair: 1992) said Geli's consorting with a Jew would have been a deep sexual wound to Hitler. "She would have been, to use his odious rhetoric, 'polluted'. The humiliation would have been a political wound as well, perhaps a fatal one: Hitler's sweetheart chooses a Jew over the champion of Aryan supremacy. It would have been unbearable."

There was also another kind of political danger, according to Rosenbaum: "Sexual intimacy might have led to confessional intimacy, an intimacy in which Geli might have told her Jewish lover exactly what kind of aberrational practices Hitler demanded of her. If Geli told just one Jew, and if, in Hitler's eyes, all Jews were linked in an implacable conspiracy against him, she would be placing in the hands of all Jews (and their journalist allies) enough sensational material to destroy him." (Ibid.)

Final argument

Several informed sources have said that on Friday, September 18, 1931 Hitler and his niece had a fierce quarrel. What was the cause? Geli wanted to go to Vienna and Hitler was decidedly against this.

Anni Winter, Hitler's housekeeper claimed she overheard the argument.

Geli was very upset because Hitler had originally given his permission but then changed his mind.

"You say you have to go to Vienna? Is it to see that filthy Jew, the one who claims to be a singing teacher? Is that it? Have you been seeing him secretly again? Have you forgotten I forbade you to have anything to do with him? Tell me the truth now. Why do you want to go to Vienna?"

Apparently she replied: "I have to go to Vienna, Uncle Alf, because I'm going to have a baby."

Ronald Hayman, author of Hitler & Geli (1997) said: "It is quite likely that the other Nazi leaders were putting pressure on him. Though they would all have been glad to get rid of her, they may have told him it was unsafe to set her free; she knew too much. They may have found out that she had confided in other men about Hitler's sexual habits, and Franz Schwarz [and others] knew she had modeled for his pornographic drawings. If she talked indiscreetly in Vienna, stories might get picked up by the liberal press at the very worst."

Ron Rosenbaum (Vanity Fair: 1992) said almost every source except Hitler acknowledged the two of them quarreled over Geli's planned trip to Vienna to be with her lover.

John Toland (Definitive Biography: 1991), conducted extensive interviews with surviving members of Hitler's household staff, who said that just the week before, Hitler had already prevented Geli's attempt to leave Munich for Vienna without his knowledge.

Apparently, Geli had gotten as far as the Hitler cottage at Berchtesgaden when "she got a phone call from Uncle Alf urgently requesting her to return". After she got back, "her indignation turned to fury" when Hitler told her she was forbidden to travel while he went on his trip to Hamburg.

"The argument continued during a spaghetti lunch for two and as Geli rushed out of the dining room, the cook noticed her face was flushed." Later, the cook heard something smash and said: "Geli must have picked up a perfume bottle from her dressing table and broken it."

Rosenbaum said that even the name of the city "Vienna" could not have been pleasing to Hitler. "He hated the place, reviled it as 'the personification of incest' in Mein Kampf, viewed it as a seething nest of his mortal enemies: Jews, Marxists, and journalists."

But for Geli, Vienna was something else. It had been her only sanctioned escape from her confinement in Hitler's Munich apartment.

"He'd permitted her to go there to consult famous voice teachers, and if we believe several reports to this effect, she made the most of her brief flights to freedom, entering into a surreptitious relationship with a Jewish voice teacher, the ultimate act of defiance for her Jew-hating uncle."

And now, on the final day of her life, she was telling Hitler she was determined to go to Vienna because she was pregnant by a Jew.

Having interviewed witnesses and the relevant members of Hitler's staff, Munich journalist Konrad Heiden described what happened the morning Hitler left for Hamburg.

"As he was setting out on his trip, she called down to him from a window in the house 'Then you won't let me go to Vienna?' And Hitler, from his car, called up, 'No!

No. For the last time, no!'"

The timing of the argument may be in question but it certainly happened, but Hitler always claimed that "there had never been any argument of any kind".

HORIZONTAL REFRESHMENT: Before her death, Geli had helped her uncle to release his nervous tension in the most peculiar ways

Geli's death

On the morning of Saturday, September 19, 1931, Geli's body was found on the floor of her room in the flat she and Hitler shared. It appeared she had shot herself in the chest using Hitler's gun.

Police, when they were eventually called to the scene, were unable to give a time of death because rigor mortis had set in, therefore it was assumed that she died some time between the evening of September 18 [shortly after the argument with Hitler] and the early morning of September 19.

Ron Rosenbaum (Vanity Fair: 1992) said "There are an extraordinary number of conflicting versions of how the body was discovered. In almost all the accounts, the housekeeper couple who lived there claimed never to have heard anything suspicious, not to have noticed anything wrong until the next morning, when Geli didn't answer to a knock."

In the immediate aftermath of her death, three different people claimed to have kicked down or forced open Geli's door.

According to the official story, her door had been locked from the inside.

Some witnesses said the door was broken open in the presence of Rudolf Hess and "he was the first to inspect the death scene".

What he found inside apparently was "Geli in a beige dress and a pool of blood, lying face up on her couch, lifeless, Hitler's gun still clutched in a death grip."

Hitler's staff said that "no suicide note was found; in any case, none was there when the police were finally summoned to the death scene".

John Toland (Definitive Biography: 1991), based his version of the death scene on interviews he conducted with housekeeper Anni Winter, who said it was not Hess but party treasurer Franz Schwarz and party publisher Max Amann who arrived, found the door locked, and summoned a locksmith.

Ernst Hanfstaengl (The Missing Years: 1957) said he strongly suspected "it was made worth Anni Winter's while for the rest of her life to adhere to the official version."

Unfinished letter
One thing is certain, at some point, after Hitler left the apartment for Hamburg, Geli sat at her desk and began writing a letter.
That letter, her last known act, is the most revealing clue of all. According to the Munich Post, it was a letter to a girlfriend in Vienna.
The letter began, "When I come to Vienna, hopefully very soon, we'll drive together to Semmering an-"
It ended there, in the midst of her first sentence, in the midst of a word. That missing letter suggested an interruption that was sudden and unwelcome and compelling. She did not appear depressed or suicidal from the letter's tone. In fact, she sounded upbeat, optimistic and looking forward to her future.
Rosenbaum (Vanity Fair: 1992) said the big mistake made by the Nazi damage-control squad was "not destroying this note, because it is actually a very strong piece of evidence against the suicide theory".

Cover up
Hitler had reason to be frightened. The gunshot death of a twenty-three-year-old woman in an apartment they shared would have derailed his rise had the scandal not been suppressed.
In his wake, Hitler left his Nazi handlers, Rudolf Hess, Franz Schwarz, Max Amann and party Youth Leader, Baldur von Schirach, to handle damage control. They discussed what they should do before the police were brought in.
Ronald Hayman (Hitler & Geli: 1997) said: "We know that a top-level conference of Munich Nazis was held in his flat during the morning of Saturday September 19 though we do not know what time it began or who convened it. Eventually, von Schirach telephoned Adolf Dresler of the press department at the Brown House, instructing him to tell the press that Hitler had gone into deep mourning after his niece's suicide. But they went on arguing about whether this was the best line to take, and they decided it was not."
One of the first things this nervous group did was to say the suicide was caused by "Geli's stage fright" prior to an important singing performance. Then they immediately contradicted this story.
Ernst Hanfstaengl (The Missing Years: 1957) said: "Then the group at the flat must have got into a panic, because twenty-five minutes later, von Schirach was on the phone again asking if the communique had gone out and saying that the wording was wrong. They should announce that there had been a lamentable accident [rather than a suicide]. But by then it was too late. The word was out."
Eventually, a Detective Sauer arrived and interviewed witnesses who all insisted that Hitler had not been in the apartment at the time of Geli's death. However, the detective was able to confirm that the Walther 6.35 pistol that killed Geli belonged to him.

Hitler's alibi

According to Hitler's staff, he left Munich some time after lunch on Friday September 18, heading for Hamburg with his chauffeur Julius Schreck who was driving his Mercedes.

According to Heinrich Hoffmann (who claimed to have been with him) Hitler spent the night at the Deutscher Hof hotel in Nuremberg, ninety miles north of Munich.

Rosenbaum (Vanity Fair: 1992) said: "It was not until the next morning, the alibi goes, when he'd already departed for Hamburg that word reached him of Geli's death."

Rudolf Hess allegedly phoned the Deutscher Hof hotel from the death scene and had the hotel dispatch a motorcycle courier to overtake Hitler's car. At which point Hitler's chauffeur raced back to Munich so fast his Mercedes was stopped for speeding (going through the center of the small town of Ebenhausen) and his car was issued with a ticket - the only documentary support for the alibi which conveniently placed Hitler at a time and place remote from the death scene. But Julius Schreck was driving the car without Hitler in it. His whereabouts were unknown.

Disappearing the body

Bavarian Justice Minister, Franz Guertner [who had helped Hitler during his trial for treason in 1923] allowed Geli's body to be shipped off to Vienna after a cursory once-over by the police doctor and a hasty declaration of suicide. The body was only given a perfunctory postmortem and when a public prosecutor began his own inquiry, Guertner [later promoted to Minister of Justice for the Reich] had the prosecution quashed.

The police issued a hasty pronouncement of suicide and permitted the body to be slipped down the back stairs so it could be shipped off to Vienna for burial before the first reports of her death could appear in Monday morning's papers.

"With the body buried safely out of reach and with Minister Guertner in the [Nazi] party pocket, there were no more facts left to dig up." (The Mirror: 2006). British journalist, Murray Davies also noted that the first detective on the scene, Heinrich Mueller, later rose to a high rank in the Gestapo.

Pens dipped in poison

Ernst Hanfstaengl (The Missing Years: 1957) said Hitler "was in a state of hysteria" and left Munich the same day for the seclusion of a friend's lakeside retreat on the Tegernsee to escape press scrutiny. Apparently, he was distraught and raving over "the terrible smear campaign" against him.

He spoke wildly to his close companion Rudolf Hess about how it was all over, his political career, his very life. There was a moment, according to one story, when Hess had to leap up and grab a pistol out of Hitler's hand before he could put it to his head.

Hess later confirmed that Hitler became suicidal because of the rumors that he had shot Geli. "He was so fearfully vilified by this new campaign of lies that he wanted to make an end of everything. He could no longer look at a newspaper because this frightful filth was killing him. He wanted to give up politics and never again appear in public."

Despite the Nazi Party's threats of law suits, rumors started immediately that Hitler was involved in his niece's death and the story began to grow. Some newspapers also added dark hints about the nature of the physical relationship between Hitler and his niece.

HAPPIER TIMES: The troubled couple during a day at the seaside

By late afternoon, Saturday, September 19, the city's newspapers already knew Geli had been found shot in the apartment with Hitler's gun; that her nose bone was shattered and "the corpse evidenced other serious injuries". From a letter to a girlfriend, they knew Geli had intended to go to Vienna. They also knew that the men in the Brown House deliberated over what should be announced as the cause of the suicide and that they had agreed to give the reason for Geli's death as "unsatisfied artistic achievement".

Some newspapers gleefully discussed who should succeed Hitler as leader of the Nazi Party and Gregor Strasser's name was mentioned.

The Munich Post reported that Hitler had been involved in an argument about Geli's engagement to a man in Vienna.

"In a flat on Prinzregentenplatz, a 23-year-old music student, a niece of Hitler's, has shot herself. For two years, the girl had been living in a furnished room in a flat on the same floor on which Hitler's flat was situated. What drove the student to kill herself is still unknown. She was Angela Raubal, the daughter of Hitler's half-sister. On Friday 18 September there was once again a violent quarrel between Herr Hitler and his niece. What was the reason? The vivacious 23-year-old music student, Geli, wanted to go to Vienna, she wanted to become engaged.

Hitler was strongly opposed to this. The two of them had recurrent disagreements about it. After a violent scene, Hitler left his flat on the second floor of 16 Prinzregentenplatz."

The paper also reported that Geli's nose had been broken which cast doubt on whether it was really a suicide.

The Regensburger Echo [Regional Echo] said Geli Raubal died because what Hitler had done to her was "beyond her strength" to endure. The gossip sheet Die Fanfare, ran one article with the headline "Hitler's Lover Commits Suicide: Bachelors and Homosexuals as Leaders of the Party".

The article mentioned another woman, whose suicide attempt in 1928 [Maria Reiter but the year was 1927] followed a purported intimacy with Hitler. The paper said Hitler's private life with Geli, "took on forms which obviously the young woman was unable to bear."

According to Hitler's personal lawyer, Hans Frank, some newspapers went even further. "There was even one version that he had shot the girl himself; [the stories] not only appeared in scandal sheets, but daily in the leading papers with pens dipped in poison."

Hans Frank said Hitler "could not look at the papers any more for fear the terrible smear campaign would kill him."

Stopping the rumors

The Nazi Party moved quickly to stop the rumors circulating that he was involved in her death. Hitler's statement proclaiming his innocence was published in the Munich Post on September 21, 1931 and quoted by other newspapers in the days which followed.

"1) It is untrue that I had either "recurrent disagreements" or "a violent quarrel" with my niece Angela Raubal on Friday 18 September or previously.

(2) It is untrue that I was "strongly opposed" to my niece's traveling to Vienna. The truth is that I was never against the trip my niece had planned to Vienna.

(3) It is untrue that my niece wanted to become engaged in Vienna or that I had some objection to my niece's engagement. The truth is that my niece, tortured by anxiety about whether she really had the talent necessary for a public appearance, wanted to go to Vienna in order to have a new assessment of her voice by a qualified voice specialist.

(4) It is untrue that I left my flat on 18 September 1931 "after a violent scene". The truth is that there was no kind of scene and no agitation of any kind when I left my flat on that day."

Nazi spin doctors found a "Dr. Mueller" who issued a statement contradicting the forensic evidence already published against Hitler. Dr. Mueller's assessment was published alongside Hitler's statement of innocence:

"On the face and especially on the nose were to be found no wounds connected with bleeding of any kind. Nothing was to be found on the face except dark grayish death marks which had proceeded from the fact that Raubal expired with her face to the floor and remained in this position for about 17-18 hours." "That the tip of the nose was pressed slightly flat is due entirely to her lying with her face on the floor for several hours. The extreme discoloration of the death marks in the face is probably to be explained by the fact that death was primarily consequent on suffocation following the shot in the lung."

Police interview
Police did not interview Adolf Hitler until one week after his "statement of innocence" had been widely circulated. Here is a summary of Detective Sauer's interview with Hitler conducted on September 28, 1931:
"His niece was a student of medicine, then she didn't like that any more and she turned toward singing lessons. She should have been on the stage in a short time, but she didn't feel able enough, that's why she wanted further studies with a professor in Vienna. Hitler says that was okay with him but only under the condition that her mother from Berchtesgaden accompany her to Vienna. When she didn't want this, he said he told her, 'Then I'm against your Vienna plans.' She was angry about this, but she wasn't very nervous or excited and she very calmly said good-bye to him when he went off on Friday afternoon."
"She had previously belonged to a society that had seances where tables moved, and she had said to Hitler that she had learned that one day she would die an unnatural death. Hitler went on to add that she could have taken the pistol very easily because she knew where it was, where he kept his things. Her dying touches his emotions very deeply because she was the only one of his relatives who was close to him. And now this must happen to him."
In his book, Explaining Hitler: The Search for the Origins of his Evil (1998), Ron Rosenbaum suggested that the "strange seance story was a brilliant, if somewhat desperate, stroke on Hitler's part, a carefully calculated subtext of character assassination".
Was it suicide?
The suicide theory tends to be supported by historians who point to the number of women who attempted suicide after sexual liaisons with Hitler.
Henriette Hoffmann believed that Geli killed herself because she could not get away from her uncle's obsessive attention: "He [Hitler] fenced her life so tightly, confined her in such a narrow space that she saw no other way out. Finally, she hated her uncle; she really wanted to kill him. She couldn't do that. So she killed herself, to hurt him deeply enough, to disturb him. She knew that nothing else would wound him so badly. And because he knew too, he was so desperate, he had to blame himself." (spartacus-educational.com: 2015) Six years after Geli's death, Bridget Hitler Dowling, [the Irish woman who had married and was abandoned by Hitler's half-brother, Alois Jr.] visited Ernst Hanfstaengl who was then living in London.
She said she was convinced that it was suicide rather than murder. She claimed that "the immediate family knew very well that the cause of Geli's suicide was the fact that she was pregnant by a young Jewish art teacher in Linz, whom she had met in 1928 and wanted to marry at the time of her death."
But if Geli was pregnant, surely it would be a reason to keep on living.
John Toland (Definitive Biography: 1991) had another theory, he said that Geli had found a note from Eva Braun "in Uncle Alf's jacket pocket".

Toland's source was Anni Winter the housekeeper, who also believed it was suicide, and who claimed she saw Geli angrily tear up the note. When Winter pieced the scraps together, she maintained, it was a letter from Braun saying she was "counting the hours" until she could see Hitler again.

Others have suggested, that the "disgusting" sexual rituals she was forced to perform may have become so unbearable for her that she ended it the only way she knew how, with a bullet through her chest.

But none of the suicide theorists can explain why Geli was writing a letter to a friend in Vienna, looking forward to a holiday in Semmering.

Bushido

Anti-Nazi journalist, Konrad Heiden (Hitler's Rise to Power: 1944) had a theory - "as Geli was pregnant by a Jewish man, she was visited by Gestapo-chief, Heinrich Himmler who told her that she had betrayed the man who was her guardian, her lover and her Fuhrer, and according to National Socialist conceptions there was only one way of making good such a betrayal."

He cited the Nazi Party exaltation of the code of personal honor "Bushido" which was "proselytized by Hitler's Japanophile adviser, Karl Haushofer."

This code is why so many Nazis committed suicide rather than surrender at the end of WW2. In other words, according to Heiden, Geli's death was a forced suicide.

Former Nazi, Ernst Hanfstaengl (The Missing Years: 1957) described a similar final scene, only he placed Hitler, not Himmler, in the bedroom with Geli.

"It may well be that Hitler extracted from her the real purpose of her visit to Vienna to see her Jewish lover. "

"It is not too difficult to reconstruct the reaction of that tortured mind and body. His anti-Semitism would have caused him to accuse her of dishonoring them both and to tell her that the best thing she could do was to shoot herself. Perhaps he threatened to cut off all support from her mother. " "He had wallowed for so long in ideas about the Samurai and Bushido and the necessity, in given circumstances, of committing the ritual suicide of Hara-kiri that he may have overwhelmed the wretched girl."

Historian Ron Rosenbaum said that if he "didn't do it himself, he certainly drove her to it" and "she must at least be accorded the excuse of having been ignorant of the magnitude of the future horror breeding in the mind of Hitler".

Was it murder?

Did Hitler murder Geli because she was about to reveal his sexual perversions to the world or was it because she had fallen pregnant by a Jew? There is little or no chance that the baby was Hitler's.

"If it was indeed murder, then it could have happened at any time after the quarrel, leaving plenty of time for Hitler to manifest himself elsewhere. And since there was no police investigation to confirm whether the door had been locked from the inside and then broken open, we have only Anni Winter's word on the crucial assertion that Geli must have been alone when the gun was fired." "Three different people claimed to have broken down Geli's door." Some of them lied to cover up what had really happened but if Hitler was not involved then why tell lies about it? (The Mirror: 2006)

One of the men Geli confessed to about Hitler's monstrous sexual urges, Otto Strasser (Hitler and I: 1940) said his brother Gregor "knew Hitler shot Geli" and he was murdered during the Night of the Long Knives because he talked too much about it.

In his 1940 memoir, Strasser said: "The public prosecutor, who has lived abroad since Hitler's accession to power, wanted to charge Hitler with murder, but Guertner, the Bavarian Minister of Justice, [who was in the pocket of the Nazi Party] stopped the case."

The Strasser brothers were not the only people with suspicions.

Geli's mother, Angela, thought at first her daughter's death had been a tragic accident but as time went on she believed her death was probably carried out under compulsion.

She said of her daughter: "I can't understand why she did it. Perhaps it was an accident, and Geli killed herself while she was playing with the pistol which she got from him [Hitler]."

But she later implied that Gestapo chief, Heinrich Himmler might have had something to do with it.

Konrad Heiden (Hitler's Rise to Power: 1944)said Geli's mother "hinted at murder, or else suicide under compulsion or strong suggestion". However, she never accused her half-brother, Hitler.

On the contrary, she said, "she was sure that Adolf was determined to marry Geli."

Guilty as sin

Ronald Hayman claimed like Hanfstaengl, that none of the evidence was examined by police because what really happened was covered up. (Hitler & Geli: 1997)

"Questions should have been asked about the trajectory of the bullet, which entered above the heart and ended up above the level of the hip. The trajectory of the bullet seems inconsistent with the suicide theory."

Ron Rosenbaum (Vanity Fair: 1992) posed the question. "Should we really take Hitler's word on faith that he wasn't a murderer?"

"The young girl is in possession of the kind of knowledge the mere whisper of which could destroy Hitler. Worse, she's incapable of remaining discreet. She blurts out the truth to Strasser; she tells a talkative girlfriend that her uncle is a 'monster' and she may be talking to a Jewish lover in Vienna and God knows who else. And, according to Konrad Heiden, in their final quarrel, Geli may even have told Hitler she'd talked - confessed that in her despair she'd told outsiders about her relations with her uncle."

And thereby sealed her fate.

Rosenbaum said Geli's death may have been his first murder "perhaps the only one he committed with his own hands. Perhaps it might be argued that a single death is meaningless with so many millions to come. If what he learned from it was precisely that, with a 'Big Lie', he could get away with murder; if he could kill someone he 'loved', and escape the consequences, how much easier to go on to kill those he hated?"

"We know he quarreled with her that day and lied about it. We know he lied about her real reason for going to Vienna. We know he fled town to escape scrutiny and had her body spirited out of town. We know he exhibited hysterical grief and suicidal despair afterward. We know that as soon as he came to power he had at least four former supporters who talked too much about the death of Geli murdered. "

[Including Gregor Strasser, Father Stempfle, courageous journalist Fritz Gerlich and at least one of his sources, George Bell.]

"We know, in other words, that he acted guilty as sin."

The funeral

Geli Raubal was given a Catholic funeral and buried at the Zentralfriedhof Cemetery, Vienna on September 23, 1931. Her gravestone inscription described her as one of god's angels. Catholics who committed suicide were not normally allowed a religious service.

Fr. Pant had been the Raubal family confessor when Geli and her mother lived in Vienna, and remained a faithful family friend when mother and daughter moved to Munich.

According to Otto Strasser (Hitler and I: 1940), the priest confided to him in 1939 that he had helped ease the way for Geli's burial. He also told Strasser he "would never have permitted a suicide to be buried in consecrated ground."

He said he had information about who murdered Geli but he was forbidden to reveal anything because of the Catholic "seal of confession".

Hitler did not attend Geli's funeral but he would often tell Nazi colleagues and his secretaries that "she was the only woman he had ever really loved".

Hitler's development into a demon

Certainly Hitler went to great lengths to demonstrate his posthumous devotion.

One of Hitler's secretaries Christa Schroeder, said: "After the death of his niece, her bedroom [in the Munich apartment they shared] was kept like it was at the time of her death and Anni Winter, the housekeeper, was the only person allowed into the room."

Ron Rosenbaum (Vanity Fair: 1992) said: "Geli became for him a kind of personal cult,"

Dr. Robert G. L. Waite (Psychopathic God: 1977) said. "He locked the door to her room and would allow no one to enter except the housekeeper, who was instructed to place a bunch of fresh chrysanthemums there every day. He commissioned a bust and portraits [and] along with portraits of his mother, he kept a portrait or bust of Geli in every one of his bedrooms [Munich, Berlin and Berchtesgaden]."

And it became an unwritten law that none of Hitler's inner-circle could mention her name in conversation unless he did.

Rosenbaum claimed "On one occasion, he told Eva Braun his niece had killed herself out of love for him and told her 'We are all responsible for the death of my dear Geli.' He also said she had wrapped the pistol in a facecloth to muffle the explosion and then fired it into her mouth" which of course was a lie.

Ernst Hanfstaengl (The Missing Years: 1957) said: "The death of Geli Raubal marked a turning point in the development of Hitler's character . . . only too soon his nervous energy was to find its final expression in ruthlessness and savagery. With her death, the way was clear for his final development into a demon, with his sex life deteriorating into a sort of bisexual narcissus-like vanity with Eva Braun little more than a vague domestic adjunct."

According to Alan Bullock (A Study in Tyranny: 1962) another consequence of Geli's death was that Hitler became a vegetarian. He claimed that "meat now reminded him of her corpse".

Ron Rosenbaum (Vanity Fair: 1992) concluded his niece may have been the first person to really know and experience how monstrous Adolf Hitler really was. and "the first to subvert, or thwart his will with whatever weapon she had at hand, whether it meant defying him with a Jewish lover or firing his gun at herself, thus extinguishing his most cherished source of pleasure."

Fifteen years after her death, Luftwaffe chief, Hermann Goering said [during his trial at Nuremberg]: "Geli's death in 1931 had such a devastating effect on Hitler that it changed his relationships with all other people."

CHAPTER 17: RENATE MUELLER

RENATE MUELLER (1906-1937) was a German singer and actress. She performed in both silent films and "talkies" as well as on stage. In the early 1930s, she was considered to be as big a star as Marlene Dietrich, having already starred in a string of successful films, such as Love in the Ring (1930), Son of White Mountain (1930), The Office Girl (1931) and When Love Sets the Fashion (1932).

During her relationship with Hitler, she claimed he was a sadomasochist who enjoyed being kicked, beaten and whipped while he masturbated on the ground. Mueller's life spiraled out of control as a result of knowing the German dictator. In 1933, she collapsed in public due to the stress of his attention on her but the incident was hushed up and newspapers reported that the cause of her collapse was "too much dieting".

From 1934 onward, she reduced the amount of her film work, refusing to take the lead role in the film Enjoy Life.

Then, when she stopped playing his sexual games, Adolf Hitler ruined her career by getting her blacklisted among film producers and directors. He then ordered the Gestapo to follow her when he heard of her relationship with a Jewish man. With her career and personal life in ruins, Mueller became addicted to morphine and jumped to her death from a Berlin sanatorium window in 1937.

Renate Mueller was born on April 26, 1906 in Munich and grew up in the picturesque area of Emmering. Her father Karl Eugen Mueller, a historian and philologist, was the chief editor at the Munich Latest News. In 1914, the Mueller family moved to Gdansk, where she received singing lessons.

In 1924, the family moved again, this time to Berlin, where her father took a job at the Berliner Tageblatt [Berlin Daily News].

Renate left high school early to pursue a career as an actress and singer. She enrolled at the Reinhardt School of Drama where one of her teachers, G.W. Pabst helped launch her career.

After graduating in March 1925, she was employed at the Harz Mountain Theater in Thale, where Pabst worked as a director. She made her stage debut as Helena in A Midsummer Night's Dream.

Biggest fan
Mueller also acted on stage in Berlin and performed at the Lessing Theater as part of the so-called "young generation". She then became a star of German silent films. Her fourth film, Love in the Ring (1930), in which she played a character called Max Schmeling, received rave reviews.

As she was vocally trained, she also thrived in Germany's fledgling recording business. Her song from the film The Private Secretary (1931) "I am so happy today" [in German] was also recorded in English as "Sunshine Susie" and became a hit.

In eight of her 26 films, she played under the direction of Jewish supremo, Reinhold Schuenzel, in whose ironic comedies she expressed the funny side of her screen character.

In Viktor und Viktoria (1933) she played a young soprano, who worked as a female impersonator - to the outside world a man, but in reality, she was a woman - a character who inevitably got into all sorts of trouble.

After seeing several of Renate Mueller's films, Adolf Hitler announced to the German media that he was one of her "biggest fans".

ALL WOMAN: Renate Mueller in one of her most famous roles, Viktor und Viktoria (1933) in which she played both male and female characters

First meeting

Renate Mueller first met Hitler when she was making a film on location near the Danish coast in autumn 1932. Hitler had arrived without ceremony and watched the all-day film-shoot hardly saying a word to anyone.

Later that evening, he visited the house where Mueller was staying but according to Ronald Hayman (Hitler and Geli: 1997) "his behavior, when they were together, was distinctly odd. At forty-three, he still seemed ill at ease when alone with a glamorous woman".

She was not impressed by her first meeting with the Nazi leader and told film director, Adolf Zeissler: "He sat there, not moving at all, looking at me all the time, and then he'd take my hand in his and look some more. He talked all the time, just nonsense."

By contrast, Hitler was so impressed by the actress that he demanded to see her again and again. He began to shower her with expensive jewelry including a diamond bracelet which was "far more valuable than any of his presents to either Geli Raubal or Eva Braun". (Ibid.)

HOT PROPERTY: Mueller was as popular as Marlene Dietrich in the early 1930s

Ronald Hayman described Hitler's awkward behavior in Mueller's company. "When she was invited to a party at the Chancellery, he ignored her until everyone was leaving, but then took her arm, offering to show her around the building. He pointed out the changes he had made to the [private living] room and took her to his wardrobe, where he brought out his tail-coated dinner shirt, saying he had never worn evening dress until he came to power."

After this, he arranged frequent meetings with her but soon the demands he made of her were as unpalatable as they had been for his niece, Geli Raubal.

The Nizkor Project (1943) authors said that with Renate Mueller, Hitler did not risk revealing his true nature but contented himself with other less degrading "masochistic gratifications".

She confided what had happened on her first intimate night with Hitler to her friend and film director, Adolf Zeissler. He had asked the actress "what was troubling her" after she had spent an evening with Hitler at the Chancellery. Zeissler said: "The evening before she had been with Hitler and was sure that he was going to have intercourse with her."

"She said that they had both undressed and were apparently getting ready for bed when Hitler fell on the floor and begged her to kick him. She demurred but he pleaded with her and condemned himself as unworthy and just 'groveled around in the most agonizing manner'."

The scene became intolerable to Mueller and she finally acceded to his wishes and kicked him. "This excited him greatly and he begged for more and more, always saying that it was even better than he deserved and that he was not worthy to be in the same room with her. As she continued to kick him, he became more and more excited." (Ibid.)

Torture techniques

Ronald Hayman gave slightly more explicit details of another sexual encounter between Hitler and Mueller in his book (Hitler and Geli: 1997): "One night, for instance, at the Chancellery, he [Hitler] began by going into details about Gestapo methods of torture, comparing them with medieval techniques. After they had both taken their clothes off, he lay on the floor, begging her to hit him and kick him. She refused, but he went on heaping accusations on his own head, saying he was her slave, unworthy to be in the same room."

"Eventually giving in, she started to kick him, abuse him with obscene words and hit him with his whip. Becoming increasingly excited, Hitler started to masturbate. After his orgasm, he suggested quietly that they should both put their clothes on. They drank a glass of wine together and chatted about trivialities. Finally he stood up, kissed her hand, thanked her for a pleasant evening and rang for a servant to show her out."

The strange affair between them continued even though Mueller told her close friends and associates that she was repulsed by what was going on.

According to one of Hitler's maids at Berchtesgaden, Pauline Kohler (The Girls Who Knew His Love: 1940) propaganda minister, Joseph Goebbels arranged for Mueller's first holiday weekend with the Fuhrer at his country home in the Bavarian mountains [Berchtesgaden].

She arrived on a Friday in time for dinner, after which Hitler suggested a tour of the house and grounds.

"Hitler suddenly looked for a few moments at her, then stretched out his arm in the Nazi salute. 'I can hold my arm like that for two solid hours,' he declared. 'I never feel tired when my Storm Troopers and soldiers march past me and I stand at the salute. I never move. My arm is as if of granite! But Goering can't stand it. He has to drop his hand after half an hour of the salute. That means I am four times as strong as Goering. He's flabby. I am hard. I marvel at my own power', Hitler said. And with that he turned and walked out of the room." According to Kohler, Renate Mueller was stunned.

On the last night of Mueller's stay, he invited her to see herself on screen in his private cinema. He had ordered her latest film to be shown and half way through it he "indulged in an orgy of petting".

It seems Mueller sat passively and must have endured rather than enjoyed what was going on.

Kohler said the following morning, the actress was flown back to Berlin in Hitler's private plane.

"For several weeks, he sent her flowers every day. There were other more costly presents, diamonds and furs. Articles appeared throughout the Nazi press praising her as Germany's greatest actress."

PUBLICITY STILL: Mueller in a still from The Office Girl; Hitler became besotted by her after seeing the film

Cinemas were ordered to show revivals of her earlier films.

Again according to Kohler, as Mueller acted in the theater as well as film studios, she was obliged to base herself in Berlin for work. She visited Hitler at the Chancellery and he visited her at her Berlin apartment.

Kohler said Mueller never loved Hitler; "at first she liked him and the celebrity he could offer dazzled her but of course that was not enough".

For the next few years, the actress was expected to be available "to facilitate Hitler" whenever he required her company for sadomasochistic sessions. She needed his permission beforehand if she wanted to travel outside Germany.

Also, the Gestapo began to monitor her relationships with other men and reported the details, including photographs, back to their Fuhrer.

Under the pressure of Hitler's attention on her, Mueller tried to rebel against him. Unlike the teenage women Hitler liked to manipulate and dominate, Mueller was already in her late 20s; was financially independent, did not believe in Fascism and could not be easily bullied.

Several sources claim she refused to renounce her Jewish friends and she repeatedly refused to act in films promoting Nazi Party propaganda.

Eventually, she asked for and was granted permission to visit London, but while she was there, the Gestapo continued their surveillance of her. (spartacus-

Jewish lover

In London, the actress spent time with a former lover, Frank Deutsch, who was Jewish, and when she returned to Germany, she discovered she had been completely blacklisted, on Hitler's orders, in Germany's film and theater world. Directors were ordered not to employ her and theater owners were warned not to show any of her films.

Then, Mueller was horrified by rumors that she would be put on trial for "race defamation" for having sexual relations with a Jew.

As with his niece, Geli Raubal, having to share his woman with a Jewish man was the ultimate humiliation for Hitler; he had spent a fortune on the actress, yet she had decided to follow her own heart.

Despite the threat of a race defamation trial, Mueller continued her liaisons with Jewish men and started a new relationship with a man referred to only as "Herr R-".

Apparently, he was the only son of a millionaire whose family had lived in Germany for years.

Pauline Kohler (The Girls Who Knew His Love: 1940) said: "It was in the Tiergarten in Berlin that he met Renate Mueller, riding a horse that had been given to her by Hitler. It was not long before she and this young man were madly in love. There were secret, long motor drives, dinners in country beer gardens. But always the shadow of persecution hung over them. Renate finally persuaded her lover to leave Germany. He crossed into Czechoslovakia, at that time still free and independent, and went to Paris."

Kohler said Mueller confided in her during one of her visits to Berchtesgaden: "The two lovers, Renate and Herr R- spent a glorious month in Paris. Hitler was forgotten. They were seen in public together and did not try to hide it. So it was no wonder that the Gestapo heard of them. Its agents shadowed them with cameras. Leader Heinrich Himmler made a special trip to Berchtesgaden with the [recorded] material."

Apparently, Hitler went "white with fury" when he read the dossier and viewed the photographs. He ordered that the actress be brought to him the moment she crossed the border into Germany on her return trip.

Kohler [who was a Berchtesgaden maid at the time] and two SS men were dispatched to collect Mueller at Aachen station.

Kohler said: "I was given a strict warning not to discuss the Fuhrer with her and to forget everything she might say to me."

When Mueller arrived at Berchtesgaden, she was obliged to wait several hours, until almost midnight, before being summoned into Hitler's presence.

He knocked over a chair in anger when he started to speak.

Kohler described what happened next; Hitler yelled: "Slut! That's how you spend your time! You're wasted on the screen! You should be on the streets of Berlin, that's your real place! Picking up men from the gutter!"

He screamed the words at her.

"Yes, I know all about your Paris trip. But I'm not to be insulted like that. I am the

Fuhrer!" He threw the Gestapo documents and photographs at her head. Then, suddenly, he burst into tears. He cried like a hysterical child.

This behavior certainly fits with what has already been revealed about Hitler. When he felt slighted, humiliated or he wanted to manipulate a situation, he used hysterics to make his point.

DRUG PROBLEM: She became addicted to morphine under the pressure of Hitler's attention; the Gestapo followed her when she holidayed outside Germany

Mueller told Kohler afterward that she had promised Hitler she would never see Herr R- again but she had no intention of keeping her word.

Kohler then predicted correctly that the Fuhrer would never let the matter rest. "Mueller left Germany again, this time for Monte Carlo. And Herr R- was there with her. The Gestapo was still active. Renate reached Berlin before they could put the new material they had gathered into [Heinrich] Himmler's hands".

But according to a Channel 4 (UK) television documentary, when she returned from Monte Carlo, Hitler's virtual torture of the actress continued.

Mueller and Hitler had one final three hour meeting alone in a Berlin hotel bedroom [in late 1935).

During this meeting, armed guards were positioned in the hotel lobby and also outside the bedroom door "so they would not be disturbed".

It was the last time they would ever meet.

Morphine

Historian Cate Haste (Nazi Women: 2001) said what happened next was really tragic. "With her career in ruins, she became addicted to morphine and was sent to a sanatorium. Having asked for, and been refused, permission to see Hitler in 1936, she remained in the sanatorium." She told her friends that the situation was hopeless and that she could never have a normal life again.

A few weeks before her death, Mueller contacted several German newspapers and radio stations to say that the Fuhrer liked "to be beaten and kicked while on his bended knees".

She told journalists that her refusal to continue their sadomasochistic relationship had meant the end of her acting career.

Without a doubt, Hitler must have known of her attempts to undermine him - as he had eyes and ears everywhere - and her sensational story was never broadcast or published.

Death

On October 7, 1937, Mueller was looking out the Berlin sanatorium [balcony] window when a car pulled up outside and four SS officers got out.

Most historians agree that in a state of panic and fear, believing the SS men had come to arrest her, she jumped off the balcony to her death. She was 30 years old. (spartacus-educational.com: 2015)

Ronald Hayman said: "Had she survived, she could possibly have been dangerous to Hitler in the same way Geli Raubal could, either of them could have damaged him by revealing the truth about his sexual habits."

When her death was reported in German newspapers, there was no mention of her association with Hitler.

The Nazi Party newspaper, Volkischer Beobachter [National Observer] said "it had been known for some time that Renate Mueller was no longer in the best of health" which was a sly way of saying she was a drug addict.

Another newspaper claimed she had died "from an epileptic fit".

Yet another claimed she had become addicted to diet pills.

According to Pauline Kohler when "the news of her death was flashed to Hitler in Berchtesgaden, he behaved like a madman, screaming hideous threats against the Jews".

He did not attend her funeral and when he was asked by journalists about his relationship with the actress, he claimed he had never even met her.

Nazi propaganda minister, Joseph Goebbels apparently sent a wreath to the ceremony but did not attend.

Renate Mueller's life story was filmed in 1960 and given the romantic title, Favorite of the Gods, with Ruth Leuwerik playing the title role.

In the film, the cause of her death was left unclear and her strange relationship with Adolf Hitler was "normalized" for the viewing public.

CHAPTER 18: UNITY MITFORD

UNITY MITFORD (b.1914-d.1948) was an English aristocrat and Hitler devotee who became besotted by the glamour of Fascism: the uniforms, the insignia and the Nazi rallies. She left her comfortable home in England to stalk the German dictator until she met him. Witnesses said Hitler behaved like an adolescent in her company but was only interested in using her for propaganda purposes.

In the 1930s, the Mitford family knew many of the people who mattered in Britain including Winston Churchill, Anthony Eden, Lord Chamberlain and Lord Rothermere. Hitler may well have used the young English woman for propaganda purposes but he also enjoyed listening to her stories about the orgies she had with his Storm Troopers and SS men.

Unfortunately she, like so many others, fell in love with the image of the "manly Fuhrer", the fake personality he presented to the German people. When she discovered she had deluded herself and that he had nothing to offer her, Unity Mitford committed suicide by shooting herself in the head with the gun Hitler had given her. It took nine years for her to die from the infected head wound.

Unity "Valkyrie" Mitford was named after Richard Wagner's Die Valkyrie, when her father Bertie struck up a friendship with the right-wing composer. She and her sisters had been presented at Britain's royal court and Unity attended some of the best British schools, including briefly, Queen's Gate School in London from where she was expelled for drawing pictures of people having sex - including graphic images of Adam and Eve in mid-orgasm.

Elizabeth Powell who became a close friend in 1932 said "Unity used to stay in our house in Hyde Park Gate; she was always rushing off to the East End to meet boys. It wasn't allowed by her parents, they tried to stop her, that's why she came to us."

In his book, Hitler's Valkyrie: the uncensored biography of Unity Mitford (2014), David Litchfield claimed she had a fascination with all things sexual from an early age.

"Growing up at Swinbrook House, near the Oxfordshire village of Burford, one of her favorite artists was Hieronymus Bosch, famous for paintings of Purgatory featuring explicitly sexual and violent images."

Soon, she was producing similarly shocking artwork of her own.

According to Litchfield's mother, Kathleen, Unity showed her a notebook, on the front of which, were two copulating figures.

On another occasion, the teenager raised her skirt in the local post office "to demonstrate her preference for not wearing knickers".

The author also claimed that Unity lost her virginity to British Fascist leader, Oswald Mosley on a billiard table when she was only18. This apparently happened at her debutante's ball, even though Mosley had already started an affair with her older married sister, Diana.

When she was 19, Unity Mitford seized the opportunity to travel to Germany to attend the now infamous Nuremberg rally in 1933. In no doubt as to where her destiny lay, she persuaded her parents to let her attend a finishing school in

Munich, not to be "finished" but to learn German in preparation for the meeting with Hitler which she was determined would happen.

In June 1933, she had joined the British Union of Fascists (BUF), founded by Mosley the previous year. He described her as "full of enthusiasm and stage-struck by the glamour of national socialism and the mass admiration of Hitler".

MAD ABOUT SEX: Unity Mitford wearing her debutante's gown

First trip to Germany

She saw Hitler in action for the first time when she traveled as part of a British Fascist delegation to watch the Nazis "Rally of Victory" over the Weimar Republic in Nuremberg in August 1933. The Nazi rally, which can be seen on old newsreels, was a striking demonstration of Hitler's power in Germany with thousands of Storm troopers and legions of his adoring followers displaying their unquestioning loyalty to their Fuhrer.

Though she never got to meet Hitler, Unity Mitford was immediately bewitched by him.

On her return to England, she told the London Evening Standard: "The first moment I saw him, I knew there was no one I would rather meet."

In spring 1934, she left England to live in Munich so she "could be near him".

In her book, Hons and Rebels, (1960) her sister Jessica remembered: "It was the year of Hitler's accession to power. Unity announced her intention was to go to

Germany, learn German, and meet the Fuhrer. My parents put up much less opposition than might have been expected. Perhaps the thought of another London season of sham tiaras and tame rats let loose in ballrooms was a bit more than my mother could contemplate with any pleasure."

BROWNSHIRT: Mitford became besotted by the pomp and ceremony of Germany's Nazi regime and joined the British Union of Fascists with her older sister, Diana

Stalker

Once she had set herself up in Munich, Unity Mitford began to stalk Hitler. She told her friends, she would not stop until she had met him. Once she found out where he was dining or where he was staying in Munich, she would arrive and flaunt herself in front of him.

In 1934, she became friends with former Nazi, Ernst Hanfstaengl (The Missing Years: 1957).

Hanfstaengl admitted that Unity and her sister Diana were outstanding Nordic beauties: "They were very attractive but they were made up to the eyebrows in a manner which conflicted directly with the newly proclaimed Nazi ideal of German womanhood."

As a result, he suggested they remove some of the make up and lipstick: "My dears, it is no good, but to stand any hope of meeting him [Hitler] you will have to wipe

some of that stuff off your faces." (spartacus-educational.com: 2015)
Another Munich friend, Rosemary Macindoe described the first time they saw
Hitler up close.

NAZI FAITHFUL: Unity Mitford at a Nazi rally with Ernst Hanfstaengl

"In October 1934, Unity had not yet met Hitler in person. Every Friday, he lunched
at the Osteria Bavaria, and she used to go there in blind adoration. One day, he
came in with a raincoat, an Alsatian, and a whip in his hand, and Unity said, 'Don't
you think his eyes are marvelous?'."
Jessica Mitford (Hons and Rebels: 1960) described her sister's devotion:
"Within six months, she came home for a brief visit, having accomplished both her
objectives. She already spoke fairly fluent German, and had met not only Hitler, but
Himmler, Goering, Goebbels, and others of the Nazi leaders. Unity explained that it
had been fairly simple; she had reserved a nightly table in the Osteria Bavaria
restaurant, where they often went. Evening after evening, she sat and stared at
them, until finally a flunky was sent over to find out who she was. On learning that
she was an admirer of the Nazis, and a member of the British Union of Fascists,
Hitler invited her to join them at their table. Thereafter, she became one of their
circle, saw them constantly in Munich, and accompanied them to meetings and
rallies. The Nazi salute, 'Heil Hitler!' with hand upraised, became her standard
greeting to everyone. Her collection of Nazi trophies and paraphernalia now
overflowed our little sitting-room including an autographed copy of Mein Kampf."
Unity also became friendly with Hitler confidant and anti-Semite, Julius Streicher
and used him to try to get closer to the German leader.
According to Mitford's biographer, Richard Davenport-Hines (Unity Mitford:
2004): "The fixity of her admiration for Nazi-dom was unreasonable: her conduct
and conversation became exaggerated. When home for a visit in England, she
saluted the post mistress of Swinbrook, Oxfordshire, with raised hand, chanted

Blackshirt rhymes about Jews, and agreed with Julius Streicher that Jews should be made to eat grass."

Perfect specimen of womanhood

Unity told her friends that her first conversation alone with Hitler on February 9, 1935 "was the most wonderful and beautiful day" of her life. In turn, Hitler told Germany's media that she was "a perfect specimen of Aryan womanhood".

Albert Speer told writer, David Pryce-Jones (Unity Mitford: 1976) that he first met her at the Osteria Bavaria in mid-1935. He claimed the dictator, who was 46 years old, behaved like a "teenager" when he was with the English woman.

"She was very romantic. She was highly in love with Hitler, we could see it easily; her face brightened up, her eyes gleaming, staring at Hitler. Hero-worship. Absolutely phenomenal. Hitler liked to be admired by a young woman."

"She was quite attractive; he was excited by the possibility of a love affair with her. Towards an attractive woman, he behaved as a seventeen-year-old would."

Speer said: "He wanted light relief. Her German was good enough to make herself understood. She was never bored and never boring."

"Her features were those of a woman with some intelligence, thinking in her own way, not the type of Eva Braun who had no serious interests. Unity was very sentimental. I'm not surprised she could say only how wonderful he was. That was his fascination which nobody can explain."

Unity introduced her sister Diana, four years her senior, to Hitler in March 1935. At the time, Diana was the mistress of Oswald Mosley, leader of the British Union of Fascists.

In April 1935, having only met Unity three times, Hitler invited her to a lunch party in honor of Mosley who was visiting Germany hoping to gain financial support for the BUF.

This was the first time the two men had met and as Mosley did not speak German, Mitford was asked to act as a translator.

Shortly afterward, Diana Mitford left her husband, Bryan Walter Guinness, [heir to the Guinness Brewery and Baron of Moyne], so she could continue her affair with Mosley which caused a scandal in England. [They set up home together and then married in the Berlin home of Joseph Goebbels in 1936. Adolf Hitler was guest of honor at their wedding.]

But despite Unity Mitford's connections, she was never invited to Hitler's summer residence, the Berghof, as Eva Braun would have been jealous.

Albert Speer (Inside The Third Reich: 1970) said: "In the Berghof there was the snag of Eva Braun, who would have been angry, in a bad mood."

The two women were rivals for Hitler's affections even though the German leader was incapable of giving either woman what they wanted – sex.

Speer also said when Mitford gate-crashed Munich's inner circle in 1935, the people who joined Hitler at the Osteria Bavaria included two doctors, Morell and Brandt.

They were there for one purpose only, to give Hitler a constant supply of injections for his growing list of ailments [he was too squeamish to inject himself]. By the mid 1930s, he had also developed a tremor in his left arm and leg which was later diagnosed as Parkinson's disease.

So in effect, Mitford and Braun were competing for the sexual attention of a burgeoning drug addict and virtual cripple. Even so, the rivalry between the two women continued until the outbreak of WW2.

DRESSED TO KILL: The dark clothing and leather paraphernalia took on a hidden sexual meaning for Mitford

Yearning for sex

According to Mitford's diary, she met Hitler once a fortnight for more than four years, about 140 times in total, mainly at the Carlton tearooms and the Osteria Bavaria [in Munich] and at least once during a Wagner festival in Bayreuth.

Hitler confidante, Princess Carmencita Wrede interviewed by David Pryce-Jones (Unity Mitford: 1976) said:

"Hitler calculated exactly the correct distance between him and Unity. She was too fine, really too aristocratic for him."

"Eva Braun was at his social level. Unity could not bear it. She was always badgering me, 'How is this Eva Braun? What does she have that I don't? How does she do it?'"

"She said to me, 'He never asks me to the Obersalzberg because Eva is always there.' There was a proper rivalry between them. Unity was thoroughly jealous."

But Eva Braun was also extremely jealous of Mitford. When Hitler announced the "Anschluss" in March 1938, the young English woman appeared with him on the balcony in Vienna and photographs of the couple appeared in all of Germany's major newspapers, much to Braun's annoyance. She was obliged to stay in the background and any photographs of her were destroyed. (spartacus-educational.com: 2015)

HIGH CLASS BEAUTY: Diana Mitford had an affair with Oswald Mosley, leader of the British Fascists while married to a wealthy business heir

According to Nazi architect, Albert Speer, Mitford "would have slept with him, of course, she was more than willing but he would not have gone to bed with her. I doubt if he ever did more than take her hand in his."

Henriette Hoffmann, who socialized occasionally with Mitford, believed Hitler was only using her for his own ends:

"He was aware of the value, for propaganda purposes, of Unity and her blind devotion to him."

Another Hitler confidant, Princess Stephanie von Hohenlohe, also believed Mitford was being used by Hitler for the specific purpose of communicating with the British establishment.

In her unpublished memoirs, the princess said:

"In 1938 during the September crisis [over the Sudetenland] Hitler sent for her. When she arrived, he told her that in view of the gravity of the situation, he wanted her to leave Germany. Though it would seem that such a gesture was prompted only by friendly concern towards one of his most ardent admirers, his intention was of a different nature."

"His real purpose in sending for Unity Mitford was to make her return to England and impress her people with the gravity of the situation. This is an example of his cunning and supreme ability to make use of even the slightest incident."

Hitler scholar, Nerin E. Gun (Hitler's Mistress: 1969) had an alternative explanation for why the Fuhrer needed the English woman in his life - quite simply, she told him exactly what he wanted to hear and proved to him that "he was always right".

She was a British aristocrat whose family "knew all the right people" and she told Hitler that the British people had a positive view of Nazi Germany and his leadership. In short, she assured him that Britain would join the Fuhrer if and when a war began.

"Unity Mitford had been acquainted with Winston Churchill, Eden, Chamberlain, Lord Rothermere, and had been presented at court. She told him exactly what he wanted to hear: that the [British] government did not represent the country, that there was a strong nationalist movement, that the young people admired the Fuhrer, that only the Jews wanted war, that they had bought the votes of the politicians, including Churchill, whom she called the grave digger of the Empire, that England and Germany, if they acted together, could rule the world."

Orgies

One of Unity Mitford's Munich flatmates, interviewed by David Pryce-Jones (Unity Mitford: 1976), said the English woman was "a bit mad".

"Unity slept next door to me, and I could hear her talking in her sleep. She'd suddenly scream out, and I complained about it, as well as about the portraits of Hitler all over her room, which she'd salute. She used to bring SA or SS men back and ask them to spend the night, I remember thinking she was a bit mad."

David Litchfield (Hitler's Valkyrie: 2014), said that Unity Mitford held orgies in her Munich apartment so she could get sexually and spiritually closer to Hitler. "Late one night in pre-war Munich, a young English woman, dressed all in black and accompanied by six SS officers in full uniform, climbed the dark stairs to her apartment. Once inside, she lit two large church candles either side of her bed, their glow revealing enormous swastika banners at its head and silver framed portraits of Adolf Hitler on side tables."

"After sliding off her boots and gauntlet-style gloves, she stepped out of her long black skirt and blindfolded herself with a Nazi armband before lying down, spread-eagled, on the bed. One man bound her hands and feet to its four corners while another, in what was obviously a familiar ritual, wound up the gramophone and dropped the needle on to a record of Horst-Wessel-Lied, the Nazi anthem." (Nazi orgies: 2013)

"This was the cue for the other officers to remove their boots, belts and uniforms. Then, as the pounding marching song broke the silence, they took it in turns to enjoy the entirely willing object of their desire. So passed another typical evening for Unity Mitford."

Litchfield said: "Later, with considerable pride and no hint of shame, she admitted that sex with the SA and SS officers was her 'Eucharist'."

"Her bed, draped with swastika flags and surmounted by iconic images of the Fuhrer, was the altar devoted to her messiah, on which she gave her body to those closest to him, his personal warriors. She explained that remaining blindfolded

minimized her personal involvement." (Hitler's Valkyrie: 2013)
And it was these soldiers who told her where Hitler would be so that she could continue to follow his every move. Once she knew his schedule, she would arrive in advance so she could get the best view of him, and when possible, the closest proximity to him.

VOYEUR: Diana Mitford (right) took occasional lovers; she became an audience for her younger sister, Unity's sexual antics

As for her sister Diana's reaction, the author has suggested that she found her role of being a voyeur to her younger sister's sex life exciting.
"By mutual consent, they would often repeat the process. From time to time, Diana also took SS lovers, but only one at a time." (Ibid.)

Hitler's arousal
According to Litchfield, the voyeuristic side of Mitford and Hitler's relationship began one night in early 1935 when the English woman was delighted to see champagne in an ice bucket and lighted candles in his Munich apartment. Convinced her beloved Fuhrer was about to seduce her, she was surprised when he asked her for details of her erotic encounters with his Storm Troopers. (Nazi orgies: 2013).
"Naively, she was shocked he knew of them, but his intimate questions suggested that, far from being angry, he was fascinated and even aroused. Particularly so, when she confessed she only thought of him during these acts, and they were a symbol of her submission to his control. On his orders, the sessions with the 'Storms' continued, as did Unity's erotic re-tellings of them in private audiences with Hitler."
These Nazi-themed orgies "were devised by Unity and carried out with Hitler's connivance on condition that she titillate him with the details afterwards.
All this was part of her sadomasochistic worship of the Fuhrer which eventually

led him to demand she "make the ultimate sacrifice and offer up her own life". (Ibid.)

Black magic

Litchfield said (Hitler's Valkyrie: 2014): "From these sadomasochistic scenarios in which she offered herself bound and helpless to his henchmen surrounded by a shrine to him, Hitler and Mitford developed a deadly fantasy inspired by her middle name, Valkyrie."

DOING THE DEVIL'S DANCE: Unity Mitford has dinner with Julius Streicher (left) after a Nazi rally in 1938

Derived from a Norse legend, the word "Valkyrie" describes the immortal female figures who decide who shall be slain in battle; the dead are then brought to the kingdom of the dead, ruled over by the god Odin. [In one of Hitler's earliest attempts to write a play in Vienna, when he shared a flat with August Kubizek, the script contained flying Valkyries.]

Litchfield claimed that with Unity Mitford, Hitler cast himself in the role of Odin, and would come to see her as his own personal Valkyrie, persuading her they could only be together [sexually] when they were both in the after-life.

This idea was encouraged by bisexual, Hungarian aristocrat Count Janos Almasy, [the former lover of Unity's brother Tom]. He soon became Unity's partner in what she described as "savage fornication".

This fornication took place in his castle on the Austro-Hungarian border. The Count was fascinated by the occult practice of black magic or necromancy, the power of being able to control life and death.

His particular thrill was to deprive his lovers of oxygen at the point of orgasm by means of a silk noose. (Nazi orgies: 2013)

Apparently, it was Mitford's enthusiasm for "gaspers" as she called them which endeared her to Count Almasy, but he appears to have had little regard for her

survival, and encouraged her to take her own life as Hitler had suggested.
For Mitford, it was to be the supreme sacrifice and the ultimate experience.
On the other side
Litchfield described a typical evening shared by Hitler and his "Valkyrie", Mitford: "After he had given one of his hysterical performances at yet another party rally, Hitler returned home exhausted. With insufficient energy even to talk, they would listen to music together, particularly recordings of Wagner's Ride of the Valkyries." (Nazi orgies: 2013)
Then Mitford would relate the latest story of her "savage fornication" with Count Almasy. Hitler always loved to gossip about the sex lives of royalty or anyone with a title.

FESTIVAL OF ALWAYS RIGHT: Hitler and his devotee at a music festival in Bayreuth in 1936

The author speculated that while Hitler yearned for the frisson of causing her to take her own life, he was undecided when this should happen, as he was still enjoying her mortal company.
"The moment appears to have come over a lunch in Munich on August 5, 1939, less than a month before his forces invaded Poland." Unity told one of her friends, Kathleen Atkins, that while the rest of the company were talking among themselves [in the Osteria Bavaria in Munich], Hitler turned to her and announced quietly that if war broke out, it would be impossible for him to spend time with her and that she must now wait for him "on the other side".
Her biographer, David Pryce-Jones (Unity Mitford: 1976) said simply that when Hitler lost interest in her, Mitford became depressed and fatalistic and told friends matter-of-factly that if war broke out between Britain and Germany, she would kill herself.
"By August 29, 1939, Unity was alone with her wireless. It became her focus. To listen in to the news became a matter of life and death. She went out for meals; she

came back for the news. Unity lunched at the Osteria Bavaria, one more time, like a shade unable to tear loose from haunts of the past. The German army was thrusting into Poland. The black-out was compulsory. As she walked home, the darkness over Munich was complete. Back in the Agnestrasse, she listened in to the English news."

"The British ultimatum to Hitler, to withdraw the German army from Poland, was not delivered until nine o'clock on the morning of Sunday, September 3, and it expired, unanswered, two hours later. The war had started." (Ibid.)

Bullet in the brain

When Britain declared war on Germany on September 3, 1939, Unity Mitford went to the English Garden in Munich, took a pearl-handled pistol given to her by Hitler from her handbag and shot herself in the head. She survived the suicide attempt and was hospitalized in Munich.

She was unconscious for almost two months. German surgeons saved her life but were unable to extract the bullet from her brain.

On Hitler's instructions, she was moved to Switzerland, and then returned to England on January 3, 1940. Her mental and physical powers were impaired and gradually her weight ballooned to almost 14 stone.

GLAMOUR PUSS: Mitford's life went downhill once she met Hitler

One friend who visited her said: "Her mind is that of a sophisticated child." (spartacus-educational.com: 2015)

Albert Speer told author David Pryce-Jones: "It was a shock to Hitler when she shot herself. He felt responsible for her committing suicide. About a year or so later, she had been forgotten. People who were no longer in his view were quickly forgotten."

Unity Mitford never recovered from her brain injuries. She died from meningitis in West Highland Cottage Hospital, Scotland in 1948.

CHAPTER 19: INGE LEY

SHE HAS BEEN described as both "a ravishing blonde" and a "gentle soul". Inge Spilcker Ley came from a musical family and enjoyed a successful career as an opera singer in Munich in her late teens.

Hitler first met her when he became German Chancellor in 1933. He was immediately smitten by the 17-year-old and said "no man could ever be bored in her company".

Before her marriage to Robert Ley, Hitler painted a nude portrait of her and displayed it in one of his private living rooms but he encouraged her relationship and marriage to the middle-aged drunkard Ley, who was head of the German Labor Front (DAF).

When their marriage got into difficulty, Inge spent many hours pouring her heart out to Hitler. Some reports suggest that she first attempted suicide [by throwing herself out a Berlin window] when Hitler rejected her sexual advances. Eventually, aged only 26, Inge Ley committed suicide by shooting herself in the head on December 29, 1942.

Inge Spilcker Ley (1916-1942) was an extraordinary beauty who impressed everyone around her with her soul-stirring voice and her gentle restrained nature (Metapedia.de: 2015). She was born on March 8, 1916 as Inge Ursula Spilcker in Wroclaw, western Poland, the daughter of opera singers Max Spilcker and his wife Lory.

In this artistic family she received singing lessons at an early age along with her younger sister Gitly. Inge had a beautiful mezzo-soprano voice and when she was just 17 years old, she was awarded the "Theater of the People" prize for her performance at the old Friedrichstadtpalast [Fredrick's City Palace] in Munich.

When Inge met Hitler

During his rise to power, Hitler became a regular visitor at the Munich home of Winifred Wagner, the English-born daughter of the famous composer, Richard Wagner. It was Winifred's daughter, Friedelinde Wagner, who had described Hitler at the family home in the 1920s as wearing "Bavarian suspenders" and having "rotten brown teeth" and "dirty fingernails".

By the time he had become Chancellor in 1933, Hitler was considered to be "part of the Wagner family".

For almost a decade, Winifred Wagner's musical soirees had been the talk of Munich society and everybody who wanted to be somebody hoped for an invitation to one of her social events.

Of course, Hitler had been a fan of Wagner's music since his days in Linz and over the years had harangued his Nazi colleagues regularly with his love and supposed knowledge of the composer's repertoire.

He once said (Portable Lair: 1942): "For me, Wagner is something godly, and his music is my religion. I go to his concerts as others go to church."

Inge Spilcker [Ley] first met Hitler when she was 17 years old at one of Winifred

Wagner's parties in 1933. Hitler was aged 44 and flushed with the success of becoming German leader while Inge had already given her first mezzo-soprano performance in Munich to great acclaim.

By all accounts, Hitler was immediately captivated by the talented teenager who he said had "great poise, beauty and an enchanting voice". Inge was 27 years younger than him and therefore suited his predilection for much younger women. Hitler and the "ravishing blonde", as Munich's newspapers described her, continued to meet at regular intervals as guests in the Wagner home. Hitler said he had become "bewitched" by her mezzo-soprano voice and attended the Munich opera regularly to hear her singing from the stage.

Over the next few years, a close bond developed between the two and the young singer confided her deepest fears and disappointments to him. She also allowed him to paint her naked.

ROSE AMONG THORNS: Inge with husband Robert Ley at a Nazi parade

Turbulent marriage

Inge Spilcker met her future husband, Robert Ley, the Nazi leader of the German Labor Front (DAF) in 1935 following one of her performances at the Friedrichstadtpalast Theater. She was 19 years old and he was 45.

At the time, Robert Ley was still married to his first wife, Elisabeth Schmidt. Normally, Hitler balked at marital infidelity but he did not try to stop the relationship between Inge and his Nazi colleague, Ley.

Some historians have suggested that Hitler was happy to see Inge "married off to a middle-aged drunk and known womanizer" as she had been putting pressure on him to start a sexual relationship which, due to his impotence and predominant homosexuality, was a demand he could never satisfy.

Hitler's nude painting of Inge Ley

In the late 1930s, rumors began to circulate that Adolf Hitler had a nude portrait of the "ravishing" Inge Ley hanging in the living room of one of his apartments. Which apartment was not known, Munich or Berlin or perhaps even his private residence in the Bavarian mountains. The rumors turned out to be true, though the existence of the painting was not revealed until the 1960s.

Hitler painted the nude portrait of Inge Ley, when she was still a single woman (though probably already Robert Ley's girlfriend) at his summer residence at Berchtesgaden, prior to August 1938.

NUDE PORTRAIT: Hitler's portrait of Inge Ley was painted before her marriage to the Nazi Labor leader, Robert Ley

The painting appears to have been completed in one of the guest bedrooms at Wachenfeld House, presumably when Robert Ley was away at work. The quilted bed cover, flowers and washbasin suggest a guest room. [The Eagle's Nest was not completed until April 1939.]

It is very unlikely to have been Hitler's own sleeping quarters as he disliked embellishments in his bedrooms and preferred to sleep in a single bed. Though there is no conclusive evidence of a sexual relationship between them, it seems that as with Princess Stephanie von Hohenlohe, Inge Ley was "physically intimate" with Hitler but they never had sexual intercourse.

Inge's husband

Robert Ley had served as a pilot in WW1 and was shot down over France. He survived, barely. Of his many injuries, the head injury he sustained was the worst. Along with swelling, his frontal lobe was damaged permanently and some of his cognitive reasoning had been hindered.

He developed a speech impediment in the form of a severe stutter. He began to use alcohol to ease the problem and it worked but it meant he became an alcoholic.

ROGER THAT: Inge Ley was used by the Nazi Party to promote worker's cruises in the mid 1930s, seen here with Hitler

By all accounts, Robert Ley abused his powers as DAF leader in a conspicuous way, even by Nazi Party standards. Indeed, the DAF was known as one of the most corrupt institutions within the Third Reich.

He embezzled funds for his personal use and by 1938, he owned an estate in Cologne, a string of villas, a fleet of cars, and a large art collection, all paid for with the compulsory dues demanded of German workers.

In November 1933, as a means of preventing labor disaffection, he established the "Strength Through Joy" [Kraft durch Freude, KdF].

The purpose of the KdF was to provide a range of benefits and amenities to the German working classes and their families, an alternative to increasing workers' wages. These included subsidized holidays at resorts across Germany and cruises to "safe countries" abroad, particularly Italy.

From circa 1936 onward, Inge Ley's image was used by the Nazi Party to promote these workers' holidays. She was photographed with both Hitler and Ley on the cruise ships and trains with the so-called "happy travelers".

As soon as he had divorced his first wife, Robert Ley and Inge Spilcker married on August 20, 1938. Two months later, the first of their three children, Lore a daughter was born (October 25, 1938). They named their second child, "Wolf" in honor of Hitler., a boy who was born 19 months later (May 14, 1940).

When he was not working, Robert Ley devoted much of his time to heavy drinking and womanizing which sometimes led to embarrassing public displays and the attention of anti-Nazi journalists.

RIDE OF YOUR LIFE: Hitler and Ley take a train to a cruise ship with other travelers

His marriage to Inge was in trouble almost from the beginning as he had become addicted to alcohol and she had become addicted to the painkillers she used to ease the pain caused by the fibroids in her womb.

Drug addiction
During the first year of their marriage, the Leys lived in their Berlin home. Many artists and prominent politicians were invited as guests, among them Adolf Hitler, who sometimes visited twice a week. (Metapedia.de: 1915) "Husband and wife attended a variety of receptions and when they met other guests, it was always Inge who drew admiring glances."
"Inge's outer beauty, however, was marred by a disease of the internal organs

[womb] that had plagued her for years. To alleviate the spasmodic pain, her doctors prescribed morphine in 1938 and she soon became dependent on the drug to deal with the constant pain. In her husband's absence, Inge had the medical support and companionship of a nurse who gave her regular morphine injections." (Ibid.)

TUNNEL PATROL: Inge is said to have poured her heart out to Hitler about her health and marital problems

In 1936, Robert Ley bought a farm called Gut Rottland located in Waldbroel near Gummersbach. At first, he was happy to live there and enjoyed the rest from his hectic schedule in Berlin. Having such a retreat meant that "his new wife could relax and express her artistic talent for both music and storytelling".
Using the pseudonym "Inge Hansen" Inge wrote children's books about dogs and illustrated them herself. But in spite of the restful effect of the farm, Berlin would remain the center of their lives. Inge was reluctant to spend time away from her husband in Berlin and she did not want to stay alone in the countryside. Also, many of the friends, theaters and concert halls she loved were located in Berlin.

Refuge in morphine
In March 1941, Inge Ley was involved in a serious accident when she was in the fifth month of her third pregnancy. She was a passenger in a horse-drawn carriage on the road near the farm in Waldbroel. Apparently, an oncoming car blew its horn as it approached the carriage which upset the horses and she was obliged to jump out onto the road.
When she fell, she lost some of the amniotic fluid in her womb and was immediately flown to a hospital in Berlin. In the course of her treatment, once

again, morphine was administered to give her pain relief. The baby survived the accident unscathed but arrived one month early on June 27, 1941.

"Based on the hitherto successful German army campaign in Russia, the Leys third child was called 'Gloria'." (Metapedia.de)

Six months later, during the Allied bombing of Berlin, she became worried about the safety of her three children and at the end of 1941, she brought them to the relative safety of the farm at Gut Rottland.

BEAUTY & THE BEAST: Inge Ley and Hitler have a chat but all is not well in her world

Apparently, she was not accepted as a farmer by the staff on the manor who resented her city ways. She missed Berlin where she had been courted by all, and she missed her husband even though she knew he had been unfaithful with other women.

In the numerous letters she wrote to him, she expressed how much she was waiting for him and how much she needed him.

The letters had a tragic air of desperation.

"I miss you...", "I need you..." and "I cannot cope without you...".

In 1941, Hitler appointed Robert Ley as Commissioner for Social House-Building, which, along with his labor leadership role, meant he had even less time to spend with his wife and children.

She continued to seek refuge in morphine injections and eventually checked herself into a rehab clinic in San Remo in May 1942.

In a letter to her mother written on May 20, she claimed all was well in her life:

"My dear mother!
I have recently returned from our visit and I thank you. I'm glad you appreciate my love for riding horseback. It's nice to know you enjoy it as much as I do.
Hopefully, you received the flowers I sent you for Mother's Day. Things are getting a little better for me; the 'discomfort' is not so strong.
Next week, I will have had no major problems for 14 days.
The weather seems to be staying completely gorgeous. Love Inge."

Obviously her stay at the sanatorium in San Remo was not a success because from August to October 1942, she was back in rehab, this time in Berlin.
"Her state of mind was seriously injured and she was still suffering from severe cramps [in her womb]." (Metapedia.de: 1915) It seems the morphine injections no longer worked to ease the pain.

Inge's suicide
Inge's life before her marriage had been privileged and she had thrived in the glamorous world of theater, singing and acting. By the time she was 25, she was the mother of three young children, had a drunken husband who was always working (or womanizing) and she had to deal with her own morphine addiction.
Apparently, she once took refuge from her husband at the Obersalzberg in Berchtesgaden to be with Hitler. On another occasion in 1941, after writing a letter to Hitler, which left him very depressed, she first attempted suicide.
One report said she was about to throw herself from a window when a member of her Berlin staff prevented her from doing so. This would have been shortly after the birth of her third child.
Adolf Hitler, who rarely stayed in Berlin at the time, visited the Leys for the last time in November 1942.
Shortly afterward, Inge departed Berlin once again and returned to the safety of the farm at Gut Rottland. By this time, Polish, Ukrainian and Russian prisoners-of-war were employed to do the heavy agricultural work (as German laborers were all at war).
Hand guns were issued to Inge and her staff so they could protect themselves against possible attacks from the workers.
A few days before her death, she was shown how to use a pistol which was later deposited in her bedroom.
The last days Inge and her husband shared at their farm were described later by witnesses as "un-harmonious". House staff said Inge's depressed mood made Robert Ley nervous and irritable. The German army's failure at Stalingrad which had left its mark on Germany had also taken its toll at the Ley's home. (Metapedia.de: 1915)
Inge's depression was exacerbated by the dreary winter weather and the fact that her husband, who spent most of December at Gut Rottland, was expected to spend the New Year at Hitler's "Wolf's Lair" in east Prussia. Robert Ley was due to leave on December 29 at six o' clock with his adjutant, Otto Marrenbach. When the

service car was not ready for the trip to the station, Inge and Robert Ley waited together with Marrenbach, Ley's other aides and a trustee on the ground floor of the house. After a brief conversation with the group, Inge went to her bedroom on the first floor and shortly afterward a gunshot rang out.

TRAPPED IN A CAGE: Inge Ley peers out a window in the Eagle's Nest

According to witnesses, Robert Ley and Marrenbach ran to the upper floor and tried to open the bedroom door but it was locked. When Marrenbach kicked it down, they found Inge Ley, who had taken her own life with a gunshot to the head. (Ibid.)

There has been speculation over the years that her husband shot her in a drunken rage, but there is little evidence to support this. His wife left a short suicide note: "For my Bobsy. Please forgive me, I can not-".

The Ley family's Berlin housekeeper, Hedwig Schroeder gave a statement to police on the day of Inge's suicide [December 29, 1942]. "I stood with Otto Marrenbach and his adjutant beside Robert Ley in the foyer on the first floor when the shot rang out. Robert Ley was just on his way to the Fuhrer HQ. To my knowledge, Otto Marrenbach was the first in the bedroom and he took the gun away from the body. After him, Robert Ley entered the room. I was present when the corpse was found in the bedroom. Inge was lying half-back on the bed, the gun beside her. The wall to the right was full of blood, it was terrible."

Inge Ley was 26 years old.

Apparently, Hitler was deeply moved when he learned that she had committed suicide. He was already in a depressed mood in his Wolf's Lair. A week earlier [December 23, 1942] he had received the news that the German army had been defeated by the Russians at Stalingrad. This was a military disaster. For days, he had been spewing venom against the Russians and the incompetence of his own army, but even so, he wrote a letter of condolence to Inge's mother.

German newspapers said Adolf Hitler, who greatly admired and cultivated a strong friendship with the Ley family, was deeply affected by the untimely death of this "beautiful woman". Hitler described her suicide as "incomprehensible", "appalling" and "dreadful ".

In October 1945, her husband Robert Ley committed suicide while awaiting his trial at Nuremberg for war crimes. His last words in court were recorded as:
"Stand us against a wall and shoot us, well and good, you are the victors. But why should I be brought before a Tribunal like a c-c-c- I can't even get the word out!" His stutter had returned.

On October 24, three days after receiving the indictment [for war crimes], he strangled himself in his prison cell using a noose made by tearing a towel into strips, which he then fastened to the toilet pipe.

He was 55 years old. Apparently, he warned one of his prison guards that he would come back to haunt him again after his death.

Hitler's nude painting of Inge Ley was bought by an anonymous bidder at a private auction in Germany in the 1960s and has not been viewed in public since its purchase.

Original hard copies of Inge Ley's children's books [written under the name Inge Hansen] have sold for up to $2,000. In fact, her books about dogs, which she illustrated herself, are republished regularly in Germany.

CHAPTER 20: EVA BRAUN

"A highly intelligent man should take a primitive and stupid woman," Adolf Hitler [to his Nazi colleagues in the presence of Eva Braun]

EVA BRAUN (1912 -1945) was Adolf Hitler's longtime companion, and for 40 hours, his wife. During their 16 year relationship, she became so sexually frustrated that she begged Hitler's doctor, Theodor Morell, to give him medicine to increase his sexual appetite.

Having sex with Braun did not seem to appeal to him and Hitler managed to be unfaithful to her with both sexes. He enjoyed sadomasochistic and voyeuristic sex with several actresses, had regular casual sex with his bodyguards and chauffeurs and enjoyed a long term physical relationship with his Munich chauffeur, Julius Schreck until his death in 1936.

During this time, Eva Braun attempted suicide twice in the hope of "getting his attention".

In the end, she seems to have settled for a platonic style friendship with little or no physical contact.

In 1940, when Unity Mitford returned to England (with a bullet still lodged in her skull), Braun knew she had won the battle for the man she had told friends she would one day marry. Her perseverance, her loyalty and willingness to stay in the shadows had won the day. Perhaps she was his ideal Aryan woman after all.

From the very beginning, Hitler had ordered her to stay in the background of his life. Taking photographs of her was forbidden.

Though she became a regular fixture in his life toward the end of the war, the German public did not know of her existence.

Forty hours after their wedding in the Berlin bunker, Eva Braun committed suicide (using a cyanide capsule) with Hitler (who shot himself in the temple) to prove her love and loyalty to him.

But a few weeks before her death, she told her girlfriends she wished she had left him ten years earlier when she had the opportunity.

First meeting with Hitler

Eva Braun was born in Simbach, Germany on February 6, 1912, the middle child of Friedrich and Franziska Braun.

In 1929, when she was 17 years old, she first met the 40-year-old Hitler while she worked as an assistant to Nazi Party photographer, Heinrich Hoffmann in Munich. She had just completed her Catholic convent education, and was living at home with one of her sisters and their protective parents.

Braun described meeting the "old man with the funny mustache" for the first time [in her diary] in 1929.

"I stayed on after closing time to file some papers and climbed up a ladder to fetch the files kept on the top shelves of the cupboard. At that moment, the boss came in accompanied by a man of uncertain age with a funny mustache, a light-colored,

English-style overcoat and a big felt hat in his hand. They both sat down on the other side of the room, opposite me. I tried to squint in their direction without appearing to turn round and sensed that this character was looking at my legs. That very day I had shortened my skirt, and I felt slightly embarrassed because I wasn't sure I had got the hem even."

TOO YOUNG TO KNOW: Eva Braun aged 16

Hoffmann sent her out to buy beer and sausages, and then invited her to join them. In her diary, Eva claimed that Hitler ravished her with his eyes:
"The elderly gentleman [Hitler] was paying me compliments. We talked about music and a play at the Staatstheater, as I remember, with him devouring me with his eyes all the time. Then, as it was getting late, I rushed off. I refused an offer of a lift in his Mercedes. Just think what Papa's reaction would have been!"

When Eva told her father, a master craftsman, that she had met the Nazi leader, he was hostile and dismissive. He disapproved of any potential relationship between them because the Nazi chief was 23 years older than his daughter.
Also, in 1929, Hitler had already moved into a large flat in the Prinzregentenplatz in Munich, and his niece Geli Raubal had moved in with him. The rumors about uncle and niece having a sexual relationship had already appeared in local and national newspapers so it is no surprise that Braun's father did not want Eva to associate with the Nazi leader.
In any event, there is little sign that Hitler paid more than passing attention to Braun while "the love of his life" Geli Raubal was still alive.

SLAP & TICKLE: Braun and Hitler in the Bavarian mountains; Hitler liked to feed his young girlfriends cream cakes from a spoon as though they were his children

Feminine wiles

Heinrich Hoffmann's daughter, Henriette became friends with Eva Braun at about this time and said, even at the tender age of 17, Braun already knew how to get a man's attention.

"Eva had pale blonde hair, cut short, blue eyes, and although she had been educated in a Catholic convent, she had learned feminine wiles, a certain look, and swaying hips when she walked, which made men turn their heads. She was given theater tickets like I was [by Hitler], and she thanked him with a curtsy." (spartacus-educational.com: 2015)

It is not known whether Henriette divulged Hitler's "indiscretions" with her to her female friends but in Eva Braun's case, it probably would not have mattered, as very early on, she decided her aim was "to get and keep Hitler's attention and to one day make him marry her".

The Nizkor Project (1943) noted that the relationship between Braun and Hitler took a long time to develop and that for many years it was not exclusive on Hitler's side.

Indeed, Braun did not see him very often after their first meeting, unless he called in to speak to her boss Hoffmann on matters relating to photography or Nazi Party publicity. When they did meet at her workplace, their conversations amounted to nothing more than a mild flirtation.

Even when his niece Geli died in late 1931, the way was not yet clear for Braun to participate in his life in a meaningful way. Hitler took comfort in the arms of his Munich chauffeur Julius Schreck [until his death in 1936] and he had strange dalliances with actresses Jenny Jugo [a few months], Renate Mueller [a few years] followed by a "public fling" with the gullible English aristocrat, Unity Mitford [four years].

During this time, Eva Braun was obliged to stay in the shadows pining for the man she already adored.

LASTING IMPRESSION: An early Hitler drawing of Eva Braun but she could not hold his attention for long

Eva's sister, Ilse Braun said she knew nothing about the relationship in the early years, probably because it did not amount to anything at the beginning: "We Braun girls were not very communicative when it came to the details of our private lives. Even among ourselves, in the sanctum of our bedroom, we rarely spoke about our relations with men. There was a very strong barrier of puritanism, perhaps because of our convent education, perhaps because of the Victorian ideas of our parents. I knew Eva sometimes went out with Hitler, but I knew nothing about the state of her feelings."

In his book, Hitler: A Study in Tyranny (1962) Alan Bullock said the effort was always on Eva Braun's side to keep some kind of relationship going.

"She was a pretty, empty-headed blonde, with a round face and blue eyes, who worked as a shop girl in Hoffmann's photographer's shop. Hitler met her there, paid her a few casual compliments, gave her flowers, and occasionally invited her to be one of his circle on an outing. The initiative was all on Eva's side; she told her friends Hitler was in love with her and she would make him marry her."

Things changed slightly after his niece, Geli's death - once he got over his depression – and he gradually began to pay more attention to her. It was far from a passionate relationship and he ignored her for months at a time, always saying he was too busy for a serious relationship.

But both Eva Braun's diary and her letters to him reveal her own infatuation and determination to stay in contact with him.

"Dear Herr Hitler,

Thank you again for the wonderful invitation to the theater. It was a memorable evening. I am most grateful to you for your kindness. I am counting the hours until I may have the joy of another meeting.

Yours, Eva."

Eva's despair

Hitler's housekeeper, Anni Winter, remembered that Braun often visited his Munich apartment: "She was there often when Hitler was in Munich. She was always running after him, insisting on being alone with him. She was a most demanding woman."

According to Cate Haste, author of Nazi Women (2001) from the start, their relationship was conducted in secret as Hitler did not want to be associated in public with any one woman.

"Eva lived at home, and her parents were strict. Hitler, almost totally preoccupied with politics, was rarely in Munich. Eva was kept firmly in the background of his life. The pattern of secrecy that began their relationship suited Hitler, and continued to its end. And so did the pattern of despair for Eva."

In his book, The Rise and Fall of the Third Reich (1960) William L. Shirer said though Hitler found relaxation in her unobtrusive company "he had always kept her out of sight, refusing to allow her to come to his various headquarters where he spent almost all of his time during the war years, and rarely permitting her even to come to Berlin."

Shirer said: "She remained immured at the Berghof [Hitler's country residence] on the Obersalzberg, passing her time in swimming and skiing, in reading cheap novels and seeing trashy films, in dancing, which Hitler disapproved of, and endlessly grooming herself, pining away for her absent loved one."

Braun's suicide attempts

Eva Braun first attempted suicide on August 10, 1932, three years after meeting Hitler when she shot herself in the neck with her father's pistol. Historians believe this suicide attempt was not very serious, but merely a bid to get Hitler's attention. According to Cate Haste, (Nazi Women: 2001), "she then rang Hitler's doctor [Morell], who came to save her and the whole thing was hushed up. Hitler came to visit her with flowers at the clinic where she was recovering. Eva, the shadowy, loyal figure at the periphery of Hitler's life, continued to be frustrated by his neglect. Hitler would turn up at unpredictable times, and his moods shifted between gushing charm and indifference."

On her twenty-third birthday, Eva Braun again tried to kill herself. It was 1935 and Hitler was publicly flirting with Unity Mitford; this relationship was widely publicized in the German media which was devastating for Braun.

According to Eva's sister Ilse, she suspected that her sister had, to some extent, staged this second suicide attempt.

She told friends "Eva had taken only twenty tablets of Vanodorm [sleeping tablets], an amount that had little chance of killing her".

Hitler was shocked by this second suicide attempt and turned up at her home asking for forgiveness. She recorded in her diary on February 18, 1935, that he promised to buy her a house.

"Dear God, please let them [Hitler's promises] come true and let it happen in the near future. I am infinitely happy that he loves me so much and I pray that it may always remain so. I never want it to be my fault if one day he should cease to love me."

However, in her diary on May 28, Braun complained: "Is this the mad love he promised me, when he doesn't send me a single comforting line in three months?" One of Hitler's secretaries, Christa Schroeder regarded Eva Braun as a schemer: "When he no longer had much time for her because of the electioneering, she pursued him cunningly with suicide attempts. And of course she succeeded, because as a politician Hitler couldn't have survived a second suicide from someone close to him. The only woman he loved and would certainly have married later was his step-niece, Geli Raubal." (spartacus-educational.com: 2015)

Cate Haste (Nazi Women: 2001), agreed with Schroeder's assessment: "In a perverse way, Eva Braun had shown her steady loyalty to him, the thing Hitler craved most from people. She was rewarded by being allowed to play a small part in his private, but never his public, life."

Primitive and stupid

Albert Speer (Inside The Third Reich: 1970) recalled that on one occasion, in front of Eva Braun, Hitler said: "A highly intelligent man should take a primitive and stupid woman. Imagine if, on top of everything else, I had a woman who interfered with my work! In my leisure time, I want to have peace."

Nazi political aide, Reinhard Spitzy [aide to Joachim von Ribbentrop] met Eva Braun on several occasions and said:

"Hitler wanted to be absolutely free, and his woman should give him a small bourgeois home with cake and tea. Hitler didn't want to have a socially high person. He could have had them, but he didn't want to have a woman who would discuss political questions or who would try to have her influence, and that Eva Braun never did. Eva Braun didn't interfere in politics."

Even though Nazi architect, Albert Speer (Inside The Third Reich: 1970) believed Hitler and Braun rarely if ever had sex, he thought Eva was the Fuhrer's ideal partner: "Eva was very feminine, a man's woman, incredibly undemanding of herself, helpful to many people behind the scenes, nobody ever knew that, and infinitely thoughtful of Hitler. She was a restful sort of girl. And her love for Hitler was beyond question."

Above all else, Braun accepted Hitler's shabby treatment of her.

Speer said: "Eva was never seen in public with him. Any photograph that showed her face was stamped 'Publication Forbidden' by Nazi Party censors. It is the reason why the German public never knew about her."

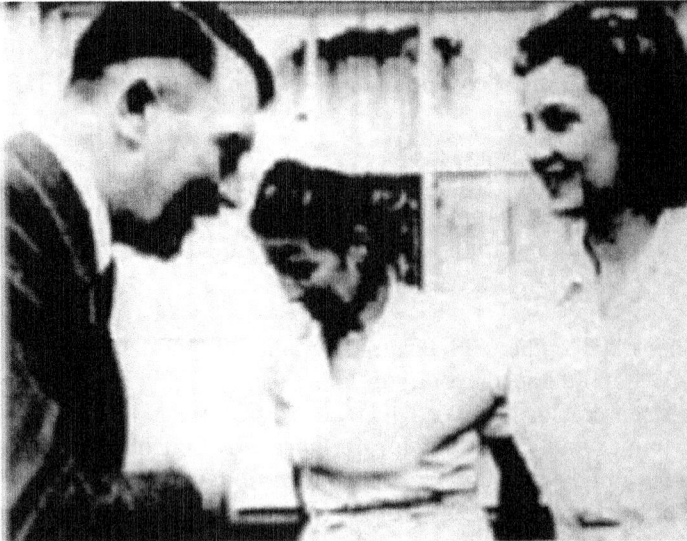

NOW HE LOVES ME: Hitler bends to kiss Braun's hand at his summer residence, the Berghof

Jealousy

Meanwhile, Hitler continued to be photographed in public with Unity Mitford which really upset Braun. She was also jealous of another of Hitler's intimates, Princess Stephanie von Hohenlohe.

According to historian and editor, John Simkin (spartacus-educational.com: 2015) Braun was extremely jealous of Princess Stephanie von Hohenlohe who admitted in her unpublished memoirs that her relationship with Hitler upset many of the people around him:

"Every visit of mine to the Reich Chancellery seemed to them an impudent encroachment upon their sacred privileges, and every hour that Adolf wasted upon me was an hour which he might have spent to so much greater advantage in their devoted company."

Apparently, both Braun and Unity Mitford pointed out the obvious, that the princess was Jewish, in an attempt to end Hitler's association with her, but to no avail.

[In 1939, Stephanie von Hohenlohe escaped Jewish persecution by going first to England and then to the USA. After WW2, the FBI continued to keep a file on her as they believed she was both "extremely intelligent and extremely dangerous".]

A gift of her own apartment

Meanwhile, Eva Braun put pressure on Hitler to marry her but he refused.

According to the Fuhrer, (Hitler Speaks: 1939): "The bad side of marriage is that it creates rights. In that case, it is far better to have a mistress. The burden is lightened, and everything is placed on the level of a gift. Of course, this only holds true in the case of exceptional men."

He did eventually give Braun her own apartment in the Reich Chancellery in Berlin. However, he insisted that she enter it through the servants quarters so she would not be seen by photographers or journalists.

WASTED GLAMOUR: Eva Braun posing at Hitler's retreat in the Bavarian mountains; she liked to imitate the movie stars from the celebrity magazines she read

Her friend, Henriette Hoffmann said: "It was furnished like a guest house, deep armchairs covered in rustic material, pots of flowers, cupboards painted with gentians, whole years editions of film magazines. Eva had film stars clothes copied, knew which star sign they were born under, and was interested in their lives." She added that Braun often had her two dogs by her side and "was smoking fast and nervously, as she always did when she knew that Hitler was not nearby".

Nazi aide, Reinhard Spitzy claimed that Braun had some privileges that enabled her to do what was forbidden to others: "She was allowed to sing, to dance, to paint her nails with red paint, and she was allowed to smoke a cigarette outside."

"Meanwhile, we had to go to the loo to smoke. Hitler had a very good nose, and it was forbidden to smoke. But Eva Braun was allowed everything."

Hitler tried to persuade Eva and her sister Gretl to stop. When Gretl refused to even try, Hitler apparently offered to buy her a villa but she still said 'No'."

Nerin E. Gun, author of Eva Braun: Hitler's Mistress (1969) said he "promised the ladies who went for a month without smoking a gift of a Swiss gold watch and some jewelry".

Apparently, Eva Braun stopped smoking for a month, and then started again once she had received her Swiss watch and other gifts.

The Nizkor Project (1943) said: "In the course of time, Hitler has bought her [Braun] many things including high-powered automobiles and a house between Munich and Berchtesgaden".

HOLIDAY BLISS: A rare snap of Braun and Hitler smiling

Did Braun and Hitler ever have sex?

Herbert Dohring, the Fuhrer's manservant at the Berghof, recalled: "She [Eva] was friendly, elegant, but she was sometimes moody and morose. Those who knew how the relationship was between them couldn't hold this against her. It was not a love affair, never. This was apparent to my wife before and after we married. She was convinced it was a friendship, a forced, necessary one."

Hitler's photographer, Heinrich Hoffmann agreed and said he was not sure Hitler and Braun ever had a sexual relationship. (Hitler Was My Friend: 1955)

"Eva moved into his house, became the constant companion of his leisure hours and, to the best of my knowledge, that was all there was to it. Not at any time was there any perceptible change in his attitude towards her which might have pointed to more intimate relations between them; and the secrecy which surrounded the whole affair is emphasized by the profound astonishment of all of us in his most intimate circle when, at the bitter end, the marriage was announced."

Nazi architect, Albert Speer also agreed with Hoffmann's assessment in his own memoirs (Inside The Third Reich: 1970) and said Braun never slept in the same room as Hitler; she had her own rooms at the Berghof summer residence, and also in the Berlin bunker.

CAMERA READY: But this photograph of Braun and Hitler only emerged after WW2; photographs of her were stamped "Verboten" on Hitler's orders

And again, Hitler's valet, Heinz Linge who was devoted to both Hitler and Eva Braun, agreed with Hoffmann and Speer in own his book, With Hitler to the End (2009). He said "Hitler and Braun had two bedrooms and two bathrooms. Public displays of affection or physical contact were non-existent, even in the enclosed world of the Berghof summer residence."

Drugs to boost Hitler's sexual appetite
If Dr. Theodor Morell's medical records are to be believed, Hitler was having up to 82 types of drugs injected into his body from the late 1930s to deal with his many medical and psychological complaints.
These medical complaints included Parkinson's disease, which meant that the Fuhrer was unlikely to have been sexually active. In any case, he did not seem interested in having sex with Eva Braun and more than once, he encouraged her to find sexual happiness with other men, but she always refused.
Albert Speer (Inside The Third Reich: 1970) recalled that in 1943, Eva Braun came to him in tears, sobbing that "the Fuhrer has just told me to find someone else; he [Hitler] said that he can no longer fulfill me".
Speer said: "There are no two ways of interpreting this. She made it quite clear: Hitler had told her that he was too busy, too immersed, too tired, he could no longer satisfy her as a man."

WOOF AS A LOVER: But Braun and Hitler shared a love of dogs

The lack of sex in their relationship left Eva Braun very frustrated.

Dr. Morell admitted in several post war interviews that she had asked him several times to "give Hitler drugs to boost his sexual appetite".

According to a Washington Examiner article (2013) under the heading "Hitler was definitely gay according to doctors", Hitler's medical records detailed how he was "shot up" or injected with bull semen especially when Braun was with him.

"The new notes add that bull semen shots were used to regulate his level of testosterone and prove beyond doubt that his doctors used many experimental treatments on the Fuhrer."

Herman Merl's medical assessment mentioned that the Fuhrer was also receiving female hormones to "treat various ailments which were dangerous and often interfere with male sexual functions". (Ibid.)

Hitler also suffered a minor heart attack in 1944, which would not have helped his sexual prowess. Apart from anything else, he had grown prematurely old.

Dr. Karl Brandt who replaced Morell in 1944 said the Fuhrer needed to sleep late almost every day; and even then, he had very little energy and looked much older than his 56 years.

"His hair had gone white, his body was stooped, and he had difficulty walking. His voice had become feeble and his eyesight was so poor that he needed special lenses to read documents from his Fuhrer typewriter. People who had not seen him for months were shocked by his appearance." (spartacus-educational.com: 2015)

Bunkered

At the beginning of 1945, Soviet troops entered Nazi Germany from the east and Hitler moved into the Fuhrer bunker in Berlin (on January 16). He was joined there by Eva Braun and her sister Gretl, the Goebbels and their children, Martin Bormann, one of his physicians, Dr. Ernst-Gunther Schenck, three personal secretaries: Johanna Wolf, Traudl Junge, Christa Schroeder, and two personal assistants, Heinz Linge and Otto Gunsche.

When Soviet troops first entered Berlin, Joseph Goebbels suggested that Hitler should try to escape with the help of the Hitler Youth but Hitler rejected the idea as he feared the possibility of being captured. (spartacus-educational.com: 2015) He had heard stories of how the Soviet troops planned to parade him through the streets of Berlin in a cage. To prevent this humiliation, Hitler told Goebbels he had decided to commit suicide.

Hitler was very near death in any case.

One Berlin witness said: "It was a ghastly physical image he presented. The upper part of his body was bowed and he dragged his feet as he made his way slowly and laboriously through the bunker from his living room."

"If anyone happened to stop him, he was forced either to sit down or to catch hold of the person he was speaking to. Often saliva would dribble from the corners of his mouth, presenting a hideous and pitiful spectacle." (Ibid.)

TOO TIRED: The couple had one of the shortest marriages in history; it lasted just 40 hours

Other men

In the film of Hitler's final days, Downfall (2004), based on the war diaries of Traudl Junge (Hitler's Last Secretary: 2002). it is implied that Braun was allowed to have sex with other men so long as she was "discreet in her night time pleasures".

Braun confided to her friend, Marion Schonmann, [the daughter of opera singer, Maria Petzl whom Hitler admired]:

"A few years ago, the boss [Hitler] said that if I fell in love one day with another man, then I should let him know and he would release me. If I had only known

[Hermann] Fegelein ten years ago, I would have asked the boss to let me go!" (spartacus-educational.com: 2015)

Eva's sister, Gretl eventually married Hermann Fegelein, a decorated SS-officer, after Hitler arranged to bring them together.

Traudl Junge said that he was a notorious womanizer and even after his marriage to Gretl Braun, "Fegelein continued to seduce Hitler's secretaries".

Christa Schroeder [another Berlin bunker secretary], said the SS officer had a very close relationship with Eva Braun.

"Hermann Fegelein was frequently amongst those who danced with Eva Braun. Today, I can recall clearly the unforgettable scene. After a dance, Fegelein would lift Eva chest high. At eye level, they would gaze at each other full of tenderness and loving: Eva was obviously strongly attracted to Fegelein. I am convinced that her feelings for him went well beyond those feelings for a brother-in-law." (spartacus-educational.com: 2015)

Beginning of the end

By the beginning of April 1945, Red Army soldiers were only 300 yards away from the underground Fuhrer bunker. Even though defeat was inevitable, Hitler insisted his troops fight to the death and he sent out orders for the execution of any military commanders who retreated.

Albert Speer said Hitler's addiction to amphetamines was the reason for this, that no matter how many casualties were involved, he would not allow any retreat.

STUFFING THE MUFFIN: Braun and Hitler in the Berlin bunker living room where they would commit suicide together

Meanwhile, Hermann Fegelein [married to pregnant Gretl Braun] was arrested with his mistress on April 27, 1945 while carrying a large sum of money and just about to leave the country.

His briefcase contained documents suggesting that he had been in peace negotiations with the Allies. There was nothing Hitler hated more than disloyalty. In his book, With Hitler To The End (2009), Heinz Linge said: "On Hitler's order, he [Fegelein] was arraigned immediately before a court-martial and sentenced to death for treason. Eva Braun, though clearly fighting an internal struggle, would not enter a plea for mercy for her brother-in-law even though Hitler indicated that he would commute the sentence to atonement at the front."

Hermann Fegelein was executed by firing squad the day before Eva Braun's wedding to Hitler.

Wedding with champagne, tea and sandwiches

On April 29, 1945, as Red Army troops fought their way through east Berlin's streets, Braun and Hitler were married in a brief civil ceremony. She was 33 and he was 56. Forty hours later, they would both be dead.

Heinz Linge (With Hitler To The End: 2009) described Hitler and Eva's wedding ceremony which was held in the bunker conference room:

"I had imagined the Fuhrer's marriage differently in earlier years. There were few people present. When registrar Walter Wagner, clad in Volksstrum uniform, arrived shortly before one o'clock on the morning of 29 April, everything was ready. Hitler had the situation conference room set up for the ceremony. At one side of the table were four chairs, one each for Hitler, Eva Braun and the witnesses Goebbels and Bormann."

"After the witnesses had been advised as to their role they waited with the guests. Registrar Wagner, as excited as Eva Braun, had a two-page typed document from which he requested the contracting parties to declare that they were of Aryan origin and free of any hereditary disease which would present an impediment to the marriage. Then Wagner said in trembling tones: 'In the presence of the witnesses I ask you, mein Fuhrer Adolf Hitler, if you are so willed as to enter wedlock with Fraulein Eva Braun? In this case I request that you answer with Yes'." Hitler did this, and then Eva Braun did so, after Wagner had continued.

"After the signature of Hitler, Eva Hitler, Goebbels, Bormann and Registrar Wagner to the certificate, the ceremony was over. Hitler and his bride accepted our best wishes and retired 90 minutes later. We celebrated with the Goebbels family, Bormann et al. Champagne, sandwiches and tea were served in a fitting atmosphere."

The Fuhrer's favorite dress

Traudl Junge (Hitler's Last Secretary: 2002), described the moments before Hitler and Braun's double suicide. She said Eva Braun smiled, then embraced her for the last time and said with a sob in her voice: "Please do try to get out. You may yet make your way through. And give Bavaria my love."

"She was wearing the Fuhrer's favorite dress, the black one with the roses at the neckline, and her hair was washed and beautifully done.

The heavy iron door closed. Like that, she followed the Fuhrer into his room, and to her death."

Heinz Linge (With Hitler To The End: 2009) recalled: "After the meal, Eva Hitler came to me to take her leave. Pale, having remained awake all night but careful to maintain her composure, she thanked me for 'everything you have done for the Fuhrer'."

"With a sad look she begged me at the finish: 'Should you meet my sister Gretl, do not tell her how her husband, Hermann Fegelein, met his death'."

He said then Eva Braun went to say farewell to Frau Goebbels while Hitler tried to retire to his study but Magda Goebbels wanted one last "personal conversation with the Fuhrer".

"When I entered, Hitler was thanking her for her commitment and services. He asked me to remove the gold Party badge from one of his uniforms and pinned it on her in 'especial recognition'."

Hitler, who had already tested out a cyanide capsule on his pet Alsatian, Blondi, asked to see Heinz Linge privately.

He described their final conversation in his memoirs: "My mouth was dry. Soon I would have to carry out my last duty. Anxiously, I gazed at the man whom I had served devotedly for more than ten years. He stood stooped, the hank of hair, as always, across the pale forehead. He had become gray."

"He looked at me with tired eyes and said he would now retire. It was 15.15 hours. I asked for his orders for the last time. Outwardly calm and in a quiet voice, as if he were sending me into the garden to fetch something, he said: 'Linge, I am going to shoot myself now. You know what you have to do. I have given the order for the break-out. Attach yourself to one of the groups and try to get through to the west'."

The coming man

Heinz Linge said: "To my question what we should fight for now, the Fuhrer answered: 'For the Coming Man'. I saluted. Hitler took two or three tired steps towards me and offered his hand. Then for the last time in his life, he raised his right arm in the Hitler salute. A ghostly scene."

Traudl Junge remembered the exact moment when Hitler locked himself in his room with Braun: "Suddenly there was the sound of a shot, so loud, so close, that we all fell silent. It echoed on through all the bunker rooms."

Hitler shot himself in the temple with a hand gun. He had another pistol at his feet in case the first gun failed. He wanted to be certain he did not survive. Braun killed herself by biting down on a cyanide capsule.

Heinz Linge described what he saw in Hitler's private quarters: "I smelt the gas from a discharged firearm. Thus it had come to pass. Although I was beyond surprises, everything in me resisted opening the door and entering alone. I went to the map room where a number of people were gathered around Martin Bormann. I gave Bormann a signal and asked him to come with me to Hitler's room. I opened the door and went in, Bormann following me. He turned white as chalk and stared at me helplessly."

"Adolf Hitler and Eva Braun were seated on the sofa. Both were dead. Hitler had shot himself in the right temple with his 7.65-mm pistol. This weapon, and his 6.35-mm pistol which he had kept in reserve in the event that the larger gun misfired, lay near his feet on the floor. His head was inclined a little towards the wall. Blood had spattered on the carpet near the sofa. To his right beside him sat his wife. She had drawn up her legs on the sofa. Her contorted face betrayed how she had died. Cyanide poisoning was marked in her features. The small box in which the capsule had been kept lay on the table."

HITLER'S BERLIN CHAUFFEUR: Erich Kempka was known as "Queen of the Reich"; he helped to dispose of Hitler's body

Traudl Junge described the room after the bodies had been removed:"There is a bottle of Steinhager standing there, with an empty glass beside it. Automatically, I pour myself a drink and swallow the strong liquor. So now it's over. Eva's little revolver is lying on the table with a pink chiffon scarf beside it, and I see the brass case of the poison capsule glinting on the floor next to Frau Hitler's chair. It looks like an empty lipstick. There is blood on the blue-and-white upholstery of the bench where Hitler was sitting: Hitler's blood. I suddenly feel sick. The heavy smell of bitter almonds is nauseating "

Burning the bodies
Hitler had ordered his personal assistants to burn his body until there was "nothing left but ashes" so that Russian soldiers, already a few hundred yards away, could not parade his dead body on Berlin's streets.
His Berlin chauffeur, Erich Kempka (I Was Hitler's Chauffeur: 1951) said between 180 and 200 liters of petrol had been placed in readiness at the bunker exit.
"Hitler's body was wrapped in a dark field blanket. His face was covered as far as the bridge of his nose. Below the graying hair the forehead had the waxy pallor of death. The left arm was dangling out of the blanket as far as the elbow. [Martin]

Bormann had the dead Eva Hitler in his arms."

"She was dressed in a black dress of light material, her head and blonde tresses inclined backwards. Eva had hated Bormann. He had caused her a great deal of aggravation. Now in death her greatest enemy carried her to the pyre. I said to Gunsche: 'You help carry the chief, I will take Eva!' Then without speaking, I took Eva's body from Bormann's arms. There were twenty steps up to the bunker exit. I had not reckoned with the weight. Halfway up, Gunsche hurried to assist me, and together we carried the body of Eva Hitler into the open. The Reich Chancellery was being shelled by the Russians. The air was filled with mortar dust."

Kempka continued: "In haste, the dead Hitler was placed on the ground about three meters half-right of the bunker exit, very close to the giant cement mixer which was to have been used to thicken the Fuhrer-bunker roof by one meter. Now he lay there still wrapped in the gray blanket, legs towards the bunker stairway. The long black trouser legs were pushed up, his right foot turned inwards. I had often seen his foot in this position when he had nodded off beside me on long car drives. Gunsche and I lay Eva Hitler beside her husband. In the enormous excitement of the moment, we put her at an angle to him. Then I seized a canister of petrol, ran out again and placed it near the two bodies. Quickly, I bent low to place Hitler's left arm closer to his body. His untidy hair fluttered in the wind. Shells exploded close by, spattering us with earth and dust, metal splinters whirred and whistled above us. I was trembling as I poured the contents over the two bodies, conscious of it being Hitler's last order and my sense of duty overcame my sensitivity." (Ibid.)

In his book, I Was Hitler's Chauffeur, (1951) Erich Kempka described Eva Braun as "the unhappiest woman in Germany".

According to Nazi architect, Albert Speer: "Eva's love for him, her loyalty, were absolute as she proved unmistakably at the end." But he also said she would prove a "great disappointment for historians" because of her lack of intimacy with the German leader.

Lothar Machtan (Hidden Hitler: 2001) simply said that she brought a sense of normality to Hitler's life and "he used her as a smokescreen".

"Her presence, however subdued, helped suppress the rumors of his homosexuality. Hitler and Eva lived in an illusion of a self-denying love affair. It was a relationship meant only to keep the public at rest."

PART SIX – HITLER'S CHILDREN

CHAPTER 21: HITLER'S SON

"I shall never make such a mistake [to be forgotten]. I know how to keep my hold on people after I have passed on. I shall be the Fuhrer they look up at and go home to talk of and remember. My life shall not end in the mere form of death. It will, on the contrary, begin then." Adolf Hitler (The Foe We Face: 1942)

In his last will and testament, dictated to his secretary Traudl Junge (Hitler's Last Secretary: 2002) he stated that "in spite of all setbacks the war will one day go down in history as the most glorious and heroic manifestation of a people's will to live".

ADOLF HITLER'S descendants by his half-brother, Alois Jr. and half-sister, Angela Raubal can be found today living in obscurity in Florida, New York and Austria. Some of them have had the temerity to seek royalties from Hitler's bestselling book Mein Kampf (1925) without success.
But what of Hitler himself? Since his death by suicide in the Berlin bunker in 1945, rumors regularly surfaced that he never really died but escaped like Holocaust mastermind, Adolf Eichmann and Auschwitz doctor, Josef Mengele, who both fled to South America.
Other tittle-tattle speculated that Hitler returned to Austria to live out his days unnoticed. Many of the rumors were fueled by the fact that Hitler's body was never found.

Hitler's son
Other gossip about "Hitler's son" had circulated in France and Germany since the early 1960s. Then in the 1970s, more specific rumors emerged around the Saint-Quentin district in France and were published prominently in illustrated magazines such as the German scandal sheet, Bunte [Colorful] and more respectable papers, such as the historical journal, Zeitgeschichte.
Could Adolf Hitler have fathered a child with an 18-year-old peasant girl he met during WW1? Hardly likely.
Then a man called Jean-Marie Loret (b.1918-d.1985) stepped forward to say that he was the illegitimate son of the German Fuhrer and that his mother, Charlotte Lobjoie (b.1898-d.1951) had an affair, aged 18, with a 30-year-old soldier called Adolf Hitler in the summer of 1917.
[Charlotte's age, reported elsewhere as 16, is incorrect, given her date of birth].
Jean-Marie Loret's autobiography, Ton pere s'appelait Hitler (Your Father's Name was Hitler) caused a sensation in France, Germany and Austria when it was first published in 1981. Newspapers in other countries also ran with the story and it eventually became worldwide news.
Apparently in 1948, Charlotte Lobjoie (who thought she was dying) told her son

Jean-Marie that the "unknown German soldier" - his father - with whom she had an affair during WW1 was Adolf Hitler.

When the reputable German magazine Der Spiegel [The Mirror] wrote a detailed story on Loret called "Love in Flanders", the wider world began to believe the story was authentic.

HITLER'S MISTRESS? Charlotte Lobjoie aged 18

Since Adolf Hitler and his regiment had stayed in the localities of Seclin, Fournes, Wavrin, and Ardooie during the years 1916 and 1917, and according to certain witnesses, had a relationship with Charlotte Lobjoie, the story seemed credible and became the subject of heated debate.

Naturally, there were many people in the media, academia and elsewhere who did not want to believe it was true. The idea that the most evil man in history "had issue" was too repulsive to even contemplate. But of course, there were others who wanted to profit from the possibility.

In June 1978, historian Werner Maser moved Jean-Marie Loret to his own house in Speyer, Germany to seclude him from the intense media interest in Loret's home town, Saint-Quentin.

Maser and Loret visited several places, including the former concentration camp at Dachau, where Loret apparently said, "I didn't choose my father".

The historian also took Loret on a lecture tour highlighting his parentage but the Frenchman was reluctant to give interviews and the two men eventually fell out.

Undaunted, Maser then wrote a Hitler biography focusing on the supposed relationship between Hitler and Lobjoie called Adolf Hitler: Legend, Myth, Reality (1975).

Maser said: "At the beginning of 1916, the young woman had met the German soldier Adolf Hitler for the first time. She stayed first in Premont, allowed herself to fall into a sexual relationship with him, and followed him until autumn 1917 to, among other places, Seboncourt, Fournes and Wavrin in Northern France and in May, June and July 1917, also to Ardooie in Belgium [where Charlotte fell pregnant]".

Did Werner Maser and others get involved in the story merely for financial gain? Is there any truth in it?

Jean-Marie Loret was born illegitimately in 1918 in Seboncourt, in north-eastern France as Jean-Marie "Lobjoie".

His mother, Charlotte Lobjoie was the daughter of a local butcher. According to the birth registry in Seboncourt, her new-born's father was an "unidentified German soldier".

A few months after the birth, Charlotte left her son with her parents and went to Paris to become a dancer.

MONEY IN MIND: Did Charlotte Lobjoie-Loret invent a story about her son's parentage to help him out of bankruptcy?

In his book, Jean-Marie Loret said he spent his first seven years with his grandparents who "treated him badly" and with whom his mother had no contact whatsoever.

In May 1922, Charlotte Lobjoie married Clement Loret, a lithographer, who agreed to support his wife's illegitimate son and to allow him to bear his own last name.

From then on, Jean-Marie Loret attended Catholic boarding schools in Cambrai and Saint-Quentin. In 1936, (aged 18) he joined the French army and was promoted to staff sergeant.

During WW2, he worked as a charge de mission for the French police in Saint-Quentin, Aisne. He claimed in his book that he got the job by Hitler's order, though there is no evidence to support this.

However, Loret was considered by those who knew him to be only "an average individual" so it would have been unusual for him to gain such a high rank on his own merit while still only in his early twenties.

Loret also claimed he had collaborated with German Gestapo units in France even though no charges of collaboration were ever brought against him after the war. He said Hitler ordered all material on him to be destroyed.

After WW2, he became a trader in glass welding, but had to give that up in 1948 due to bad debts and eventual insolvency.

Arguments against Hitler having a son

The year 1948, was the year Charlotte Lobjoie-Loret chose to reveal the sensational identity of her son, Jean-Marie's father which was the same year her son's business went bankrupt. Is that a coincidence?

Many of the people who knew Hitler and survived WW2 had already profited by selling their stories about him. Was Lobjoie-Loret merely adding herself to the long list of money-makers?

Was the revelation about "Hitler-the-Daddy" a mother's "invention" to help her son and his growing family out of financial difficulty?

Jean-Marie claimed that his mother thought she was dying in 1948 when she made the startling revelation, yet she managed to make a miraculous recovery and did not die for another three years.

Alice Lobjoie, Loret's aunt and Charlotte's sister, stated that her sister had indeed had a love relationship with a German soldier during WW1, but she vehemently disputed that this soldier was Adolf Hitler. She stated that she could remember the man's face quite well and knew that this face had no resemblance to Hitler's.

She also stated for the record that her nephew was a fantasist. "Jean is a nutcase. Only the Germans talked up that Hitler story to him."

Also, all of Adolf Hitler's WW1 comrades said that he was absolutely against any relationships between German soldiers and French women.

In his 1932 memoir, Two Dispatch-Runners, Balthasar Brandmayer said Hitler had reacted in the most violent terms against the intent of his regiment-mates to get involved with French girls and had reproached them for having "no German sense of honor". Also, at this time in his life, all his army comrades agreed that Hitler showed absolutely no sexual interest in women.

Critics have also shown logical inconsistencies in Werner Maser's biography of Hitler. These critics have said that it is highly improbable that any soldier in the war, let alone somebody ranked as low as a lance corporal, would have been able to take a young woman with him through all the relocations of his regiment, as Hitler had supposedly done with Lobjoie. Free movement would not have been possible in the occupied areas.

In 2008, the Belgian journalist Jean-Paul Mulders traveled to Germany, Austria, France and the United States to collect DNA from the Loret family and from the last living relatives of Hitler in Austria and New York.

By comparing the DNA, Mulders claimed he had proof that Jean-Marie Loret could not be Adolf Hitler's son. The results of his research were published in Het Laatste Nieuws, [The Latest News], Belgium's most popular newspaper.

Then in February 2009, a book on the same subject was published by Herbig Verlag in Munich: Looking for his son, a preparatory inquiry.

If Mulder's DNA investigation was conducted in a valid scientific manner, then, without question, no other arguments would be pertinent, Adolf Hitler was not the father of the French claimant. So the only question remaining concerns the validity of Mulders' DNA investigation.

If it is accurate, all other explanations and claims are false.

Though scientists and biologists have been unable to agree on the DNA evidence, the predominant view of historians is that Hitler's paternity of Loret is either unlikely or impossible.

THREE GENERATIONS: Adolf Hitler, Jean-Marie Loret and one of Loret's nine children, Philippe Loret who told people he was Hitler's grandson

Arguments for Hitler having a son

On February 17, 2012 the French magazine Le Point said there had been new developments in the investigation, reporting that a study by the University of Heidelberg showed Hitler and Loret were of the same blood group and that another study showed they had similar handwriting.

But DNA or genetic certification of Jean-Marie Loret's "biological inheritance" conducted at the university resulted in the finding that "at best, Loret could be Hitler's son", but that "he need not be such".

More importantly, the article also stated that official German Army paperwork proved officers brought envelopes of cash to a "Miss Lobjoie" during Germany's occupation of France.

Historian Werner Maser has claimed that evidence for Hitler's paternity included Charlotte Lobjoie's incarceration in a French sanatorium (allegedly on Hitler's orders) after Germany's occupation of Paris and a protracted interrogation of Jean-Marie Loret by the Gestapo in the Hotel Lutetia, the Gestapo's headquarters, also in Paris.

Werner also cites Loret's alleged collaboration with the Gestapo while he worked as a military policeman.

DOG'S LIFE: Philippe Loret walking his Alsatian

Perhaps the most damning evidence confirming Jean-Marie Loret as the German dictator's son is that apparently Hitler himself admitted to a few close associates that he had fathered a child some time during WW1.

In his book, With Hitler to the End: The Memoirs of Adolf Hitler's Valet (2009), Heinz Linge stated that Hitler had told a number of people "his belief that he had a son, born in 1918 as the result of a relationship with a French girl while he was a soldier in 1916-1917 in northern France and Belgium." [Linge died in 1980 but his memoirs were not published until 2009.]

A word of caution here is required as Heinz Linge remained a Hitler devotee until his death and his memoir of Hitler was written only after Jean-Marie Loret first revealed in interviews [in the 1970s] who he believed his father to be. In other words, Heinz Linge, who was loyal to the Fuhrer to the very end, may merely have repeated the rumors that had already been published in newspapers and magazines to deliberately perpetuate the Hitler myth.

Hitler's alleged son, Jean-Marie Loret died in 1985 aged 67. During his lifetime, he married twice and fathered nine children. One of these children, Philippe Loret, has also claimed to be the direct descendant or grandson of Adolf Hitler.

WORKS CITED

Essays, articles, reports and websites

"Adolf Hitler Took Cocktail of Drugs Reveals New Documentary" by Tom Porter, Daily Mail, August 2013 (Porter: 2013)
"Adolf Hitler's Time in Jail: Flowers for the Fuhrer in Landsberg Prison" Spiegel international by Jan Friedmann translated from German by Christopher Sultan,2010
(Hitler's Time in Jail: 2010)
"Hitler Foresees His End" by Karl von Weigand, Cosmopolitanmagazine 1939 (Hitler sees his end: 1939)
"Hitler Gave Nazi Soldiers Blow Up Sex Dolls To Combat Syphilis: Book", Huffington Post, 2012 (Huffington Post: 2012)
"Hitler tries to get out of speeding ticket" by Alan Hall, September 2011 Daily Mailonline (Hitler's speeding ticket: 2011)
"Hitler was definitely gay according to doctors" by Ryan Lovelace, Washington Examiner, 2013 (Lovelace: 2013)
"Hitler's Doomed Angel" by Ron Rosenbaum, Vanity Fair magazine, 1992 (Vanity Fair: 1992)
"Hitler's First Murder" by Henry Makow Ph.D. online article, March 19, 2012
(Hitler's First Murder: 2012)
"Hitler's mentally ill relative was sent to gas chamber" by Stephen Castle, The Independent (UK) January 2005 (The Independent: 2005)
"Journal reveals Hitler's dysfunctional family" The Guardian newspaper, 2005 (The Guardian: 2005)
"Mein Kampf, a translation controversy" by Michael Ford, 2009 online (Controversy: 2009) Metapedia.de(Metapedia.de: 2015)
"Purple Velvet" in Der Spiegel, June 17, 1959 (Purple Velvet: 1959)
"Uncle Adolf: The Incestuous Coprophiliac" by Murray Davies The Mirror, September 16, 2006 (The Mirror: 2006)
"The Psychological Development of Adolf Hitler" by Adrea Antczak 2010 online (Antczak: 2010)
"Was Adolf Hitler a Pedophile?" by Siobhan Pat Mulcahy Yahoo contributor network, July 2013 (Hitler a pedophile: 2013)
Interview with Paula Hitler; Modern Military Records (NWCTM) (Military Records: 1946)
Jewish Virtual Library online (Jewish Virtual Library: 2015)
US Holocaust Memorial Museum (Holocaust Memorial Museum: 2015)
Various online academic articles by John Simkin available at spartacus-educational.com updated 2015; (spartacus-educational.com: 1997-2015)
History Learning Site by C.N Trueman (2000-2015) (History Learning Site: 2015)
"Ten things you never knew about Adolf Hitler" by Siobhan Pat Mulcahy, CrimeMagazine.com, June 2013 (CrimeMagazine.com: 2013)
"Unity Mitford: English debutante staged Nazi orgies" Daily Mail, October 11, 2013 (Nazi orgies: 2013)
Hans Mend interview with German counter-intelligence agent, Friedrich Alfred Schmid-Noerr, in December 1939 (Schmid-Noerr: 1939)
The French Yellow Book, a collection of French diplomatic papers by Francois-Poncet (1938-9) (French Yellow Book: 1938-9)
"Atheist and gay: Frederick the Great more radical than today's leaders" by Philip Mansel, Spectator Online 2015 (Atheist and gay: 2015)

Newspapers and magazines:
Germany: Der Spiegel (various dates); Stern (1959), Bild (2015); Munich Observer, Munich Illustrated, Munich Post, Berlin Daily News, The Right Way, National Observer, Frankfurt News,

Bavarian Echo, Bunte, Zeitgeist, Die Fanfare, Regional Echo (various dates)
Britain: London Evening Standard (1933), The Spectator magazine (1934), SpectatorOnline (2015) The Guardian, The Independent, The Daily Mail, The Mirror, MailOnline (2015); News Chronicle (1937), Look magazine (various dates)
USA: Time, Newsweek, Washington Examiner, Vanity Fair, The New Republic, Literary Digest, Chicago Times, Pittsburgh Press (various dates)
Miscellaneous: Linz Post, Belgium Daily News, Pour Vous magazine, Belgium's Daily News, Le Point magazine, Vienna Daily News (various dates)

ABRAMS/ LIVELY, The Pink Swastika: Homosexuality in the Nazi Party by Scott Lively, Kevin Abrams (1995)
AMIS, Zone of Interest by Martin Amis (2014)
BAYLES, Caesars in Goose Step by Will D. Bayles (1940)
BINION, Hitler Among the Germans by Rudolph Binion (1976)
BLOCH/ KUBIZEK, The Young Hitler by Eduard Bloch and August Kubizek (2013)
BLUEHER, The German Wandervogel Movement as an Erotic Phenomenon by Hans Blueher (1912)
BRANDMAYER, Two Dispatch Runners by Balthasar Brandmayer (1932)
BROMBERG/ VOLZ-SMALL, Hitler's Psychopathology by Verna Volz-Small and Dr. Norbert Bromberg (1983)
BULLOCK, Hitler: A Study in Tyranny by Alan Bullock (1962)
BURLEIGH/ WIPPERMAN, The Racial State: Germany 1933-1945 by Michael Burleigh and Wolfgang Wipperman (1993)
CANTARELLA, Bisexuality in the Ancient World by Eva Cantarella (2002)
CARRUTHERS, Hitler's violent youth: how trench warfare and street fighting molded Hitler by Bob Carruthers (2015)
DAVENPORT-HINES, Unity Mitford by Richard Davenport-Hines (2004)
DONALD, Mussolini's Barber by Graeme Donald (2010)
DUNNING, Psychological Effects of Child Abuse M.M. Dunning, (2004)
EBERLE/ NEUMANN, Was Hitler ill? by Henrik Eberle, Hans-Joachim Neumann (2012)
EBERMAYER, Personal and political diary1933-5 by Erich Ebermayer (1959)
EBING, Psychopathia Sexualis by Richard von Krafft-Ebing (1886)
FOTIS-KAPNISTOS, Hitler's Doubles by Peter Fotis-Kapnistos (2015)
GOESCHEL, Suicide in Nazi Germany by Christian Goeschel 2009
GRAVEN-HUGHES, Getting Hitler into Heaven by John Graven Hughes (1987)
GUN, Eva Braun: Hitler's Mistress by Nerin E. Gun (1969)
HAMANN, Hitler's Vienna: a portrait of the tyrant as a young man by Brigitte Hamann (2010)
HANFSTAENGL, Hitler: The Missing Years by Ernst Hanfstaengl (1957)
HANFSTAENGL, Unheard Witness by Hanfstaengl (1957)
HANISCH, I was Hitler's Buddy by Reinhold Hanisch (1939)
HASTE, Nazi Women by Cate Haste (2001)
HAYMAN, Hitler and Geli by Ronald Hayman (1997)
HEIDEN, Der Fuhrer Hitler's Rise to Power by Konrad Heiden (1944)
HEIDEN, Hitler: a Biography by Konrad Heiden (1936)
HITLER, Mein Kampf [My Struggle] by Adolf Hitler (1925)
HOFMANN, Hitler Was My Friend by Heinrich Hoffman 1955)
HOOK, The Madmen of History by Donald Hook (1976)
HUSS, The Foe We Face by Pierre Huss (1942)
INFIELD, Eva and Adolf by Glenn Infield (1974)
JUNGE, To The Last Hour: Hitler's Last Secretary by Traudl Junge (2002)
KEMPKA, I Was Hitler's Chauffeur: The Memoirs of Erich Kempka by Erich Kempka (1951)
KERSHAW, Hitler 1889-1936 by Ian Kershaw (1998)
KOHLER, Hitler's Sex Life: The Girls Who Knew His Love, and then the Kiss of Death

by Pauline Kohler (1940)
KUBIZEK, The Young Hitler I Knewby August Kubizek (1953)
KUBIZEK/ BLOCH, The Young Hitler by Eduard Bloch and August Kubizek (2013)
KUDECKE, I Knew Hitler by Kurt Kudecke (1937).
LANGER, The Nizkor Project: A Psychological Analysis of Adolf Hitler: His Life and Legend by Walter C Langer et al(1943)
LEWY, The Drug Policy of the Third Reich, Social History of Alcohol and Drugs, Volume 22, No 2, by Jonathan Lewy (2008)
LINGE, With Hitler to the End: The Memoirs of Adolf Hitler's Valet by Heinz Linge (2009)
LITCHFIELD Hitler's Valkyrie: the uncensored biography of Unity Mitford by David Litchfield, (2014)
LIVELY/ ABRAMS, The Pink Swastika: Homosexuality in the Nazi Party by Scott Lively, Kevin Abrams (1995)
LOCHNER, What about Germany? by Louis P. Lochner (1942)
LORET, Your Father's Name was Hitler by Jean Marie Loret (1981)
MACHTAN, The Hidden Hitler by Lothar Machtan (2001)
MARACIN, The Night of the Long Knives: Forty-Eight Hours that Changed the History of the World by Paul R. Maracin (2004)
MASER, Adolf Hitler: Legend, Myth, Reality by Werner Maser (1975)
MITCHELL, Hitler's Mountain by Arthur H. Mitchell (2010)
MITFORD, Hons and Rebels by Jessica Mitford (1960)
MOLLO, To The Death's Head: The Story of the SS by Andrew Mollo (1982)
MURRAY, Analysis of the Personality of Adolf Hitler by Henry Murray et al (1943)
NEUMANN/ EBERLE, Was Hitler ill? by Henrik Eberle, Hans-Joachim Neumann (2012)
NICHOLSON, Richard and Adolf by Christopher Nicholson (2007)
OLDEN, Hitler the Pawn by Rudolf Olden (1936)
PEIS/ WIGHTON, Hitler's Spies and Saboteurs by Gunter Peis and Charles Wighton (1973)
PIETRUSZA, Rise of Hitler & FDR by David Pietrusza (2015)
PLANT, The Pink Triangle by Richard Plant (1988)
POPE, Munich Playground by Ernest R. Pope (1941)
PRYCE-JONES, Unity Mitford by David Pryce-Jones (1976)
RAUSCHNING, Hitler Speaks by Herman Rauschning (1939)
RAUSCHNING, The Voice of Destruction by Herman Rauschning (1939)
ROSENBAUM, Explaining Hitler: The Search for the Origins of his Evil by Ron Rosenbaum (1998)
SHIRER, The Rise and Fall of the Third Reich by William L. Shirer (1960)
SIMKIN, spartacus-educational.com, edited by John Simkin (2015)
SNYDER, Encyclopedia of the Third Reich by Dr. Louis L. Snyder (1994)
SNYDER, Hitler and Nazism by Dr. Louis L. Snyder (1932)
SNYDER, Hitlerism: The Iron Fist in Germany by Dr. Louis L. Snyder (1932)
SPEER, Inside The Third Reich (A Memoir) by Albert Speer (1970)
STRASSER, Gangsters around Hitler, by Otto Strasser (1942)
STRASSER, Hitler and I by Otto Strasser (1940)
PONCET, The French Yellow Book, a collection of French diplomatic papers Francois-Poncet (1938-9)
TOLAND, Adolf Hitler, the definitive biography by John Toland (1991)
TYSON, The Surreal Reich by Joseph Howard Tyson (2010)
VOIGT, Unto Caesar by F. A. Voigt (1938)
VOLZ-SMALL/ BROMBERG, Hitler's Psychopathology by Verna Volz-Small and Dr. Norbert Bromberg (1983)
WAITE, The Psychopathic God: Adolf Hitler by Dr. Robert G. L. Waite (1977)
WIGHTON/ PEIS, Hitler's Spies and Saboteurs by Gunter Peis and Charles Wighton (1973)
WIPPERMAN/ BURLEIGH, The Racial State: Germany 1933-1945 by Michael Burleigh and Wolfgang Wipperman (1993)

Printed in Great Britain
by Amazon